C000132328

Captain or Colonel

Captain or Colonel

The Soldier in Milton's Life and Art

Robert Thomas Fallon

University of Missouri Press
Columbia, 1984

University of Missouri Press, Columbia, Missouri 65211
Printed and bound in the United States of America

Library of Congress Cataloging in Publication Data

Fallon, Robert Thomas.
Captain or colonel.

Bibliography: p.
Includes index.
1. Milton, John, 1608–1674—Knowledge—Military sciences. 2. Milton, John, 1608–1674—Characters—Soldiers. 3. Soldiers in literature. 4. War in literature. 5. Great Britain—History, Military—Stuarts, 1603–1714. I. Title
PR3592.M55F34 1984 821'.4 84-2308
ISBN 0-8262-0447-3

To Max

Acknowledgments

In its long gestation this book has engaged a legion of debts: To Marjorie Hope Nicolson, who read one of its pages to her class on a summer's day and persuaded me of its value. To Edward Tayler, who guided its uncertain beginnings. To Jacques Barzun, who trimmed the lard from the ribs of its prose. To John Shawcross, the conscience of us all. To Michael Lieb and Al Labriola, who insisted on its value when I most doubted. To those who have read it, in part or whole, and given of their wisdom: Roland Frye, James Sims, William B. Hunter, James Butler, and James Freeman. To historians: Christopher Hill for his generous concern, Austin Woolrych for his challenging and genial debate, and Gerald Aylmer for his advice on a seminal afternoon. To Jerry Sherwood for her faithful advocacy. To the Keeper of the Public Record Office, London, and the Steward of the Honourable Artillery Company, who extended a warm English welcome to an unknown American. To the American Council of Learned Societies for their most helpful grant. To the Christian Brothers and my colleagues at La Salle College, whose generosity made the work possible. To many who bore with me and encouraged: Roger Rollin, Kenneth Hill, Claude Koch, and Beth.

But the debt is deepest to J. Max Patrick, who cared so fully and demanded so much, as he has with all who aspire.

Several essays published over the years appear in the text variously condensed, revised, or excerpted. I am grateful to the editors for permission to use them: Roy Flannagan of *Milton Quarterly* for "John Milton and the Honourable Artillery Company," *MQ* 9 (1975) and "Milton's 'defenseless doors': The Limits of Irony," *MQ* 13 (1979); James M. Simmonds of *Milton Studies* (Pittsburgh: University of Pittsburgh Press) for "Filling the Gaps: New Perspectives on Mr. Secretary Milton," *MS* 12 (1979) and "Milton's Epics and the Spanish War: Toward a Poetics of Experience," *MS* 15 (1982); Fredson Bowers of *Studies in Bibliography* for "Miltonic Documents in the Public Record Office, London," *SB* 32 (1979); and Robert L. Patten of *Studies in English Literature* for "Milton in the Anarchy, 1659–1660: A Question of Consistency," *SEL* 21 (1981).

R.T.F., Philadelphia, Pa.
June 1984

Contents

Acknowledgments, *vii*

Introduction, *1*

I.
Life and Art:
Experiential Criticism, *7*

II.
The First Response, *30*

III.
The Army of Saints, *72*

IV.
Mr. Secretary Milton, *100*

V.
The Creative Process, *134*

VI.
Satan, *167*

VII.
The War in Heaven, *202*

VIII.
Two Warriors, *235*

Afterword, *251*

Works Cited, *253*

Index, *265*

Note on Texts and Abbreviations

The following editions have been used for quotations from the works of Milton: *The Complete Prose Works of John Milton*, ed. Don M. Wolfe et al. (New Haven: Yale University Press, 1953–1982), 8 vols., cited throughout as *YP*; *The Works of John Milton*, ed. Frank A. Patterson et al. (New York: Columbia University Press, 1931–1938), 18 vols., cited throughout as *CW*.

In the text and notes, the following abbreviations are employed: *PL, Paradise Lost; PR, Paradise Regained; SA, Samson Agonistes*; HAC, The Honourable Artillery Company; *DNB, Dictionary of National Biography; OED, Oxford English Dictionary; CSPD, Calendar of State Papers, Domestic Series, Commonwealth.*

Introduction

This is a book about, among other things, the relationship between history and literature; thus, it risks falling through the crack between the two disciplines to be dismissed as not entirely satisfactory to either, the historian finding that there is not enough history and the literary scholar that the art is slighted. To avoid the oblivion of that crack these pages will be addressed primarily to students of literature. The book will recommend itself to many historians, however, as a study of the *relationship* between the two disciplines, an effort to explore the influence of events, in this case warfare, on an extraordinarily creative imagination. Events, therefore, are not always presented exactly as they happened, it being more important to suggest how a citizen of John Milton's London would have perceived them to happen. Rupert's cavalry raids in 1643, for example, may have in fact posed no substantial military threat to the city; nonetheless Londoners lived in constant fear of being burned and plundered by the "Devil Prince." Of course, the literary community has not been known for its passionate interest in the intricacies of strategy and campaigning, but it is hoped that scholars will find much of interest here. There is a minimum of military jargon and no description of battle, since it is assumed that Milton himself would not have had an intimate knowledge of such matters.

The seed of this study germinated almost twenty years ago when, during my first readings in Milton criticism, I found myself vaguely uneasy with the commentary on the poet's war imagery. It was not, however, until I came upon B. A. Wright's analysis of the war in Heaven that this formless discontent began to take on more substantial shape. Wright proposes, "The war in Heaven is an opportunity for Milton's satire not only on epic battles but on war in general." He goes on:

> Satan, as we have seen, is representative of the traditional epic hero, seeking glory by force of arms; one of Milton's aims therefore in the war in Heaven is to make Satan and his warriors look ridiculous. But the mockery goes beyond that, being aimed at warfare in general. It is

> all an extravagant satire on the belief in war as preeminently heroic. The book [6] is filled with mockery: "laughter was in heaven" . . . The ridiculous effects that result are deliberate; the fighting is intended as a parody, not only of epic battles but of warfare in general.[1]

I came upon Wright's remarks having only recently turned to literature after a long period of historical studies, which had focused on the seventeenth century; and his interpretation seemed to jar with what I had learned about the men of the Commonwealth and about the Puritan sensibility in general. He provided no rationale for his conclusions, aside from quoting lines from *Paradise Lost*; and so I was left with two troublesome questions: Why would Milton want to write a mock epic? And why would he want to write a parody of war?

During further studies stimulated by the immensely varied scholarship of Marjorie Hope Nicolson, I encountered these same sentiments with some frequency but was never able to find a persuasive discussion of the historical basis for the reading, except for the often-repeated conviction that Milton, like any sensible man, hated war and loved peace. In our own turbulent age, of course, parodies of war lie at every hand, inspired by that same fervent conviction; but in the absence of historical evidence I had to question the assumption that the sensibilities of the 1650s resembled so closely those of the 1960s and that a seventeenth-century Puritan like Milton, whose causes prospered through the force of arms and who was the loyal servant of a military regime for a decade, would share the sentiments of twentieth-century pacifist thought. Thus those two questions continued to trouble me until that first faint disquiet became the focal inquiry of this study: What role did the figure of the soldier and of warfare play in the life and the imagination of John Milton?

A word or two about method is perhaps appropriate at the outset. The approach is based on the rather self-evident observation that experience shapes the imagination, which in turn shapes the art. Once this premise is accepted, one can argue two related positions that flow from it. First, the imagination may either transfigure the experience or simply translate it with little change, but the art that results from the process will neither negate nor contradict the essence of that experience. Second, although there are surely unconscious forces at work, the artist in the act of creation

1. *Milton's "Paradise Lost,"* p. 129.

is in conscious control of his faculties; that is, he knows what he wants to do and he knows what he is doing. On this basis the inquiry can proceed along fairly rational lines. The first step is to examine the quality of the experience, in the present case Milton's encounter with warfare in England during his mature years, in order to come to some understanding of the poet's response to it. The scholar can call on a number of resources at this stage, the most important of which are the historical chronicle and the poet's own words, here Milton's prose and the early poetry composed at the time of the encounter. When such evidence is meager, as it often is with figures from the distant past, the scholar must fill in, with some caution, by reference to the works and lives of contemporaries who can be said to have shared the same general sensibility, social background, ideological orientation, and physical environment as the artist in question.

One must then evaluate the artist's imaginative perception of the experience; and this is somewhat more tricky ground, for that perception can change as new experience intrudes. In this regard, Milton's military imagery is a subject rather uniquely suited for such an inquiry, since his great works seem to have been written toward the end of his life, when he had no further contact with the military, and it can be assumed that the figure of the soldier had become rather firmly shaped in his imagination.[2] One can arrive at a tentative hypothesis about that shape by examining the products of his creative faculty before he wrote his great works, in this case the early poetry and the more highly figured passages from his prose. Thus informed, the scholar can address the major poems with some assurance that his reading of the function of military imagery in them will be rooted in a sound evaluation of the life and mind of John Milton and will not be unduly influenced by his own late-twentieth-century aesthetic and ideological orientation.

2. Over the past three decades there has been a lively debate over the chronology of composition of Milton's works, a controversy which I shall take pains to stay out of. See especially Allan H. Gilbert, *On the Composition of "Paradise Lost": A Study of the Ordering and Insertion of Material*; John T. Shawcross, "The Chronology of Milton's Major Poems" and *With Mortal Voice: The Creation of "Paradise Lost,"* appendix; Mary Ann Radzinowicz, *Toward "Samson Agonistes": The Growth of Milton's Mind*, appendix E; and J. Max Patrick, "Milton's Revolution against Rime, and Some of Its Implications." Despite interesting textual evidence that portions of the major poems may have been written earlier, this study will adhere to the conventional dating of Milton's labors: *Paradise Lost* was composed roughly between 1658 and 1665, *Paradise Regained* and *Samson Agonistes* thereafter.

Discussion of the major poems, which constitutes the second half of the book, focuses on two issues: the influence of experience on art, and the function of martial imagery. It is argued that Milton's experience is reflected in the poems, but in ways not formerly considered. The discussion includes a theoretical analysis of the process whereby the creative imagination transforms experience into art, and an examination of all the martial figures in the great works to determine the extent to which event influenced image. Of course, one should not expect to find parallels in Milton's life for all his martial figures, since he drew on his readings for so many; but in discussing the function of military imagery, they all must be considered. Further, the political and diplomatic figures must be examined as well. The 1640s in England were years of civil warfare, when political allegiances and actions were shaped by the conflict. In the 1650s the country was seldom at peace, and diplomatic missions were largely preoccupied with matters that either led to or derived from warfare. Hence it should not be surprising that passages in Milton dealing with political and diplomatic affairs should be either directly related to warfare, like the congress of devils in book 2, or laced with references to armed conflict, as in the encounter between Jesus and Satan in *Paradise Regained*. Such passages must be considered if one is to arrive at a full appreciation of the image of the soldier in Milton's mind and an understanding of its function in his poetry. Finally, it is proposed that his martial figures serve, not as an ideological testament against war and the military, as some argue, but as a poetic representation of the causes and consequences of evil.

This approach will necessarily precipitate disagreement with some long-standing interpretations of the man and his works. In order to preserve the text as a unified and fairly straightforward exposition of the argument, I have relegated to the notes discussion of alternate readings of isolated phrases and familiar cruxes when they are not germane to the matter at hand. This practice runs certain risks, not the least of which is the danger that the notes may prove more interesting than the text; but it seems a necessary expedient to avoid plaguing the reader with a series of distracting digressions.

As luck would have it, hardly had I punctuated my last footnote when the presses rolled out four works devoted in varying degrees to Milton and war. Rather than scatter numerous references throughout the fine print, it would be best to acknowledge them here, where the discussion may serve to underline the sudden stir the subject has created. Two are book-length works on the subject, Stella P. Revard's *The War in Heaven* and James A. Freeman's *Milton and the Martial Muse*, and both have been received warmly by Miltonists.[3] Revard's work was awarded the Milton Society's prestigious James Holly Hanford Award for the most distinguished book on Milton published in 1980, and Freeman's book was the subject of a long, laudatory review in *Milton Quarterly*.[4] While admiring the immensely learned scholarship of both, I cannot accept the conclusions drawn from that scholarship. Revard examines the tradition of the Christian epic of the Renaissance and finds that poets of the age universally praised the virtues of the martial hero. Freeman examines the military literature of the time and finds that it did the same, though in more practical terms. Both argue persuasively that Milton drew on such works for his own military imagery; but both conclude that he rejected the sentiments of his contemporaries, that in his great poems he turned their praise of martial values about, finding their works a fertile source of image and allusion with which to mock the very virtues they are said to celebrate. As evidence, Revard and Freeman cite Milton's lines, hearing in them various levels of irony, satire, parody, and burlesque to support their reading of a poet who, they argue, found in the soldier a figure worthy only of scornful laughter and derision. He emerges from their pages as a man much in sympathy with those in the late twentieth century who passionately hate war and disparage the soldier. Many in our own time, contemplating the grim specter of modern warfare, are persuaded that this is the only appropriate response to our peril. This is not, however, a suitable forum to discuss the merits of such sentiments; I seek only to demonstrate that they have little in common with the convictions of the John Milton who walked the streets of London and Westminster in the mid-seventeenth century, and that consequently it is unlikely he would have expressed such views in his poetry.

If two other recent works bear any witness, biblical scholars are inclined to attribute to the poet a more serious intent. These are not studies exclusively devoted to the subject, but they include long, important chapters on book 6 and martial imagery. Murray

3. *The War in Heaven: "Paradise Lost" and the Tradition of Satan's Rebellion*; *Milton and the Martial Muse: "Paradise Lost" and European Traditions of War.*

4. By Philip J. Gallagher in *Milton Quarterly* 15 (March 1981): 19–24.

Roston is deaf to the derisive "laughter in Heaven"; as he says, "the interpretation of Milton's War in Heaven as farce has no basis in the text."[5] Michael Lieb is a scholar who has ably demonstrated a fine ear for parody and burlesque and an appreciation for Milton's devastating ability to demean a figure satirically, as his discussion of the scatalogical allusions in Satan's voyage through Chaos will attest.[6] Yet in his superb *Poetics of the Holy*, a consummate work of biblical scholarship, he observes that while the Omnipotent may indeed mix scorn with his wrath, those less endowed do not. Raphael, Adam, and the narrative voice, he insists, all respond to war "not with laughter and contempt, but with reverence and awe," and Milton himself "was imbued with the fervor of what he considered to be a just war undertaken in a righteous cause."[7]

5. *Milton and the Baroque*, p. 121.
6. *The Dialectics of Creation: Patterns of Birth and Regeneration in "Paradise Lost,"* pp. 28–34.
7. *Poetics of the Holy: A Reading of "Paradise Lost,"* pp. 266, 277.

I

Life and Art: Experiential Criticism

> It is a rare critic who can resist the tendency to reduce an admired figure to his own image.—Joseph Summers

The biographical criticism of the nineteenth century has passed from the scene, though perceptive readers will not have read this far without entertaining faint misgivings that the ghost of that discredited methodology, which they had thought safely laid to rest, may be haunting these pages. They are not to worry; the biographical critic still lies in his obscure grave, and his spirit has long since been exorcised from the corridors of the academy. The pedagogic practices that numbed the sensibilities of the youth of that age are no more, or so we fondly hope. Jacques Barzun, in his incisive and engaging way, has described a professor steeped in that tradition, one who after a lengthy discussion of the poet's life and times finally came to the work itself, which he dismissed with a shake of his sage head and a sigh of "A gem, gentlemen, a gem," its beauties, it would appear, incommunicable to the uninitiated, to be appreciated only by a select, learned brotherhood. Those who endured his tutelage may recall him occasionally lingering over a work, but only to dwell upon its veiled autobiographical allusions, the art thus serving as a means to an end, a source for searching out the secrets of the artist's life, filling in gaps left blank or inconclusive by an incomplete chronicle. His young scholars, as Barzun puts it, "were in no danger of becoming esthetes."[1]

The eclipse of this rambling pedagogue with his recitals of the loves, dates, and diet of the poet—"What porridge hath John Keats?"—is mourned by few. His passing, however, has left something of a hiatus in the spectrum of responses recommended to modern students of literature. While most scholars will accept the suggestion that poets weave into the pattern of their art some threads from the experience of their days, there remains an understandable concern about how to discuss this influence without being identified with that earlier tradition. For many years biographical criticism was so unfashionable that no aspiring scholar

1. "Biography and Criticism—A Misalliance Disputed," pp. 479–80.

would have been so foolish as to attach that label to his efforts; and if he did feel the compulsion to interpret a work in its biographical or historical context, he would have been wise to keep his remarks brief or relegate them to the safe obscurity of a footnote.[2] There are encouraging signs that this reluctance is fading,[3] yet many scholars remain sincerely apprehensive that by interpreting the art in terms of the artist's life one may diminish the aesthetic appreciation of a work, that in weighing down a poem with such a burden of stolid fact, one may retard the critical imagination intent on searching out its meanings and beauties. Many of the critical theories currently in favor restrict their attention to the text alone in isolation from the poet who composed it, a practice which certainly leaves the imagination free to wander where it will. These systems, among others constructionism, semiotics, deconstruction, and reader-response, have produced brilliant studies of the art itself but they cannot be relied upon to accurately reflect the mind of the artist.

The chief obstacle to further acceptance of the study of experience and art is a lack of method. In their enthusiasm for the New Criticism, early twentieth-century scholars threw the methodological baby out with the bathwater, and until recently scholarship has in general chosen to ignore the subject. Thus, there is presently no language available for those who might wish to discuss the art in terms of the life, save for that left over from a discredited method. As a critical approach, it doesn't even have a respectable name, since "historical criticism," which might seem most appropriate, is widely accepted today as a reference to *literary* history.

This book, then, will proceed on the premise that the life can be a valuable key to a reading of the art, and in the conviction that

2. For example, in *Milton Studies VII*, ed. Albert C. Labriola and Michael Lieb, which was published in 1975, each of the ten essays illustrated a critical approach that was currently in use to study Milton's works. Biographical criticism was not included in that very useful volume, except for an essay on psychobiography. Again, the *MLA Newsletter* of November 1973 reported the results of a survey of members in which only 236 of 42,383 (0.5 percent) responses indicated "biographical study" as an area of interest. "Literary criticism" and "literary history and criticism" combined polled 50 percent of the responses.

3. The works of Leon Edel and W. Jackson Bate are encouraging, as both include critical passages in their biographies. Bate, in *Samuel Johnson*, p. xx, proposes that we "try to heal the split between 'biography' and 'criticism.'" See also Richard Locke's "The Literary View," *New York Times Book Review*, 10 January 1978, p. 3; and 26 February 1978, p. 3.

when reading a work of the scope and complexity of a *Paradise Lost*, we need all the keys we can cut. It will propose means of filling the gap left by the eclipse of the biographical critic but without resort to the more simplistic resolutions of his discredited method, in the hope that such an effort will encourage further analysis of the process whereby life is transfigured into art. A change in terminology will fool no one, of course, but I am suggesting that the hermeneutics of such a study be identified as a *poetics of experience* and the method itself as *experiential criticism*, if only to distinguish it from its ill-famed antecedent. The influence of experience on art is only infrequently discussed today, in literary circles at any rate; hence it will be useful at the outset to propose a theoretical justification for considering a work of art through the study of the artist's life. These pages will make only passing reference to Milton's reading, though reading is, of course, as much a part of the experience of life as are working, loving, and eating. Milton, like most poets, obviously drew his inspiration from books, and chiefly from other poets. The last half-century of critical effort has mined this rich lode diligently; one scholar, drawing on that effort, has gone so far as to catalogue the works that Milton seems to have read, a list which runs to over fifteen hundred titles, many of them multivolumed.[4] Most of these studies are apt, sound, and valuable as keys to the understanding of his great works. Even those that suggest the more bizarre and obscure sources may be forgiven, for Milton was a passionate bibliophile, even after his blindness had denied him the visual joys of the printed page. Nothing can really be dismissed, for it seems at times that he must have read everything and forgotten nothing; and no one would dare propose limits to that incredible mind.

Hence the possibilities for sources of any single episode in *Paradise Lost* are legion. Models for Satan abound in Homer, Genesis, Job, Revelation, Grotius, Ariosto, Marlowe, and in theatre, masque, painting, music, sermon, and sculpture; but no one proposes any single source to the exclusion of the others. They do not contradict, but overlap and reinforce. The present study suggests yet another source as part of that store of inspiration from which the poet drew to compose his great poems—Milton's Europe in that tumultuous seventeenth century. In that time, perhaps, may be found further models for Satan—Charles I, Oliver Cromwell,

4. Jackson Campbell Boswell, *Milton's Library*.

Pope Urban VIII—and, once more, these suggestions do not question the validity of other sources. They are offered as yet another aid to prepare us better for the encounter with that soaring intellect and to enrich our understanding of his art.

The Critical Backdrop

These pages will examine parallels between Milton's experience of war and the martial figures in his works. Certainly, to explore his military imagery itself is not to enter virgin territory. Over fifty years ago, James Holly Hanford traced the striking similarity between the maneuvers of the angels and the tactics described by Milton's contemporary, Robert Ward, in his *Animadversions of Warre*.[5] About the same time Donald Dorian formulated Milton's philosophy of war from the evidence of his works.[6] Satan's cannons have been often discussed, and more than one scholar has suggested that the image derives from Valvasone's *L'Angeleida* or Ariosto's *Orlando Furioso*.[7] Roland M. Frye finds Satan frequently depicted as the inventor of gunpowder in the iconography of the period;[8] Christopher Hill calls the practice so common as to be a cliche.[9] More recently, James A. Freeman has traced the poet's martial figures to the military literature of the age.[10] Some scholars have suggested that we can flesh out our sketchy knowledge of his life by catching at hints in his works. David Masson, for example, concludes from a passage in *An Apology Against a Pamphlet* that "Milton, it seems, has for some time been practising drill."[11] G. Wilson Knight, always vigorous if at times misguided, finds the Satan of book 1 to be "a Cromwell casting an 'experienced eye' over his ironside warriors," a spectacle which we can be fairly confident Milton never witnessed.[12]

The present study will adopt a quite different orientation. Rather than search the art for keys to his thought and life, it will search the thought and life for keys to the art. This, again, is not entirely untrodden ground. Most students of Milton's political

5. "Milton and the Art of War," pp. 192–95.
6. "A Study of Milton's Ideas of War."
7. Watson Kirkconnell, *The Celestial Cycle*, p. 81.
8. *Milton's Imagery and the Visual Arts: Iconographic Tradition in the Epic Poems*, pp. 48–49.
9. *Milton and the English Revolution*, p. 362.
10. *Milton and the Martial Muse: "Paradise Lost" and European Traditions of War*.
11. *The Life of John Milton*, 2:402.
12. *Chariot of Wrath*, p. 127.

thought will permit themselves an occasional aside about the influence of specific experiences on his art. Of late, there have been encouraging signs that scholars are beginning to turn, once again, to the chronicle of the times to place an artistic achievement in its historical context. Annabel Patterson's splendid *Marvell and the Civic Crown* is such a work. In her book on Milton, Mary Ann Radzinowicz finds the "intentional fallacy" itself a fallacy, and in one section considers "*Samson Agonistes* as political teaching and the protagonist as a Commonwealth hero."[13] In his recently published *John Milton: The Inner Life*, James Thorpe refers frequently to the "outer" life in his graceful description of the "inner" one.[14] It remained for a historian, however, to provide Miltonists with the first full-scale study of the poetry as a reflection of his life. In his challenging *Milton and the English Revolution*, Christopher Hill interprets the great works against the background of the failure of the English Republic, drawing on evidence of Milton's association with and sympathy for the radical elements of English society at the time. One may find much to disagree with in his reading (and I shall below); but we owe Hill a great debt for breaking this ground with such authority, bringing to the task the many resources of his long and distinguished career.

In the search for sources of Milton's art and thought, however, modern scholarship is more comfortable in using the poetry itself as a point of departure and then moving back into the earlier works of Milton and his literary models to seek analogues or echoes for the lines. This is a valuable endeavor, giving the student a reasonably sound grasp of what Milton read, but it is not as valid when one wants to know what he *did*, or what he thought of his own life and times. For one thing, this approach lends itself to the practice of citing lines out of context, glossing over their function in the passage from which they are extracted. Milton's works are highly dramatic in form, and to assume that the thought or feeling expressed by any single figure in a specific dramatic situation reflects without qualification the poet's deepest convictions is to ignore the context of the lines. Thus Milton cannot be accused of the heresy of mortalism in *Paradise Lost* simply on the basis of a brief passage from a soliloquy by a fallen Adam who is wondering what is going to happen to him and is ticking off all the possi-

13. *Toward "Samson Agonistes": The Growth of Milton's Mind*, p. 113.
14. See, for example, pp. 26–29, 77–83, 99–101, 150–54.

bilities, among which the death of the soul is but one![15] Further, poetry is a product of the imagination expressed in the language of paradox and ambiguity, hence a questionable source for historical evidence. *Paradise Lost* surely reflects Milton's life, but only in a very veiled way; and since we have some reasonably reliable accounts of that life, judgments arising from the evidence of the poetry must be squared with what we do know of his days. The poetry "may help to thicken other proofs / That do demonstrate thinly," but it must be used with great caution for such a purpose.

Having proposed the influence of certain experiences on Milton's art, these pages will go on to suggest ways in which those experiences shaped the *function* of the imagery in his poetry. An artist may derive an image from a literary source, but this does not necessarily mean that he will apply it to the same purpose as his predecessor. Milton used the tradition of the pastoral elegy for purposes other than those intended by Bion and Moschus; St. Peter is one of the customary procession of mourners but the poet uses the figure to reflect his own experience with the English church in the 1630s. In like manner Ariosto may have had a comic intent in his account of the invention of the arquebus, as Merritt Hughes suggests;[16] but if Milton used Ariosto as a source, it does not necessarily mean that he had the same purpose in mind in his description of the invention of the cannon. The war in Heaven is a part of *Paradise Lost* because this is an epic poem and epics are traditionally about wars, and it is evident that book 6 is heavily indebted to its antecedents; but the function of war in Milton's poems is very different from its function in Homer's poem, or in Virgil's.

An analysis of the works of John Milton in terms of the experience of his days does, it is true, present some special problems. In the first place, we know so much less about him than we do of later poets, whose lives were more generously documented in correspondence and the works of contemporaries. Some of the essential facts of Milton's life are still open to question: How was he spending his time during those shadowy years, 1645–1649 and 1652–1658? And which wife was his "late espoused Saint"? An even more formidable obstacle to this effort is Milton himself, for what we do know of his life and associations is not always entirely

15. *PL* 10.782–93. See Merritt Y. Hughes, ed., *John Milton: Complete Poems and Major Prose*, p. 425n, and Hill, *English Revolution*, p. 317.

16. *Complete Poems*, p. 335n.

agreeable. It may be unsettling, for example, to be reminded that he was a loyal and active servant of a government that can only be described as a military dictatorship, that he supported the wars of the Commonwealth of England, including the sack of Drogheda, and that he had great admiration for the soldiers of the New Model Army. If it is further suggested that his works may reflect some of these sentiments, one can sympathize with those Miltonists who insist that biography is one thing and art quite another. "Milton the man" has been much disparaged by T. S. Eliot, Robert Graves, F. R. Leavis, and many others, in whose eyes he assumes the distasteful shape of the dour Victorian *pater familias*.[17] They see him as a fundamentalist zealot, preaching the punishments of eternal damnation and the rigors of the straight and narrow, an unyielding father, demanding husband, and unprincipled political polemicist, in brief, a figure from a stiff and colorless age[18] who could not be expected to elicit much sympathy from a forward-thinking twentieth-century poet, critic, or student.

In an effort to make the poet more acceptable to our age and to correct some of these critical excesses, sympathetic scholars have tried to soften this austere image, an effort which culminated in William Riley Parker's brilliant biography, where he dwells at length on Milton's humor, his humanity, and his wide circle of friends and admirers. The poet emerges from those pages as a fond family man, a delightful host and companion, and a wise counselor somewhat disappointed that his advice is not more frequently sought. Parker attempts to disassociate Milton from the Puritan government he served as secretary for foreign languages by diminishing him to a minor political figure who, untouched by the tainted ebb and flow of dictatorial power,[19] performed his slight function on the periphery of events. Others, such as Austin Woolrych, go even further, suggesting that Milton deliberately chose to be remote from events, particularly during the Protectorate, because he strongly disapproved of the policies of his government.[20]

17. The list is long. The sentiments seem to be summed up in Eliot's confession that he entertained "an antipathy toward Milton the man" in "Milton (1947)," from *The Proceedings of the British Academy, Vol. XXXIII*, as published in *Milton Criticism*, ed. James Thorpe, p. 312.

18. This view of life during the Interregnum has been corrected somewhat by Lady Antonia Fraser in her superb *Cromwell, the Lord Protector*, pp. 455–83.

19. *Milton: A Biography*, 2:95, 481.

20. *YP*, 7:2–3, 47. See also his "Milton and Cromwell: 'A Short but Scandalous Night of Interruption'?"

The effort to restore Milton to his former stature has been resourceful and wide-ranging. James Holly Hanford drew attention to the pervasive literary and philosophical influence of Christian humanism in Milton's works, an influence which, Hanford argued, overshadows that of the Puritan sensibility.[21] When the New Criticism appeared, it was by nature ready-made for the cause: disregard the man and focus on his words. But the dicta of Eliot and Leavis still rankled, and in response scholars shaped a "new" Milton, one derived largely from the evidence of his works. Out of the ashes of the disagreeable Puritan there arose Milton the Whig,[22] Milton the Radical,[23] and finally Milton the Pacifist.[24] Evidence for these more satisfactory alternatives was found either in his works or in the books from which he drew his inspiration, and persuasive indeed was the argument mounted on the basis of his wide reading and remarkable mind. So a very different Milton emerged, one whom Eliot would have found more agreeable and one with whom the modern academician and his students could be more comfortable. Joseph Summers's observation about the close relationship between a critic and his "admired figure," quoted in the chapter heading,[25] may help explain the emergence of the "new" Milton, for he resembles no other figure so closely as that of a late-twentieth-century, liberally oriented university don, who, safely insulated from the dust and heat of the race, is free to pursue his studies, surrounded by his beloved books and admiring students—a very comfortable figure, indeed. This is not to imply that the effort went without protest. Logan Pearsall Smith was rather blunt: "They seem deliberately to close their eyes to the fact (though it stares them in the face) that Milton was a Puritan, an English Puritan of the age of Cromwell, and (as far as is possible

21. *John Milton: Poet and Humanist*, passim.

22. George F. Sensabaugh, *That Grand Whig, Milton*.

23. Hill, *Milton and the English Revolution*, passim.

24. Aside from B. A. Wright (in Introduction above) see Edward Wagenknecht, *The Personality of Milton*, p. 93, where he observes that *Paradise Regained* "is certainly one of the great pacifist books of all time"; Stella P. Revard, "Milton's Critique of Heroic Warfare in *Paradise Lost* V and VI," for whom the two books represent a "full length critique of war, both earthly and heavenly" (p. 122); and Michael Wilding, "The Last of the Epics: The Rejection of the Heroic in *Paradise Lost* and *Hudibras*," who proposes that Milton wrote a parody of war because he was a pacifist (p. 113).

25. "Milton and the Cult of Conformity," p. 30. E. M. W. Tillyard says of another group of scholars, "People are so fond of Shakespeare that they are desperately anxious to have him of their own way of thinking" (*Shakespeare's History Plays*, p. 204).

to a poet) more a Puritan than anything else." He went on with some heat, "They have imagined an incredible Milton, a humanist son of the Renaissance and of the civilization of Greece."[26]

The emergence of this more attractive figure has excited no new interest, however, in identifying Milton's works with the life of the man who walked the streets of London in the mid-seventeenth century.[27] Modern critical attention focuses almost exclusively on the books he read, or on other forms of art. Scholars today accept almost any suggestion for a source or analogue of a great work if it comes from literature, painting, music, theater, sermon—any product of the human imagination. At the moment there is a lively interest in iconography, and it is not difficult to find interesting and persuasive commentaries on paintings and illustrated manuscripts that Milton may have had an opportunity to see, which therefore might possibly have inspired his work. Studies abound suggesting sources in the Talmud, Cabalistic texts, little-known philosophers, obscure European epics, and archaic musical forms with which the poet was "probably" familiar, and each is heard with the sympathy and respect it deserves. Modern scholars are fascinated with the many voices that emerge from the text of *Paradise Lost*. We may be entirely deaf to these several tongues, but we accept the sincerity of a colleague who hears them and will listen with sympathy while he tells us what they mean to him. Structuralists find forms and shapes in the work to which we may be blind, yet we will sit patiently and strain to see.[28]

This study asks the reader to assume that same openness of mind when it is proposed that art does not always arise from art alone, that a poet is something more than the sum of the books he

26. *Milton and His Modern Critics*, p. 45.

27. As Arnold Stein puts it, "The range and power of his learning persuade some that he must have learned everything from books, almost nothing from life, and nothing at all from acquaintance with the peculiar language of the human heart" (*The Art of Presence: The Poet and "Paradise Lost,"* p. 4). Response to Hill's *Milton and the English Revolution* will serve as an example of the reluctance to consider such an approach. Reception was mixed, reviewers in general praising the history but dismissing his analysis of the poetry in the light of that history; see, for example, Frank Kermode, "A Moderate New Notion." Some, however, were quite alarmed at this apparent effort to disinter the long-discredited methodology. In "Milton among the Radicals," Blair Worden warns that "Hill wants to redirect the whole course of Milton studies. If he succeeds, we shall know that literary criticism has lost its nerve." I once argued the case for a biographical approach from the floor at an MLA forum (not a Milton session); a panelist replied summarily that there was no relationship whatever between an artist's life and his art.

28. Of recent interest is Galbraith Miller Crump, *The Mystical Design of "Paradise Lost."*

has read, and that the artistic vision can be inspired as well by events that take place beyond the walls of his library. In brief, it is requested that the method I have chosen to call experiential criticism be permitted to take its place among the many critical systems that provide keys to the understanding of Milton's art. In his vivid portraits of warfare the poet was certainly indebted to Tacitus, Homer, the Bible, Robert Ward, and the iconographic traditions of the Renaissance. It should not be too difficult to accept the further suggestion that his imagination was as deeply moved by Oliver Cromwell and the wars of his country. It is proposed, simply, that life and art are symbiotic spheres of experience that a powerful imagination can encompass in a single vision, and that when the artist records that vision in the pages of a book he is not limited for his inspiration to the pages of another book.

If the reader finds himself uneasy with this proposal, he will be even further disquieted by the suggestion that the "new" Milton, with whom he may have become quite comfortable, is perhaps not an entirely accurate representation of the historical figure. One is most reluctant to disturb that very agreeable image of the sequestered scholar by intruding upon his quiet study with all of this distasteful talk of politics and warfare. The unquestioned acceptance of that figure, however, has given rise to interpretations of his works that seem clearly inconsistent with the historical Milton, specifically that commentary on the function of the military imagery in his works—the figure of Satan, the war in Heaven, the warrior angels—which has suffered by neglecting to consider the role that the soldier played in his life. Thus, these pages will submit that John Milton was deeply affected by the wars raging about him and by his experience in the embattled government he served, and that, through the subtle chemistry of creation, some part of his vital life emerges as an element in the priceless alloy of his art.

The Unconscious and the Creative Process

One wonders, of course, about that chemistry, about what is going on in the artist's mind as he shapes his vision; for his experiences seem at times to make their way into his works by some unconscious means. In the heat of composition the poet cannot be said to be in a normal state of mind; he is surely drawing on resources which, it would seem, are not available to ordinary mortals; and the presence of these unusual forces has been recognized from ancient times, when a common explanation for the poet's extraordinary powers was that he is possessed by the gods. "Inspiration" is a capricious master, for as any writer knows there are days when the words seem to flow and others when they simply refuse. Those who "tend the homely slighted Shepherd's trade," being a superstitious lot as a whole, have various explanations for the fickle and erratic behavior of the Muse. Milton's methods were surely interesting; he composed lines in his head during the early morning hours while awaiting the arrival of an amanuensis to "milk" him, as he is said to have put it. According to Aubrey, Milton was convinced that he could compose only between the autumnal and the vernal equinox.

The fact that there are enigmatic forces at work here suggests the psychological sciences as a fruitful field for inquiry into the relationship between life and art.[29] Miltonists have certainly been attracted by psychological criticism, many taking their cue from Blake's famous remark that the poet was of the Devil's party "*without knowing it*," the implication of the phrase being that the unconscious somehow surfaces in the act of creation, inspiring the poet to pen lines he otherwise would not, were he in full control. This study will make small use of this method, however, and perhaps a word of explanation is appropriate.

What few contributions these pages make to critical theory will have to do with process, not motivation; hence they must mirror the humility of Freud and Jung, both of whom admitted that their methods could never explain the creative imagination. Freud denied that psychoanalysis could ever throw light on the nature of the artistic gift, and for Jung the creative act would "forever elude the human understanding."[30] Psychology focuses on the man, its purpose to discover why he acts as he does. Much of psychological criticism is similarly oriented; it studies the poetry to discover why the poet writes as he does. This study, however, will approach the relationship between life and art from the opposite direction, examining the life for keys to the art; therefore any assumptions

29. An important work of psychoanalytic criticism by a distinguished Milton scholar appeared while this book was in proof, William Kerrigan's *The Sacred Complex: On the Psychogenesis of "Paradise Lost."* It is a major contribution to the field.

30. Silvano Arieti discusses Freud's doubts in *Creativity: The Magic Synthesis*, p. 23. For Jung, see his "Psychology and Literature," in *Modern Man in Search of a Soul*, p. 153.

about Milton's psychological makeup will be based on historical evidence, not an interpretation of the poetry. They will be based, further, on the premise that an enlightened understanding can arrive at reasonable conclusions about a human being's emotional response to the events of his life, even those as traumatic as spousal desertion, the threat of armed assault, or blindness, and that those conclusions can be satisfactorily expressed in layman's terms.

On the other hand, a study of the process whereby experience is transfigured into art certainly cannot ignore the unconscious. Indeed, modern psychologists have given the mysteries of creativity considerable study, though they seem more concerned with such practical matters as decisionmaking, problem-solving, and brainstorming techniques than with the inspired leaps of genius.[31] A handful, notable among them Frank Barron of the Laboratory for the Psychological Study of Lives at the University of California, Santa Cruz, and Silvano Arieti, have produced valuable insights into the workings of the creative imagination of great artists; and perhaps we may look to scholars like them for light in the future.[32] Meanwhile, it would be well for the literary scholar to be cautious, for the field is crowded today with many conflicting systems—behaviorism, holism, psychobiology, group dynamics, Gestalt, and Heinz Kohut's narcissism—and in examining creativity one must be wary of fixing on the abstractions of one or the other of the teeming progeny of Freud. (It might brighten the scene a bit, also, to forgo describing the creative act in pathological terms, those used in identifying symptoms of mental illness, a practice most distressing to those who consider that act the su-

31. Frank Barron, *The Shaping of Personality: Conflict, Choice, and Growth*, pp. 176–84. The first efforts to measure creativity were those of J. P. Guilford in the early 1950s (p. 181). See also "Compendium of Research on Creative Imagination," in *A Source Book for Creative Thinking*, eds. Sidney J. Parnes and Harold F. Harding, appendix A, which is an annotated bibliography of early studies of creativity during the 1950s. More recently, *The Creative Experience*, eds. Stanley Rosner and Lawrence E. Abt, reports on interviews with creative minds of all kinds, from scientists to poets. Questions about creativity, however, are limited to such matters as what mood they are in when at work, how ideas arise, and what problem-solving and revision techniques they use.

32. Frank Barron has conducted classes in which his students read the works of such figures as William Carlos Williams and William Butler Yeats while studying the forces at work in the artist's life at the time of composition. See his "Diffusion, Integration, and Enduring Attention in the Creative Process." In his *Creativity and Personal Freedom*, pp. 225–36, Barron's explanation of the creative process makes some sense of the Freudian synthesis. For Arieti, see *Creativity: The Magic Synthesis*, pp. 135–91.

preme achievement of the human spirit.)[33] Again, the imagination obviously draws on the unconscious for some of the materials it works with; but until the process is better understood, it would be prudent for the common reader to continue to fall back on his common sense. Thus, this study will not explore the complexities of repression, regression, fixation, or projection, but will presume that the reader can identify the correspondences between subliminal influences and figures they give rise to without the aid of specialized knowledge or vocabulary.

Meaning and Intent

The following pages are liberally sprinkled with references to Milton's "meaning," "intent," "purpose," and "message," which seems positively foolhardy in an age when poems "should not mean / But be" and during which an entire generation of scholars has matured under the impression that "intentional fallacy" is one word. One risks being labeled an archaic curiosity in suggesting that a poet writes a poem for any reason other than simply to write a poem. It is considered most indecorous today for a poet to entertain a conscious intent of imposing a particular meaning on readers, or to influence them to think or act in any certain way. Such a posture, it is said, smacks of propaganda; it robs the work of its aesthetic universality, questions its integrity, and diminishes its value. Thus in an age when didacticism is inartistic, it is considered advisable to ignore Milton's statement that he intended to write a poem "doctrinal and exemplary to a nation," since such a soaring achievement as *Paradise Lost* could not possibly have been composed to such a pedestrian end. Beyond question, the principle of aesthetic theory that any explicit statement of meaning or intent should be disregarded can prompt luminous studies of the inner workings of a poem. In *The Art of Presence*, for example, Arnold Stein imagines an almost completely isolated Milton, stripped of flesh, blood, psyche, or emotion, stripped almost of thought itself, a figure detached from the organic world with no history and no intent except to wrestle with the difficulties of the hexaemeral tradition and to delight himself and his readers

33. Jacques Barzun, in *Clio and the Doctors: Psycho-History, Quanto-History & History*, p. 135, notes George Bernard Shaw's objection to the theory "that artists were mental degenerates." He quotes Shaw: "What in the name of common sense is the value of a theory which identifies Ibsen, Wagner, Tolstoy, Ruskin, and Victor Hugo with the refuse of our prisons and lunatic asylums?"

with his ingenuity in overcoming them. For Stein, the ideal reader is equally detached, severed from any influence of his "individual history" and advised to disregard his own experiences as fallen man in order to fully appreciate the artistic achievement of *Paradise Lost.* We are asked to forget our sins, which we are only too happy to do, and delight in the accomplishment. Using these premises, Stein has written a brilliant and engrossing book, though it is not quite clear whether he thinks that such a poet and such a reader do indeed exist in nature or is simply using them as a critical device to narrow the focus of attention.[34]

As an aesthetic principle, then, the notion that a poem "should not mean" and that a poet should not intend anything but art can enhance the appreciation of a work; but it can only obscure a study of the poet's mind. When employed outside the aesthetic arena to examine Milton's theology, his philosophy, or his politics, the principle can lead one astray; for such studies are inclined to take the argument a step further, suggesting that the poet is not fully aware of the "true" meaning and intent of what he says and that if he does express himself on these matters, his judgment is not entirely to be trusted. These studies find in the unconscious a useful resource to help explain away some of the more puzzling or disturbing implications of a work in terms more agreeable to modern sensibility—Milton's overly attractive figure of Satan, for example, or his less-than-flattering image of God, or his apparent rejection of classical learning. E. M. W. Tillyard was among the first to explore the possibilities of "unconscious meanings" in Milton's lines, and he explained the troublesome figure of Satan by suggesting that he was an "insubordinate creature of Milton's imagination," not really the poet's fault.[35] Again, A. J. A. Waldock has suggested that Milton got carried away and had to catch himself every time he put a rousing speech in Satan's mouth; the poet found it necessary to follow each with a qualifying tag to remind the reader, and perhaps himself, that this was indeed the Devil "Vaunting aloud, but rackt with deep despare" (1. 126) or delivering "high words, that bore / Semblance of worth, not substance" (1. 528–29). In brief, he didn't "intend" to write those speeches so well, they just happened that way.[36]

34. *The Art of Presence*, pp. 67, 141, 161. Stein opens with the premise that "the man who lived his other [i.e., physical] life . . . has no direct presence in the poem" (p. 1).

35. *Milton*, p. 289.

36. *"Paradise Lost" and Its Critics*, pp. 78–79.

Many of these readings lean heavily on Freudian analysis, which suggests that the poet, while composing, loses control on a conscious level as the unconscious surfaces, carrying with it all the dark baggage of repressed emotions. If he had a conscious meaning or intent, it doesn't really matter since the unconscious, once it assumes command, has purposes of its own. The confusion that can result from the unrestrained pursuit of this theory is best illustrated by the recent interest in the various "voices" to be heard in Milton's poems. In the early 1960s, Anne Davidson Ferry wrote a very important book, *Milton's Epic Voice: The Narrator in "Paradise Lost,"* a graceful work of rare insight. It has inspired a number of studies, however, that might give her pause. At a Milton conference of recent memory, for example, several papers took up the subject where she left off, arguing that there are in fact a number of voices to be heard in his poems. One suggested that the poet himself speaks in the invocations while the narrator speaks in the balance of *Paradise Lost*, which seems reasonable enough. But another went on to maintain that the poet and the narrator, as personae, are in a constant state of strife throughout the poem; and yet another that the characters themselves are struggling with the narrator for supremacy in the lines, particularly Satan in book 6.[37] If one adds to this noisy scene Tillyard's suggestion that it is the poet who is at odds with his figures, there emerges the inescapable impression that the poem has become a battlefield on which discordant voices everywhere struggle to be heard. The poet becomes an embattled arbiter who must make his way among conflicting forces broiling within him, and this not always successfully as one voice after another seizes control of his pen. The poetic sensibility takes on all the appearance of a schizophrenic derangement, symbols out of control, which psychologists like Silvano Arieti have gone to great pains to explain is *not* to be associated with the creative process.[38]

37. The University of Wisconsin–Milwaukee Milton Tercentenary Conference, 14–19 November 1974. The papers were: John R. Mulder, "The Narrator in *Paradise Lost*"; Roger B. Rollin's reply to Mulder; James G. Mengert, "Styling the Strife of Glory: The War in Heaven"; and Roger H. Sundell, "The Prologues in *Paradise Lost*: Progress of a Prophet and His Vision." All were immensely interesting and each became the basis for a later publication. It was somewhat unsettling, however, to hear them in close succession.

38. See Arieti, *Creativity*, pp. 139, 142, 145. Arieti uses schizophrenia and daydreaming, concerning which there is considerable data, to develop his theory of the creative process; but he makes a careful distinction between pathological delusion and creative perception. In his field he is probably best known for his *Interpretation of Schizophrenia*.

As a principle of critical interpretation, then, the questioning of conscious intent and meaning lends itself wonderfully to the free play of the critical imagination; but in that very freedom lies its limitation as a means of inquiry into the mind of the poet. Having placed in doubt the author's own statement of purpose, it is an easy next step for the critic to substitute political or philosophical intentions more agreeable to his own particular vision. The process can lead to conclusions like that of William Empson, who turns *Paradise Lost* on its ear by proposing that Milton actually thought God "wicked."[39] And it is at least partly responsible for that popular figure, Milton the antimilitarist.

Experiential Criticism

The experiential approach assumes that the poet consciously intends to convey a deliberate meaning and that in the great works of literature, at any rate, he does so successfully. Further, a knowledge of the passage of his days will aid the reader in understanding both. But the question remains—how is that passage of days transfigured into art? Of course, the substance of that magic interval between thought and motion can be but dimly seen, yet the mystery of it only prods the scholar on. We do know something of the way in which the poet creates art out of art. As the fruit of a half-century of critical effort, scholars can now turn to a wealth of theoretical studies that define the process whereby a poem is made out of a myth, music, painting, or poetry itself. But how does the poet create art out of material that is not by its nature artistic, that is not the product of another creative imagination? This book can only begin to explore the complex question of the relationship between life and art, but this seems a most propitious moment to start. Materials for such an endeavor multiply at every hand; the past two decades have witnessed a flood of publications by and about past literary figures—diaries, letters by the volume, newly discovered and revised manuscripts, biographies, and encyclopedias. It is indeed a curious contradiction of our time that even with so many new historical and biographical works crowding the bookshelves, the life of the poet is still considered by many as irrelevant to an appreciation of his poetry. As K. K. Ruthven observes, the discrepancy between this "contempt for biographical

39. *Milton's God*, pp. 9–11.

information and the actual accumulation of it in vast quantities can only mean that impersonalism has influenced critical theory much more than it has critical practice."[40] Miltonists have been very much in the van of this wealth of publication, with William Riley Parker's biography, the *Yale Prose* with its exhaustive historical introductions, and the *Milton Encyclopedia*; and in the 1970s alone, a number of distinguished seventeenth-century historians—Christopher Hill, Gerald Aylmer, Robert Ashton, Antonia Fraser, C. V. Wedgwood, Godfrey Davies, Valerie Pearl, Brian Manning, D. H. Pennington, Blair Worden, and David Underdown, among others to be cited below—have published volumes packed with new insights and information about the age of Milton.

To begin, then. In a broad sense, there are three ways in which the artist makes use of the passage of his days to enrich his art. The first occurs when the work is quite clearly written about a historical event, and an explicit one-to-one relationship between art and life is both intended and expressed. The second involves the use of an event as the point of departure for reflection of a more general nature, though here the identification between the occasion and the work is somewhat less definite. The third is a broader and more persistent influence, one which makes itself felt throughout the entire canon of an artist's works, as he weaves into the fabric of his art the entire substance of his life. Here the scholar enters uncertain waters; for though this is a more pervasive influence, it is more amorphous and will defy clear identification between historical incident and creative act.

Some works are clearly rooted in an event, one to which the poet consciously and explicitly refers for one reason or another in his poem. His purpose may be to celebrate it, as in Milton's poem to Fairfax after the siege of Colchester, or to condemn it, as in his sonnet "*On the Late Massacher in* Piemont." The poem may be a response to an anniversary or a recurring event, as in "On the Morning of Christ's Nativity," which, though written about an occasion of cosmic importance, also records Milton's response to the Christmas of 1629. The poet may wish to satirize a group, as Milton does his uncomprehending readers in "I did but prompt the age"; to praise a quality of life, as in "Lady that in the prime of earliest youth," or a person, as he does Lady Margaret Ley; or to respond to a death, as in his sonnet to Catharine Thomason.

40. *Critical Assumptions*, p. 99.

These are works unequivocally about a person, a place, or an occasion, to which the poet is responding in the historical context; and it is necessary to have some knowledge of that context in order to appreciate them fully. One must have some understanding of just what the "*new Forcers of Conscience*" were forcing to appreciate Milton's distaste for the Westminster Assembly.

Another group of works records a personal experience but may or may not highly particularize it. The poet's purpose may be quite simply to share the experience with his reader. It may be a relatively unremarkable one; and though Milton was not much given to writing about the unremarkable, we do have his graceful expression of the simple desire for human companionship in "*Lawrence* of vertuous Father vertuous Son." He may assume a philosophical or didactic tone about the experience, as he does in "How soon hath time" on the occasion of his twenty-third (or twenty-fourth) birthday, or in the sonnet and invocations in *Paradise Lost* about his blindness, or in "Lycidas" about Edward King's death. Though he may not particularize the incident, the reader is still aware that the poet is writing in a historical manner. In this latter group it is less essential that the reader be familiar with the particular event or condition that gave rise to the poem; but how incomplete would be our response to those lines on blindness in the invocations, for example, if we had no knowledge of Milton's moral and physical suffering after the Restoration. He is a man reaching out to touch other men, not some disembodied voice singing in an aesthetic void.

Of greater significance, however, than any specific event, condition, or person are the more extended experiences of life—time spent in work, war, marriage, or aging—which become part of the very fabric of the artist's being and which, having passed through the forge of his imagination, are transformed by some process into poetic images that are often but a shadow of their original form. The poet in describing a woman draws on his experience of many women. When he defines a political leader, he has in his mind's eye an image of all the leaders he has encountered. When he conveys the scourge of despair, he calls upon the memory of his own despondency to enrich his lines. The influence of such experiences is of great importance; but it is not so clearly defined, nor is it so easily identified, since we have so little understanding of just what that process of transformation entails. An analogy with a more familiar literary influence may serve to clarify the distinction. Plato's presence is felt throughout *Paradise Lost*; his is not, however, as direct an influence as, let us say, that of Homer or Genesis.[41] The works of Plato may be said to "inform" the poem, but *Paradise Lost* is not *about* Plato in the same sense that it is about the epic tradition or "Mans First Disobedience." Similarly, Milton's experience of the world may be said to "inform" *Paradise Lost*, but the poem is not about the life of John Milton in the same way, that is, in which "Cromwell, our cheif of men" is *about* the lord general.

When a poet describes an abstraction—be it emotion, belief, or spiritual vision—by perceptualizing it in a concrete image, he draws the image from experience. That figure may have lodged itself in his mind as the result of an experience at second hand, from reading, viewing, or hearing of it in the works and words of others, or it may impress itself upon him as a consequence of a personal encounter. Milton, as far as we know, never saw a battle; hence, his image of the war in Heaven was derived from what he heard or read of battle accounts. He did have extensive contact with soldiers, however; thus at least a part of his imaginative concretization of warriors was shaped by that encounter. In his perception of a scene, he may have been struck by the aptness of both experiential and nonexperiential images, as with those he uses to describe the army of fallen angels, prostrate in "that inflamed Sea." He had seen, presumably, the "Autumnal Leaves that strow the Brooks / In *Vallombrosa*" but not, of course, "*Busiris* and his *Memphian* Chivalry" (1. 300–307). Such images present themselves to the creative mind, singly or in clusters, in ways that remain a mystery; but once they have emerged at the conscious level the poet must then employ the cognitive faculty to select among them for final transmutation to the page. What we know of Milton's methods of composition strongly implies that he went through such a culling and sifting process. Jonathan Richardson tells us that Milton would dictate "perhaps 40 Lines as it were in a Breath, and then reduce them to half the Number."[42] Thus we cannot know how many images he discarded before hitting upon Vallombrosian leaves and Memphian Chivalry, the one from life, the other from literature, as the most decorous and appropriate to

41. Irene Samuel, *Plato and Milton*, passim.
42. *The Early Lives of Milton*, ed. Helen Darbishire, p. 291.

his purpose; but if those lines represent but half of the original inspiration, then surely the careful craftsman was making conscious choices.[43] But where are those images stored and how is that magic connection made? Freudians would have them in the subconscious, rising like a dream, unbidden, in a release of repressed energy. Jungians have them in the collective memory of the race, forcing themselves on the poet in ways that they do not venture to explain. B. F. Skinner might have the poet simply responding to his environmental conditioning, making the correspondences a reflexive response to "contingencies of reinforcement."[44] If composition is a conscious act, however, it would seem that these images are more readily accessible, perhaps stored in what Ernst Kris called the "preconscious," from which the imagination can draw them into the conscious arena with relative ease, ready to be transformed into words.[45] If a poet compares a woman to a rose, it is because he has seen a woman and a rose, and one of them, in all likelihood, quite recently; or he is simply drawing on the long literary tradition that associates romantic love with flowers; but both the images and the tradition are close to the consciousness of the poet at the time of composition.

The issue becomes more complex, of course, when one considers the poet's emotional response to the image itself, since the way

43. The impression of conscious intent is reinforced by other figures which, in describing the devils, repeat the pattern of similes drawn alternately from the natural world and the realm of literature and myth. Satan is compared in size to creatures from "the Fables"—Titanian, Typhon, and Leviathan (1. 197–201)—but his shield is like the moon, his spear a pine (1. 284–92). The devils in Pandaemonium are first like bees, then dwarfs and "Faerie Elves" (1. 768–81). Milton had presumably seen autumnal leaves, the moon, pines, and bees, but he of course had only read of the "Memphian Chivalry," the fabled Leviathan, and "Faerie Elves." Another pair departs from the pattern, the Egyptian locusts and the barbarian hordes from "the populous North" (1. 341–51), both from his reading. The locusts are again, however, from the natural world, though Milton had probably never seen "a pitchy cloud" of them, and the barbarians are from history. The bee image has received some attention. James A. Freeman, in *Martial Muse*, pp. 186–99, cites the possible literary sources. Marjorie Nicolson, in *John Milton: A Reader's Guide to His Poetry*, p. 198, suggests experience, however, citing Milton's familiarity from his Italian trip with the coat-of-arms of the Barberini Pope, Urban VIII. I would point out simply that the poet had surely experienced bees "in spring time" much before encountering them in any other context.

44. Skinner summarizes his views in two essays, "Creating the Creative Artist" and "A Lecture on 'Having' a Poem," in *Cumulative Record: A Selection of Papers*, pp. 333–55. See also his *About Behaviorism*, pp. 113–15.

45. Arieti, *Creativity: The Magic Synthesis*, pp. 24–25. Kris conceived of the primary process of creative thought as "a regression in the service of the ego." See also Barron, *Creativity and Personal Freedom*, p. 228, on the preconscious.

he feels about women and roses strongly influences his perception of the relationship between the two, or he probably would not have written the poem in the first place. The human race almost universally responds to vultures, rats, and murderers with varying degrees of horror, fear, or disgust, and to babies with some measure of delight. When such archetypal figures appear as images in a poem, it can be assumed that the poet's perception of correspondences arises from similar responses.

The particular concern of these pages is the image of the soldier, and the first thing that can be said of soldiers is that they are not archetypal figures that elicit a common response from the bulk of the human race. Reactions to a knight-in-arms, a terrorist, or a major general can vary widely, from nostalgia to fear, disgust, humor, or pride (one man's terrorist is another man's freedom fighter), or to a complex mixture of them all. (It is evident that I am making a distinction here between one engaged in the profession of arms and a primitive killer, who may well be generic to the race, as the image of Cain implies.) Except with those children touched directly by the bitter consequences of battle, the image of the soldier is, in general, one formed during late childhood or early youth; hence it is relatively unaffected by the very early precognitive traumas that form so much of the material for Freudian and behaviorist analysis. This suggests that the experience shaping that figure takes place during a developmental period when the cognitive faculty plays a prominent role in one's response to life. Therefore, that experience can be expected to lie close to the surface of the unconscious, easily accessible to the creative imagination.

This image is subject to change, like any other, as a result of subsequent experience. Both literature and life record a wealth of accounts in which the young man enlists to tunes of glory, only to become rapidly disenchanted by the mundane boredom of the camp or the brutish horror of the battlefield. But even here the memory plays tricks, as in later years one tends to forget the toil and hardship and recall with some nostalgia only the camaraderie and the challenge of that sudden thrust into manhood. At a distance, one can grow to appreciate the qualities of a once-despised disciplinarian, even to the almost affectionate admission that he was "hard but fair." But if nothing occurs in the passage of time to alter that initial perception, then it must be assumed to prevail, an image waiting in the barely conscious levels of the mind for a poet, painter, or composer to draw upon to express his vision of the world.

Something may be said here concerning the general perception of the figure of the soldier for seventeenth-century Puritans, leaving to later pages the task of recreating the image as it evolved in the mind and art of John Milton. For most Reformation Christians, both the spiritual and the temporal worlds were arenas of conflict where unseen forces contended for possession of man's soul and very real armies struggled for control of his faith and his life. The Puritan did not conceive of this conflict as evil in itself, but rather as an unfortunate legacy of the fallen world; and he was required to engage in the struggle in order to prove himself worthy of eternal salvation. He accepted the conflicts within and the battles without as his tragic inheritance from that "First Disobedience." Thus, while the Puritan imagined the conflict in terms of temporal warfare, he did not attach any intrinsic evil to those engaged in the struggle. They were to be condemned no more than was the war itself, which was part of God's inscrutable plan. Indeed, the soldier was generally perceived as an admirable figure, for in a world destined to conflict by Adam's sin, the man who engaged in battle was to be applauded and he who shunned the field condemned. There were good soldiers and evil soldiers, to be sure, even as there were good and evil men. The Turk was evil, not however because he was a soldier, but because he was a Turk; and the same may be said of a Royalist. The Puritan did not attach to the profession of arms that same universal disapprobation that he did, for example, to priests and usurers. If he saw papist armies as instruments of the Devil, he did not see armies themselves as agents of evil.[46] The admirable image of the soldier, moreover, was not buried deep in the repressed unconscious of the people, nor was it an archetypal figure of violence, like the tempest or the claw, but a ready metaphor close to the surface of Puritan sensibility, on every preacher's tongue, available to the most prosaic or the most exalted of imaginations to use in describing the struggles of the spirit.

In short, the poet in the act of composition draws on the accumulated store of the experiences of his time. They may be forgotten or half-remembered, found in the unconscious or precon-

46. William Haller, *The Rise of Puritanism*, p. 142. See also Jackie DiSalvo, "'The Lords Battells': *Samson Agonistes* and the Puritan Revolution."

scious mind, but they do not appear in lines of poetry as conflicting forces over which he has lost control. The inventive genius is rather characterized by an unusually strong mind, one that can synthesize contradictions and resolve contending emotions by imposing upon them the ordering principles of form, structure, and syntax. Though he does seem to have a mind that dwells apart, it is still governed by forces accessible to human comprehension; and our understanding of that mind is not enhanced when its processes are reduced to the level of neurotic impulses or exalted to some Jungian vision mysteriously in touch with a cosmic life force. A genius is a unique human being, but he *is* a human being, living a life packed with moments much like those that fill our own days. He may live it with greater intensity and see it with greater clarity than do we, but that life remains the source of all his art. Furthermore, when a poet writes, he has a reader in mind, one to whom he is addressing his most deeply felt convictions and emotions in the hope that he will be understood; and I suspect that the reader he has in mind is one living in his own age and city, one with whom he has shared his time on the globe and who can therefore read in the poet's lines the chronicle of his own life. If in addressing that particular reader at that particular historical moment, the poet pens a message that all men in all times can read and treasure, this is the mark of his genius; for it is a measure of the artist's scope that he can extract the universal from the particular, eternity from a moment, all of nature from a single bud. It does not demean a work to say that it is rooted in time and place, or to picture its creator as a living being seated at a desk with pen in hand, calling on all the pain and joy of his days to speak to his neighbor or his nation. His work will carry beyond his own time only if his vision, born of that age, transcends it; but to transcend does not mean to deny. A more distant reader can surely participate in that vision, but he cannot hope to share it fully unless he knows something of that poet, living in that age.

II

The First Response

. . . in some high lonely Tower . . .

. . . the true warfaring Christian.

When John Milton was nine years old, a group of Czech noblemen tossed the representatives of the Holy Roman Empire from a window of the royal palace in Prague, a defenestration that set the spark to a savage and costly conflict that raged for three decades, warping the lives of an unhappy generation. The list of nations that added fuel to the holocaust of the Thirty Years War includes almost every major power in Europe—France, Spain, Germany, Sweden, Denmark, Poland, the United Provinces—and most of the smaller duchies, princedoms, and republics that lived in the shadow of their larger neighbors. The courts of Europe rang with such names as Gustavus Adolphus, Wallenstein, Tilly, and Turenne, and with their deeds at Lützen, Nordlingen, where twenty thousand men fell, and Rocroi, where the youthful Condé shattered the myth of the invincible Spanish infantry. These decades witnessed such widespread death and devastation that one must look back to the barbarian swarm down the boot of Italy or forward to modern warfare to find a comparable disaster. The effect of the war on Germany has been variously exaggerated but all accounts agree on the grim pictures of poverty, brutality, and destruction that marked the wake of marauding armies. C. V. Wedgwood, after cautioning against exaggeration, estimates conservatively that "the German Empire, including Alsace but excluding the Netherlands and Bohemia, probably numbered about twenty-one millions in 1618, and rather less than thirteen and a half millions in 1648."[1]

England remained relatively untouched by these events. James I had no stomach for foreign adventures, and his son, almost from the moment of his coronation, was grappling with a constitutional crisis that kept his attention so occupied and his coffers so lean that he had little choice but to stay at home. Charles did permit

1. *The Thirty Years War*, p. 516.

other powers to recruit troops in England, and in a brief war with France he sent the Duke of Buckingham on an expedition to aid the oppressed Huguenots of La Rochelle, but even this modest effort ended in dismal failure. Charles was essentially a man of peace, who preferred to spend what funds he was able to gather on Inigo Jones's elaborate masques, court painters like Rubens and Van Dyke, and his young, extravagant French queen. It was perhaps inevitable, however, that the highly contagious fever of religious strife then wasting the Continent would eventually cross the Channel. In England it took the shape of a decade of civil war, touched off, appropriately enough, by controversy over a prayer book.

Thus Milton grew to manhood in a land unscarred by marching feet; until 1639 at least, the wars and rumors of wars that characterized his times scarcely rippled the contented waters of his days. For his first thirty years he lived the quiet life of a student and scholar in London, Cambridge, and later in the self-imposed seclusion of his father's homes in Hammersmith and Horton, his studies undisturbed by beat of drum or call to arms. Like the detached observer of "L'Allegro" he viewed events from a distance, learning of war, "of Knights and Barons bold," only from his books; and this appears to have been little enough, for his interests, quite evidently, were elsewhere. Some of his contemporaries, because they were more in the world perhaps, showed a closer awareness of the impact of war on their times. The contemplative Sir Thomas Browne, after several years of travel and study on the distracted Continent, returned home to write, "I honour any man that contemns [death], nor can I highly love any that is afraid of it: this makes me naturally love a Souldier, and honour those tattered and contemptible Regiments that will die at the command of a Sergeant."[2] Even gentle George Herbert, who had been an aspiring courtier and member of Parliament, likened prayer to an "Engine against th' Almightie"[3] and relations between man and God to an artillery duel:

> Then we are shooters both, and thou dost deigne
> To enter combate with us, and contest
> With thine own clay.[4]

2. *The Works of Sir Thomas Browne*, ed. Geoffrey Keynes, 1:48–49.
3. "Prayer" (I), in *The Works of George Herbert*, ed. F. E. Hutchinson, p. 51.
4. "Artillerie," ibid., p. 139.

The aging Robert Burton, whose life was scarcely less secluded than Milton's but whose memory stretched back to the Armada, echoed Francis Bacon in placing the soldier second only to the scholar in the hierarchy of his Utopia;[5] but Milton is all but silent on such matters. He mentions the European conflict only twice in all his early works. Writing to his old tutor, Thomas Young, then in Hamburg, he alludes to the danger posed by the "grim soldiery" of the Imperial armies; and he responds briefly to a poem about Henry of Nassau by Alexander Gill.[6] Even his trip abroad, which carried him to countries where, as David Masson puts it, "the marchings and counter-marchings of the opposed armies were the subjects of talk everywhere," produced in him no heightened interest in the military events of his day.[7] His writings from the trip and for some time after bear no reference to the conflict going on about him, in marked contrast to the work of other poets who made similar journeys through troubled lands. Byron's travels from London to Geneva, for example, in similarly disturbed times over much of the same ground that Milton covered in the spring and summer of 1639, are described in the third canto of *Childe Harold's Pilgrimage*, an account that reads like a battlefield tour of northwestern Europe.[8]

The few military images that are scattered among Milton's early works add little to his art. They may be said to foreshadow later, more dynamic figures, but they do so very faintly indeed. The bulk of them perform three functions in his lines, all of them quite traditional, gleaned from his wide reading.[9] One group is largely

5. *The Anatomy of Melancholy*, ed. A. R. Shilleto, 1:116.

6. "Elegia Quarta," *CW*, 1:191; Letter 4 in *YP*, 1:317. A possible third reference is to *clerique ducis* and *fraterisque verendi* in lines 9–10 of the "Elegia Tertia," which has been traditionally accepted as an allusion to Christian of Brunswick and Count Ernest of Mansfield. Douglas Bush, however, in *A Variorum Commentary on the Poems of John Milton*, 1:65–68, demonstrates persuasively that the young Milton could not have had these two gentlemen in mind. Judgment must be reserved as to Bush's alternative pair, King James and Maurice of Orange, but his argument raises sufficient doubt as to prevent a clear identification of these lines as an allusion to the Thirty Years War.

7. *The Life of John Milton*, 1:743. The war had come quite close to Switzerland during the previous year with the campaign of Bernard of Saxe-Weimar for control of Alsace and the Upper Rhine. This included the important battle of Rhinefelden, near Basel, in February 1638 and the long siege of Breisach that ended in December. See Wedgwood, *The Thirty Years War*, pp. 404–13.

8. Byron's travels took him to Waterloo, the "bleak battlements" of the Rhine castles, and the battlefield at Morat in Switzerland.

9. Milton's references to archery may be noted and quickly passed over, since

decorative in purpose, another depicts conflicting abstractions in martial guise, and a third defines his intention to compose an epic celebrating the British Mars.

The military figures that function decoratively are marked by either their passivity or their impotence in the face of other, more powerful, forces that are the subject of his work. Thus the inherent strength and authority of poetry, innocence, God, or evil itself are enhanced when juxtaposed with an image of ineffectual armed might. The good Bishop of Ely, strong in his righteousness, passes among the stars with no fear of the sword of Orion (line 54). In "Ad Patrem" at the sound of the poet's song, again "savage Orion, with sword now lowered, turns gentle" (line 39); and in the Nativity Ode the authority of the Christ Child is underlined by the passivity of the world's men-at-arms:

> No War, or Battels sound
> Was heard the World around:
>   The idle Spear and Shield were high up hung,
> The hooked Chariot stood
> Unstain'd with hostile blood,
>   The Trumpet spake not to the armed throng,
> And Kings sate still with awfull eye,
> As if they surely knew their sovran Lord was by. (lines 53–60)

Though the angels are all armed, and "the spangled host keep watch in squadrons bright" (line 21), it is not they who confront the pagan gods. Their weapons are superfluous, for "Our Babe to shew his Godhead true, / Can in his swadling bands controul the damned crew" (lines 227–28).

In *Comus* there is an early reference to Wales as "An old, and haughty Nation proud in Arms" (line 33), but we read on to find that those arms are ineffective in the struggle underway. When the Elder Brother boasts of his weapon, the Attendant Spirit is quick to caution,

> But here thy sword can do thee little stead,
> For other arms, and other weapons must
> Be those that quell the might of hellish charms. (lines 610–12)

This wisdom is confirmed when "*The Brothers rush in with Swords drawn*" only to find that the battle has already been

---

they are generally allusions to Cupid, as in "Elegia Septima" (lines 5–10) and "Love's dart" in Sonnet 6.

fought and won on other grounds entirely and that the victory has gone to the gentle Lady, protected by "the Sun-clad power of Chastity" (line 781).

Milton's early warriors, then, are singularly unwarlike; indeed some of them appear off duty. In "Elegia Prima," for example, is a "soldier with his casque now laid aside" (line 30); and the "Knights and Barons bold" of "L'Allegro" are dressed for the occasion "In weeds of Peace" (lines 119–20). Even when on duty they have little enough to do. The celestial choir of the Nativity Ode is a soldiers' chorus, "The helmed Cherubim / And sworded Seraphim, / Are seen in glittering ranks with wings displaid" (lines 112–14); and the manger is carefully guarded by "Bright-harnest Angels" who "sit in order serviceable" (line 244). Again, in "Upon the Circumcision" the poet recalls the "flaming Powers, and winged Warriours bright" that had so "sweetly sung" the news of the Nativity to the watching shepherds. Thus, though Milton's angels seem to have been heavily armed from the outset, in their early appearances they are singularly static: they sit, they sing, they keep watch, or they simply stand about and by their presence serve to amplify God's glory. They quite conspicuously do not fight battles.

It has been suggested that Milton's "standing" soldiers reflect his commitment to certain Puritan beliefs; but one must be cautious in attaching ideological significance to military tactics and formations, which are shaped largely by the state of training of the troops and the characteristics of their weapons rather than by their spiritual convictions.[10] It is perhaps sufficient to say that

10. Michael Walzer, *The Revolution of the Saints*, pp. 270–97; Boyd M. Berry, *Process of Speech: Puritan Religious Writing and "Paradise Lost,"* pp. 172–85. Walzer suggests that the tactics of Puritan armies mirrored their religious convictions. Berry shows that the Puritan soldier on the drill ground and battlefield was acting out theological doctrine and that the New Model "*fought* like a gathered Church" (p. 170). Both cite Puritan sermon literature as evidence and in the process may have confused cause and effect; it seems more likely that the ministers would have been shaping their sermons on the basis of what they saw, rather than the soldiers structuring their units according to what they heard. As a glance at any contemporary print of a Civil War battlefield will confirm, the tactics and formations on either side of "the rough edge of battle" were remarkably similar, regulated largely by the capabilities and limitations of musket, pike, and horse. The most popular manual of drill of the war, William Barriffe's *Militarie Discipline* (see pp. 58–60 below), was widely used by *both sides*, quite reasonably, since the exercises were designed to make the most effective use of the weapons of the time and both sides had much the same weapons. Cromwell copied his tactics from Rupert, and if he was more successful with them, it was solely because of the superior state of training of the "Ironsides." Cromwell's trooper may have been more amenable

Milton wrote in a time of peace and that his military figures perform the customary duties of soldiers in such a time. If Milton lacked the art, or the inclination, to put his troops in motion, it may well be because he had never seen soldiers do anything more martial than escort the lord mayor, stand watch at the Tower, or parade in the Artillery Garden, activities ill designed to excite the youthful imagination.

There is one striking exception to this pattern of stasis in Milton's early military figures. In "Elegia Quarta," as has been noted, he responds to the report that the Imperial armies are advancing on Hamburg, and he imagines the dangers threatening his former, much-loved tutor, Thomas Young. The figures are so uncharacteristically extended and vigorous that they deserve special attention. Rumor has it, the young poet writes his friend, "that you and your city are girt with grim soldiery, and that the Saxon captains have now made ready their arms. Round about you Enyo is ravaging far and wide the plains, and already blood is watering the tilth-lands sown with flesh of men." Echoing the theme that armed might is impotent in the face of virtue, he reassures Young: "For, though you are overwhelmed by flashing arms, and though a thousand missiles threaten you with a violent death, yet no weapon will outrage *your* side, undefended by armor though it be, and no spear point will drink your blood." The Almighty will champion his own, Milton concludes; and his imagination invokes the vengeful, Old Testament God of war,

> He, who, under the walls of Zion's fortress, in a single, stilly night laid low so many Assyrians, and turned to flight the men that olden Damascus had sent from her ancient tilth-lands against Samaria's borders, who filled with fright the close-crowding battalions, and their cowering king as well, while through the empty air rang the clanging trump, while horny hoofs lashed the plain to dust, while the chariots driven at full speed shook the sandy ground, and there were heard the neighing of steeds as they dashed to war and the clank of iron and the deep-throated war-cries of men.[11]

---

to discipline because of his religious beliefs, as Berry suggests (p. 178), but his tactics were dictated by the speed of his horse and the length of his saber.

11. *CW*, 1:191–95. The nineteen-year-old Milton dramatizes the situation somewhat, caught up perhaps in a creative moment. His only source of information was, as he says, rumor, and it may have appeared to him that Young was in genuine peril, for Protestant Hamburg seemed to lie directly in the path of advancing Catholic armies. The city was in little danger, actually, for Wallenstein and Tilly, commanding respectively the Imperial and the Catholic League armies, had

The unusual vitality of these lines can best be explained as an intensely personal reaction to the imagined peril of his good friend. This is the single occasion in his early years when warfare even remotely touches him; and in response his martial figures, which otherwise sit or watch or stand about, spring to sudden life—arms flash, blood flows, the ground shakes, and harsh sounds of battle affright the ear. The influence of this incident upon the young poet's art foreshadows a later time when he will be further stirred, a time when other armies will threaten his own city, when other friends, preparing for battle, will stand in peril. Once the civil wars begin, his figures again come alive. They are called "by sudden alarum . . . to their military motions"; they rouse themselves, shake their "invincible locks," sally out, and "grapple" with the enemy.[12]

The second function of military imagery in Milton's early work is quite conventional, one which, in fact, it is surprising not to find more prevalent in his lines. The struggle between abstract qualities is occasionally defined in military terms. In "Prolusion V" the rise of the Romans reminds the young scholar of the strong forces that defend truth, and their fall at the hands of the barbarian hordes recalls how easily that same truth can be undermined by error. In "Prolusion VII" he mentions the warfare between death and immortality, and the battle between learning and ignorance. In "Prolusion I" night and day are at war; and in "L'Allegro" the cock, heralding dawn, "scatters the rear of darknes thin" (line 50).[13] In *Comus* the Elder Brother praises his sister's virtue, protected from evil by the "arms of Chastity" (line 439) and Minerva's "*Gorgon* Sheild" (line 446). Again:

> So dear to Heav'n is Saintly chastity,
> That when a soul is found sincerely so,

---

other purposes in mind. They had joined forces at Lauenburg, just south of the city, in order to pursue the shattered armies of the King of Denmark and were intent only upon eliminating that threat to the Empire. They had no reason or inclination to attack the heavily fortified free city of Hamburg, which had remained staunchly neutral in the war. Milton's allusion to "the Saxon captains" (line 77) is probably generic, not a specific reference to the soldiers of the Electorate of Saxony—he means simply "Germans." John George I, the Elector, was also maintaining an uneasy neutrality and his forces took no part in the campaign, though there is no reason to believe that the young Milton would have concerned himself with such detailed knowledge of the belligerents.

12. *YP*, 2:411, 515, 558, 561.

13. *YP*, 1:221–22, 257–58, 295, 305–6.

A thousand liveried Angels lacky her,
Driving far off each thing of sin and guilt. (lines 452–55)

One does not expect to find images of war in a pastoral elegy, which may explain why St. Peter's "two-handed engine" strikes such a dramatic note in "Lycidas." Whatever Milton meant by the figure, it most certainly has a martial ring to it. An "engine" in seventeenth-century vocabulary was a weapon of war, and a two-handed broadsword had all of the authority that Milton meant the image to convey in the struggle against the evil bishops. It has been observed that Milton uses the figure again in describing the "Sword of *Michael*" that

fell'd
Squadrons at once, with huge two-handed sway
Brandisht aloft the horrid edge came down
Wide wasting.[14] (*PL* 6.250–53)

It cannot escape attention, once more, that unlike Michael's "Wide wasting" blade, St. Peter's "engine" simply "stands ready."

Milton employed military imagery in yet a third way during those early years—to define his ambition to write an English epic—and the static figures of his early work have a direct bearing on the poet's search, after his return from Italy, for a suitable subject for the projected work. From the time the young Cambridge student first mentioned his desire to use his mother tongue "in some graver subject" (graver, that is, than the lighthearted "Vacation Exercise" he was reading), his mind was occupied with the problem. His first impulse, understandably, was to write in the classic tradition; and inspired perhaps by the sage and serious Spenser, he began to think in terms of a work about Arthur. In "Mansus" he announced an intention to "bring back to my songs the kings of my native land" and, spirit and art willing, to "break to pieces Saxon phalanxes under weight of Briton's warring." A year later in "Epitaphium Damonis" he repeated his desire to pipe "a British strain," and about the same time considered a number of subjects from British history and legend that seemed to him of sufficient stature for such a work.[15] Milton did not mention the

14. Edward Le Comte, *Yet Once More*, p. 151 and note. Marjorie Nicolson, in her *John Milton: A Reader's Guide to His Poetry*, after surveying the many interpretations of the image, remarks, "Personally, I do not think that Milton visualized it, nor did he intend us to" (pp. 99–100).

15. *CW*, 18:241–45.

matter after 1642, though some scholars feel that he might have clung to the idea until 1644.[16] He had surely abandoned the theme by this latter date, however, and some have wondered why.

Milton's rejection of the Arthurian legend as a subject for his work cannot be called a major turning point in his life or his art, but it has so many implications pertinent to our study that it seems worth pausing over. However an artist selects a subject, whether by long and careful choosing or in a flash of inspiration, such decisions are made while sitting in a room or walking a street on a certain day in history at a specific spot on the globe. Perhaps a consideration of the artist, the time, and the spot will cast light on Milton's decision to abandon the Arthuriad.

E. M. W. Tillyard has defined an epic as a work that draws its inspiration from the prevailing spirit of the age, from, as he puts it, "the accepted unconscious metaphysic" of a "large group of people living in and near" the poet's time.[17] An epic poem about King Arthur and the "magnanimous heroes of the table" would necessarily include accounts of the clash of arms in single and collective combat; the legendary court at Camelot was, after all, an early military institution and the Round Table, more than anything else, a council of war. Thus, in the classic tradition of the *Iliad* and *Aeneid* the poem would have been an account of wars and those who fought them. As we have seen, during the years when Milton was searching for a theme, the English people were not a particularly warlike race. He might have recalled Drake and his gallant crews, of course, as fine examples of English seamen; but to find a respectable example of English valor on the field of battle, he would have had to reach back almost two centuries to the War of the Roses or, if he were searching for figures of truly epic proportions, even further in the past to Harry of Monmouth and his "band of brothers" at Agincourt. Within Milton's memory the record of the English soldier had been anything but inspiring. James I ended the fruitless Elizabethan adventures in the Netherlands, and the reign of Charles I certainly added no new battle honors to English standards. The hopelessly mismanaged expeditions of the fumbling Duke of Buckingham can have brought no swell to British breasts, and the disgraceful performance of English armies in the two Bishops Wars was fresh in the minds of all

16. Tillyard, *Milton*, p. 107. Parker, in *Milton: A Biography*, however, suggests that he changed his mind as early as 1640 (1 : 190).

17. *The Epic Stream in the English Novel*, p. 15.

at the time when Milton was searching for his theme. Whatever the cause for these defeats, before the Civil War the English soldier in no way mirrored the epic qualities of his countrymen, not in the same way, that is, in which the sturdy legionnaire reflected the spirit of Virgil's Rome. The English soldier of Tudor and early Stuart days was more of a Pistol than a Black Prince, in no way expressing an "accepted unconscious metaphysic" of his people. By 1644 Milton could write of "a noble and puissant Nation rousing herself like a strong man after sleep,"[18] but for English soldiers, at least, it had been a very long sleep indeed.

There is an additional question of the poet's artistic development at the time, of his readiness to compose on a martial theme. James Holly Hanford has identified Milton's wide reading in Xenophon, Aelian, Polyaenus, Machiavelli, and his contemporary Robert Ward as sources for the account of the war in Heaven;[19] but there is no indication that by the year 1642 this reading in the military art had made much of an impression on the poet's muse. As we have seen, the military images in his early work are few and most unwarlike, and there is no hint of inclination or ability on his part to narrate scenes of high valor or feats of arms. Milton was a sound judge of his own powers. As a student at Cambridge he had abandoned "The Passion" as a subject "above the years he had." It would be entirely in keeping with his character to examine realistically this poetic talent he was so carefully and diligently nourishing and to find it inadequate to the task of describing the battles, wars, and violent deaths that any epic account of the Round Table would necessarily portray. Hanford has found in "Epitaphium Damonis" evidence of Milton's awareness "of the inadequacy of his style, hitherto used only to the simpler themes of pastoral";[20] and for a man who had hardly given a passing thought to the subject of war, who had wandered across ravaged Europe without so much as a glance at the conflict then tearing Christendom apart, to sing of arms and the man may have seemed a formidable task indeed.

In 1640, then, the time was not ripe, nor the poet ready, for an epic poem in the martial tradition. By the end of the decade, as we shall see, the image of a warlike English race had been restored and the poet himself was prepared for such a work. He did not,

18. In *Areopagitica*, *YP*, 2:558.
19. "Milton and the Art of War."
20. *A Milton Handbook*, p. 179.

however, return to his youthful ambition, and the reasons may be found, in part at least, in the quality of the experience of the intervening years, when he was to see the true shape of war and to realize that Arthur was but a fanciful legend, not worthy of his art. He passed on to a grander and more tragic theme in which that martial tradition would shape but a part of the vaster canvas of his art. This question of his choice of subject is of such interest, and so close to the heart of our inquiry, that we shall return to it in later pages;[21] but to appreciate that decision fully, it is first necessary to consider the effect of those years of conflict upon the sensibility of the poet, to examine what kind of war it was he lived through and how much he knew of it.

Milton returned from his idyll on the Continent to an England very different from the one he had left. The country was astir with new hopes and new fears. After his defeat in the First Bishops War, King Charles had to endure further humiliations; he was forced to call the Short Parliament in order to pay for the campaign. That body, the first to sit in eleven years, quickly proved recalcitrant and was as quickly dismissed. The Second Bishops War was a comparable disaster, and in November 1640 Charles convened the Long Parliament, precipitating a constitutional crisis that within two short years would find hostile armies of Englishmen facing each other on a field so close to London that the sound of cannon could be heard in the heart of the city.

Milton moved to London hoping to pursue the quiet life of a scholar, poet, and teacher; and he was less than happy with the "civil broils" that had cut short his Mediterranean idyll and now threatened the serenity and seclusion so necessary to his plans. Some years later in a letter to Carlo Dati, he complained that soon after he returned home he had been obliged

> to turn my mind from my studies to protecting life and property in any way I could. Do you think there can be any safe retreat for literary leisure among so many civil battles, so much slaughter, flight, and pillage of goods?[22]

The city became the scene of mounting turmoil and violence as the forces unleashed by the constitutional and religious conflicts between the Long Parliament and the monarchy propelled the nation toward civil war. In May 1640 the apprentices rioted in London,

21. See below, pp. 91–99.
22. *YP*, 2:764, written in April 1647.

demonstrating against Archbishop Laud. A year later, ten thousand citizens marched to Westminster, demanding a bill of attainder against Strafford; and the city was in arms as the rumor spread that Charles was bringing in a French army. In December 1641 there were further demonstrations, this time against the bishops. When the king attempted to arrest the five members on 4 January 1642, the city was again in arms as the Trained Bands were called out, gates were shut, portcullises let down, and chains stretched across the streets. At the end of the month another mob of fifteen thousand marched on Westminster in protest.[23] Indeed, what "safe retreat for literary leisure" could Milton expect to find in all this tumult? There is no evidence that he participated in any of these demonstrations but he obviously found it impossible to remain indifferent to events. He joined the pamphlet war raging over the structure of the English church and from May 1641 to May 1642 published five tracts attacking the power of the bishops.

Given these seemingly intractable divisions and the militancy of the time, one might expect such documents to contain a liberal sprinkling of images of armed conflict. But there are, in fact, very few. Of course, one cannot place too much weight on numbers alone, but some insight into the imagination of the poet may be gained by noting how often it occurs to him to express his thoughts in military terms and by observing how extensive such references are. For the Milton of 1641–1642 these allusions are weak and scattered.

In *Of Reformation* the poet is discussing a subject that had embroiled Europe in over twenty years of war and set hundreds of thousands of armed men on the march. Yet this work, probably the most vigorous of the antiprelatical tracts and at times a grim forewarning of civil war, remains singularly unmartial in its imagery. The figures are there, but only briefly, and for the most part they embellish pejorative references to the church. The communion table Milton describes as "fortified with bulwark, and barricado, to keep off the profane touch of the Laicks,"[24] and he refers in later pages to "the painted Battlements, and gaudy rottennesse of Prelatrie."[25] In discussing the church-state relationship he ques-

23. See Valerie Pearl, *London and the Outbreak of the Puritan Revolution*, pp. 108–228; and Brian Manning, *The English People and the English Revolution, 1640–1649*, pp. 1–98. Both are vivid and exhaustively thorough accounts of the prewar period. Crowd sizes are variously reported.

24. *YP*, 1:543.

25. *YP*, 1:583.

tions the church's assumption of authority outside its rightful sphere—"Where doth it intrench upon the temporal governor, where does it come in his walk?"[26]—and he accuses the prelates of weakening the monarchy, of opposing and laying "battery to regal safety."[27] While these tracts need not delay us further, they do illustrate one aspect of the poet's developing art. When the relative paucity of these figures in the tracts of 1641–1642 is contrasted with the number and vigor of military images that mark Milton's works from 1643 on,[28] one must conclude that something happened during the intervening years to stir the imagination of the poet and enhance his skill with martial narrative. One must not discount other influences, of course, but it cannot escape notice that these were the initial years of the First English Civil War.

* * *

John Milton's experience with military men and events falls generally into two periods. The first of these was during the civil wars, when as a citizen of London closely identified with the Puritan cause, he shared the changing fortunes of that city while the fighting raged through its outskirts and neighboring counties. The second was an experience of a very different character, when as a servant of the government he was part of an executive body directing military operations that ranged from the Mediterranean to the West Indies, and across Europe from the Baltic Sea to the sands of Dunkirk and the harbors of Spain. The earlier experience was influential in the development of his creative imagination not only because it was his first encounter with war but also because it was the more immediate and personal. This student, scholar, and teacher, who had lent the weight of his learning to the war of words against the bishops, found that the angry exchange over the issue led to divisions within society that could no longer be resolved by words. On an August day in 1642 Charles I raised the

26. *YP*, 1:575–76.
27. *YP*, 1:588.
28. *Of Prelaticall Episcopacy*, for example, has only four military images or references to war: *YP*, 1:627, 643, 650, and 651; and the first is the only one at all developed. The longer and more vigorous *Animadversions* has less than ten, and *The Reason of Church Government* no more than six. *An Apology Against a Pamphlet*, his last tract, published in April 1642, is more martial with over a dozen figures, reflecting perhaps the burning question of that spring, the militia bill. The focus of the controversy between King and Parliament had shifted to a struggle for control of the military, and armies were forming in the land.

royal banner at Nottingham, and from that moment the scene of conflict over abstract political and religious issues shifted from the halls of Westminster and the London press, where Milton's learned talents could play their part, to the field of battle, an arena alien to him. The pen gave way to the sword and for almost two years the citizens of London lay under the threat of armed assault.

It is important in our inquiry to gain an appreciation for the quality of those years, but of course it is possible to give here only a slim perception of the anxieties of a besieged city some three centuries ago. The most familiar parallel in modern history is perhaps the summer of 1940, when the air war raged over London and England prepared for a German invasion; but the seventeenth century dealt more harshly with stubborn cities that fell after rejecting quarter, the brutal sack of Magdeburg during the Thirty Years War being perhaps the most infamous example. Utter ruin threatened—burning, pillage, murder, and rape at the hands of a ruthless soldiery, their inflamed instincts unleashed upon a helpless populace; and many towns in England and Ireland suffered this fate in the decade of conflict that followed the King's dramatic gesture in the summer of 1642.

The first major battle of the civil wars was at Edgehill, where in late October two hastily organized and ill-trained armies fumbled to a draw. After the battle Charles advanced to Turnham Green, an hour's march from Westminster, there to be confronted by the Trained Bands in full array. An incident on that march brought home vividly to the citizens of London the dangers that threatened them. The King's advance brought him to Brentford, a small town on the Thames situated just west of the Green. Rupert was ordered to occupy the town; and so on 12 November he threw his forces against its defenders, two regiments from Essex's army, one of which, commanded by Denzil Holles, had been recruited in London itself. By the time Essex could send reinforcements, Holles's Londoners had been overwhelmed, many of them drowning in the river in their effort to escape Rupert's onslaught. Indeed, the regiment was so badly shattered that it was never reformed; and Holles, his brief career as a soldier of Parliament at an end, resumed his seat in Commons, where not surprisingly he became the chief spokesman for the peace party. Commanders in this age avoided battle in built-up areas, where they could expect to lose the rather tenuous control they exercised over their troops, which depended almost entirely on visual contact. Something of this nature ensued, for after the battle Rupert's troops raged out of hand in burning and sacking a town whose citizens, ironically, had expressed a strong loyalty to the King. The surviving Londoners of Holles's regiment straggled back to their homes, where they could give harsh testimony to the fate of cities that came under the Royalist sword.

The King was forced to retire from Turnham Green without a battle. He withdrew westward to consolidate his strength and evolve a plan of action, but he left behind a city grimly aware of the consequences of defeat. For the next year and a half that threat hung over the streets of London. The year 1643 saw a string of Royalist successes, as the King's armies slowly drew a ring of iron about the city. Prince Rupert took Newport-Pagnell to the north, Arundel Castle surrendered to Sir Ralph Hopton in the south, and in the center Charles occupied Reading, as the Parliamentary forces floundered under divided command. As it turned out, this proved the crest of the Royalist wave, for in January 1644 Scotland entered the war against the King and by May all his armies had been checked or thrown back. On 2 July the stunning Parliamentary victory at Marston Moor turned the war about, and by winter battle had receded from the walls of London, thenceforth to be fought on fields more distant.

The London of that first year and a half, when the Royalist cause was on the rise, is of most interest to our study, for during these months Milton had his first and most personal experience with the shape of war. He wrote very little in direct reference to events, but as we shall see, his tracts of 1644 were heavily influenced by the experience and his great works bear the mark of that time. We can perhaps gain some understanding of his response to those months by examining how the war touched London citizens of his social class and ideological commitment. The city was never, in fact, the scene of battle, nor did it come under siege or bombardment, though, as we have seen, during 1643 Londoners were never free of the fear that they would suffer the fate of Brentford. As it turned out, Turnham Green, some seven miles distant, was as close as any Royalist force came; and after that confrontation Londoners learned of the war by reading of it in broadsides, hearing of battles from returning veterans, caring for wounded, comforting families of the slain, or watching armies pass through the streets, crowned with triumph or straggling back from defeat. Soldiers were not quartered in the city; not until December 1648, when the New Model Army marched into London, would it experience what might be called an occupation. A military presence was felt chiefly through the regiments of the Trained Bands; and those who did not join the ranks contributed to the war by paying their taxes, by surrendering property, chiefly horses and weapons, to requisition, and for a time in 1643 by assisting in the construction of city fortifications. This is not to say that London was free of violence, but it took the form primarily of mob action, both before the war and during the counterrevolution of 1647–1648.

The Trained Bands of England could only very loosely be called "trained."[29] These antecedents of the Home Guard, or the National Guard in the United States, were composed largely of middle-class citizens, tradesmen, and "gentlemen," who in peacetime gathered periodically in the many artillery gardens of the kingdom (four in the area of London: at Finsbury Fields; St. Martin's in the Fields; St. Ann's, Westminster; and Horsedown, Southwark) where they practiced archery or, more frequently in the seventeenth century, drilled with the clumsy musket and pike.[30] They did not see themselves as a national reserve by any means, for their allegiance seldom reached beyond the borders of their own borough or county. Members took time off from their trades and professions to "exercise in the martial arts" and to raise a glass or two, as the meetings seem to have served as much a social as a military purpose. The Bands of London were a weak reed, certainly, for any cause to lean on; but it was these units that tipped the balance in favor of the city and the Parliamentary cause during the critical first year and a half of the war.

The London Trained Bands were superior in training and organization to others in the kingdom largely because they were fortunate in their corps of officers, who were drawn from a unit unique in English military history, the Honourable Artillery Company (HAC). Chartered by Henry VIII in 1537, this unit remains an ac-

29. For the material on the Trained Bands I am indebted chiefly to Pearl and Manning, for that on the HAC to two older works: G. A. Raikes, *The History of the Honourable Artillery Company*, and the more recent G. Goold Walker, *The Honourable Artillery Company, 1537–1947*. I am also indebted to the courtesy of L. T. C. Massey, secretary of the HAC until 1979, who offered access to the archives of the company and at one point showed me, with appropriate white-gloved ceremony, the *Great Vellum Book*.

30. The word *artillerie* in the seventeenth century referred to any weapon that discharged a missile, from the bow to the cannon. The Trained Bands were all infantry or cavalry units.

tive member in the Territorial Reserves to this day and thus has the distinction of being the senior volunteer unit in the English army. It was small in Milton's time, numbering perhaps five hundred at the outbreak of the war, and composed only of "gentlemen of means."[31] Its members were considerably more conscientious about their military exercises than their counterparts elsewhere in the country, drilling regularly in the Artillery Garden, first at Spital Field and after 1641 at Finsbury Fields, their headquarters to this day. The Garden, then, was a ten-minute walk from Milton's home in Aldersgate Street and even closer to Barbican, where he moved when the Powells extended his household, and, indeed, directly across the street from his last residence on Artillery Walk in Bunhill Fields. The company conducted weekly parades during the summer months and held several "General Days" throughout the year, which involved extended maneuvers in the city streets ending in a mock pitched battle at the Garden.[32] Members served as honor guards for the lord mayor and were generally in evidence at most city processions and ceremonies. The unit became increasingly important as war threatened, so much so that Charles I, in June 1641, saw fit to march the Prince of Wales, then eleven, and his younger brother, James, into the Artillery Garden and enroll them in the company.[33]

The importance of this unit arose from two factors, one military, the other political. As has been noted, members provided the officer cadre for the Trained Bands. In the six regular city regiments, for example, four of the colonels, five of the lieutenant-colonels, all of the "serjants-major" (then an officer rank, comparable to the modern major), and twenty-six of the twenty-eight captains were members of the company.[34] Philip Skippon, then

31. Walker, *HAC*, p. 30.

32. One, which took place on 2 May 1665, is described in some detail in Raikes, *History of the HAC*, 1:171–79. See also Walker, *HAC*, pp. 79–81.

33. They are listed, along with Prince Charles Frederick, Count of Palatine, in the *Great Vellum Book* under the date 1 June 1641. Further reference to this volume will be from G. A. Raikes's edition, *The Ancient Vellum Book of the Honourable Artillery Company*. The book lists all members who joined from 1611 to 1682.

34. These figures are arrived at by comparing names in the *Vellum Book* with those appearing on a contemporary broadside, "The Names, Dignities and Places of All the Collonells, Lieutenant-Collonels, Serjant Majors, Captaines, Quartermasters, Lieutenants and Ensignes of the City of London: With the Captaines Names according to their Seniority and places. London. Printed for Richard Thrale, 1642. By W. B. [certainly William Barriffe]." BM 669. f. 6. (10). John Melton (the other one) is listed as quartermaster in Pennington's regiment. Names

"captain-leader" of the HAC, was appointed commander of the Trained Bands in 1641 and continued to fill both positions for many years thereafter. In brief, the defense of the city depended almost entirely upon the skill and training of the "Gentlemen of the Artillery Garden."[35] The company was also immensely important in the political life of London. From 1635 to 1640, the lord mayor was chosen from its ranks, and the membership included numerous aldermen, sheriffs, and other city officials.[36] Of equal interest is the fact that the company became a center of Puritan sentiment in the city, including as members such Parliamentary Puritans as John Towse, John Wollaston, lord mayor after October 1643, and at least one regicide, Owen Rowe. When the city Parliamentary Puritans assumed control of the Trained Bands in January 1642, members of the company filled the all-important Militia Committee, and the unit became solidly identified with the cause against the King.[37]

Whatever direct experience Milton had of the war arose chiefly from his observation of or association with members of these Trained Bands. Until the late 1630s they were not much in evidence in London, there being little need for the four small regiments of the city; but after the King's aborted effort to arrest the five members on 4 January 1642, the Common Council ordered that the force be expanded to nine regiments, six from the city and three from the suburbs. In September six additional regiments were raised, so that by November Philip Skippon could lead a force of eighteen thousand men to join Essex at Turnham Green. For the next two years these units were extensively involved in the campaigns about London. In March 1643 two regiments were on active service while one manned the city outguards, in July they

---

appearing on a later broadside indicate that casualties were replaced by members of the HAC: "The Ensignes of the Regiments in the Rebellious Citty of London, both of Trayned Bands and Auxilliaries; together with the nearest number of their Trayned Soldiers, taken as they marched into Finsbury Feilds, being their last General Muster, Tuesday, Sept 26th, 1643," Guildhall Library, London, A. 6. 5. no. 6 in 14. The latter is in Raikes, *History of the HAC*, 1:136–39. Both are cited in Masson, *Life*, 2:446–47.

35. The HAC was referred to in a number of colorful ways, with "The Military Gentlemen of London," "The Ancient and Worthy Society exercising Armes in the Artillery Garden," and "The Societie of Armes, Cittizens of London" among them. See Walker, *HAC*, p. 24.

36. Raikes, *Vellum Book*, pp. 2–3.

37. Pearl, *Puritan Revolution*, pp. 170–73. An important exception was Isaac Pennington, colonel of the second, or "White," regiment of the Trained Bands, lord mayor from August 1642 to October 1643, and a leading Parliamentary Puritan.

helped put down the rising in Kent, and in August six regiments marched with Essex to the relief of Gloucester, participating with distinction in the First Battle of Newbury on the way home. In October seven regiments marched north, again with Essex, to block Rupert's effort to encircle the city, while two more joined Waller to turn back the attack in the south. In March 1644 they fought at Cheriton, where Waller finally ended Hopton's threat in the south; and in the fall six regiments joined Manchester's army at the Second Battle of Newbury. After 1644, however, the war receded from London, and, with the organization of the New Model Army, the city regiments were little used. Indeed, the HAC itself languished, to be revived in 1656. During the early months of the war, however, when the Parliamentary cause hung in the balance, these householders, merchants, craftsmen, and apprentices marched many miles from their homes and spent long months in the field in defense of their city.

While the Trained Bands were active on more distant fields, at home the citizens of London were occupied in a truly extraordinary effort. In early 1643 the cavalry of Prince Rupert, which he had quickly formed into a highly effective unit of dashing, though somewhat undisciplined, young Cavaliers, began to make damaging raids to the west and north of London. The Common Council took alarm and in March prescribed measures to protect the city, among them a directive that the entire area of London and Westminster be ringed with fortifications. Thus began six months of intense effort in which it would appear that at times the entire population participated. By May, according to the Venetian ambassador, an authoritative and relatively unbiased source, twenty thousand citizens were working daily on the project without pay. The Trained Bands were mobilized to assist, and there is a report that the clerks and gentlemen of the Inns of Court lent a hand. Whole families were involved and even the nobility did its part, the latter, we must assume, less to turn a shovel than to demonstrate moral support. In the fall William Lithgow, a visiting Scot, published a report, *The Present Surveigh of London and England's State*, in which he gave a detailed account of a walk around the entire circuit of the fortifications, which when complete included eighteen miles of trenches and twenty-four main forts.[38] These trenches were never tested and there is no evidence

38. Norman G. Brett-James, "The Fortifications of London in 1642/3." The full title of the report is *The Present Surveigh of London and England's State; con-*

of how heavily they weighed in the deliberations of Royalist leaders as they tightened the ring about the city; but the very extent of the enterprise gives some measure of the siege mentality of Londoners and of the sense of sacrifice and common purpose that seems to have inspired the citizens at the time.

This glow of hope and common purpose, however, was cast in shadow by the consistently dismal news of defeats of the regular Parliamentary forces about London and by the spectacle of discord and wrangling among their military leaders. The year following Turnham Green was a grim one for Londoners. In the spring of 1643 Rupert took Birmingham and Lichfield in the north and then returned south to throw his cavalry around the plodding Essex. In June, his sharp success at Chalgrove Field and the plundering of Wycombe filled the city with alarm; he could, it seemed, range the countryside with impunity. Essex returned in panic to the city. In July the remnants of Waller's army, which according to Gardiner had been "for all practical purposes annihilated" at Roundway Down, straggled back to London.[39] Hopes revived briefly when Essex marched off to the relief of Gloucester in August, but after the drawn battle at Newbury the King followed him closely on his retreat to London and in early October occupied Reading, a scant thirty miles from the city.

Many of these defeats were caused by the inability of Parliamentary commanders to coordinate their efforts. In the very person of Charles I, the Royalists enjoyed an immense advantage during those early months, for he with his immediate advisors gave them at least a semblance of unified command. In contrast, the Parliamentary cause suffered from deep divisions, both at Westminster and in its armies. The war effort was being directed by the House of Commons, a deliberative body composed of men with widely differing views as to war aims and the vigor with which they should be pursued. On the one hand, there was a peace party confident that an accommodation could be reached with the King without further bloodshed. On the other, a war party, led by the fiery Henry Marten, was determined to pursue the war to a total military defeat of the King's forces.[40] A large, undecided middle

---

taining a Typographical Description of all the Particular Forts, Redoubts, Brestworks and Trenches newly erected round about the Citie, on both sides of the River, with the several Fortifications thereof. By William Lithgow, London, 1643.

39. Samuel R. Gardiner, *History of the Great Civil War, 1642–1649,* 1:174.

40. Marten's turbulent career has been described recently by C. M. Williams in "The Anatomy of a Radical Gentleman: Henry Marten."

group was swayed, sometimes this way, sometimes that, by the force of eloquence and the pressure of events. The leading figure in Parliament until his death in December 1643 was John Pym, who with rare skill managed to steer a middle course and slowly build the alliances that would eventually attain the victory.[41] There were times, however, when Parliament's war effort resembled a campaign conducted by a debating society.

Further division arose from the nature of the Parliamentary army. Early in the war Parliament clustered contiguous counties into a number of "Associations" to facilitate the recruiting and organization of its forces, and appointed commanders to each of the armies thus formed, chief among them the Eastern under the Earl of Manchester, the Northern under Lord Fairfax, and the Southern under Sir William Waller. All were officially under the nominal command of the Earl of Essex, who was designated lord general by Parliament and commanded yet another army in the London area. The various association commanders were to receive their commissions from Essex's hand and were directed to act subject to his orders, but in practice this directive was little observed. Essex commanded the troops under him, those which Parliament had authorized him to raise; but as Gardiner observes,

> it was only in name that he was a general over the other armies of Parliament. Each separate force, supported by local resources, and controlled by local commanders, set his authority at nought on the rare occasions when he attempted to exercise it.[42]

Eventually, of course, if the King was to be defeated, something would have to be done about this lack of unity; but the Parliament was after all a lawmaking body, ill designed to conduct military campaigns, and it was forced to undergo a series of crises before arriving at a final solution. The first of these, in the summer of 1643, directly involved the city of London. The Royalist successes in the spring had immobilized Essex and unnerved the members at Westminster. In their alarm they turned on the man whom they considered the cause of the defeats, the lord general himself. Why, they asked, did he not do something? A story was circulated among the more radical members that his lack of industry was prompted by hidden Royalist sympathies; actually, one need not look far to discover more practical reasons for Essex's inaction.

41. See J. H. Hexter, *The Reign of King Pym.*
42. *Civil War,* 1:134.

Half his army was sick, unable to move had they wanted to, and those who were sound had neither arms nor proper clothing and had not been paid for months. Promises of funds and supplies from Parliament had produced nothing, and news of better conditions and pay in the various association armies had prompted a rash of desertions, which went largely unpunished. By July, Essex had only three thousand foot and twenty-five hundred horse effective for use against the much larger forces of the King.[43] The support Parliament had given to the other armies and the apparent lack of interest they showed to the needs of the lord general had reduced his forces to this helpless condition. And the members who sat at Westminster simply could not understand this! J. H. Hexter describes the attitude of the ordinary legislator:

> The low and sordid problems of military supply did not fascinate the average Parliament man. He might admit that the Lord General's army frequently had no shoes to march on, no food to eat, no clothes to wear, and no guns to shoot; but he did not therefore conclude that a naked, starving, unarmed force faced slaughter if exposed to the onset of Rupert's fast-riding cavalry. It was unfortunate, too, that pestilence scourged the ranks of the army and that some of the soldiers, discovering that one engaged in war with hazard of life and limb, tended to slip away when battle seemed imminent. This was indeed too bad; but admitting all of it from a well-warmed seat in the House of Commons, the fact remained that Essex had won no battles, and after all what was a lord general for but to win battles.[44]

Even the experienced Pym, in a moment of haste during the disastrous final days of June, addressed a letter of censure to Essex, criticizing his inactivity. That loyal but impolitic general chose this most inopportune of moments to recommend to Commons that peace negotiations be opened anew with the King. The reaction was immediate, and violent. The fiery spirits of the war party cried out now for the dismissal of Essex and the appointment of a more warlike lord general. In the political battle that ensued, Henry Marten came up against the stern figure of Pym, who, having returned to his senses, realized that Essex, inadequate as he was, was the only man acceptable to the bulk of the members; and Pym set out to defend the lord general in order to preserve the faint degree of unity that remained in the army.

43. Ibid., 1:182.
44. *Pym*, pp. 108–9.

In the crisis many of the middle group were swayed by Marten's eloquence, and there arose a great cry for the appointment of the popular Sir William Waller as lord general. Waller, a fine soldier, had been the most successful of the Parliamentary generals, and his attitude toward the war was thought to be more in line with the sentiments of the war party. His defeat at Roundway Down on 11 July, however, dulled somewhat the gleam of his armor, and an unexpected display of loyalty from Essex's officers doomed the plan. The distraught Parliament, having declared itself unwilling to live with Essex, found that it could not live without him and continued to thrash about in search of an alternate means of salvation. Blind to the fact that the multiplicity of armies was the very source of its difficulties, it authorized the creation of yet another. Upon the demand of the London Common Council, Parliament gave the city authority to place all troops raised within its limits under the control of its own militia commanders. And yet another was proposed! In the city a Committee for the General Rising convened, entirely independent of the council, and demanded that a new army of ten thousand men be formed to revive the cause. Neither of these forces was to be under the command of Essex, who was being haughtily ignored during the dispute. When at the height of the controversy he requested instructions from the Parliament under whose authority he served, he was told curtly to do as he pleased.[45] All of this was obviously the work of Waller's supporters; having failed in Parliament to make him lord general, they were now attempting to organize an army for him that would rival Essex's. Quite independently, both the London Council and the Committee for the General Rising designated the popular general to command their proposed forces. It was at this point that Pym returned to the debate.

During the last weeks of July the country witnessed a sorry spectacle. While the King's armies tightened the ring about London and Rupert's cavalry cut like a scythe through the country about the city, Parliament was torn by a struggle between two political leaders, each supporting a different general and a different army. The war effort ground to a halt while Marten and Pym fought it out; and it was fortunate for the cause that the struggle was so brief. Pym's prestige and superior tactical skill won, and on 1 August, Commons passed a resolution establishing a Council of

45. Ibid., p. 124.

War, which Pym was to dominate, authorized the raising of an additional four thousand foot and five hundred horse for Essex, and voted that he and not Waller would lead the troops in the fall campaigns. By the end of August, Marten was in the Tower, a victim of Pym's swift retribution, and Essex was marching west at the head of fifteen thousand men to raise the siege of Gloucester.

This resolution by no means ended the divisions in the armies of Parliament, for the crisis of 1643 was but the first of a series that drained the energies of its forces and prolonged the threat to the safety of London. The reversals continued; Gardiner's comment on conditions a year later, after Waller's defeat at Cropredy Bridge in June 1644, is certainly revealing:

> Yet so superior was the composition of [the Royalist] army to that of Waller, and so hopelessly were the councils of the Parliamentary Generals in the South divided, that, unless disastrous news arrived from the North, the Royal army could hardly fail to get the upper hand in the regions in which Charles himself was fighting [the area around London].[46]

Fortunately for Parliament, that "disastrous news" did arrive; the report of the Battle of Marston Moor reached London the following month, and with it word of the sharply rising star of Oliver Cromwell.

Some appreciation for the effect of these events on John Milton can be formed from the evidence of his early biographers and from his own words. The Milton family suffered from the tragic divisions and dislocations that mark such civil conflicts in any age. His wife, the daughter of an Oxford gentleman of definite Royalist sentiments, returned to her home in the summer of 1642 after a month of marriage. When Charles I raised the royal standard in August, the war that gesture initiated reached into the quiet chambers at Aldersgate Street with dramatic effect, for Oxford became the King's headquarters and Mary Powell remained there for the next three years. The Royalist advance in 1643 forced Milton's father to join his son in the city; and early in the conflict it became apparent that Christopher Milton, the poet's brother, would identify himself with the King's cause. Brothers divided, husband and wife separated, father dislocated—even if Milton had been so inclined he could not have escaped the war.

There is little to indicate that he was so inclined. Aside from his

46. *Civil War*, 1:363.

retrospective complaint to Carlo Dati some years later, everything we know points to a passionate concern for the Puritan cause. His antiprelatical tracts had identified him publicly with Parliament, and both his political and his religious convictions mark him as fully sympathetic with the city Puritans who seized power in London in 1642. As one who had chosen not to join the ranks,[47] he continued his teaching and studies, his principal achievement during these years being that curious body of prose, the Divorce Tracts. He was certainly less of a scholarly recluse than in the Horton days. That he moved about in society and remained in touch with events can be seen in his sonnets to the unnamed "Lady that in the prime of earliest youth" and to Lady Margaret Ley, and by Edward Phillips's intriguing comment about the "design of Marrying one of Dr. Davis's Daughters." He was well respected and apparently blessed with friends deeply concerned with his welfare, friends, for example, who made those extraordinary efforts to effect a reconciliation with Mary Powell in 1645. They must have known him very well to stage that little scene at Blackborough's.[48] In brief, it is safe to assume the image of a dedicated teacher and scholar hard at work, but one who moved freely in a circle that looked upon him with respect and affection, a man deeply concerned with the course of the war and both intellectually and emotionally committed to the Puritan cause.

Indeed, no citizen of London could have escaped the effects of the conflict, especially during those early months when the city was virtually under siege. The signs of war were everywhere—the drilling of the Trained Bands, the hasty mustering of regiments to march out in response to Royalist attacks, the constant flow of bad news, the shattered armies straggling through the streets, the crisis in command during the summer of 1643, and that astonishing effort to fortify the city. There were at least two total mobilizations of the city forces, one before Turnham Green in November

47. Masson (*Life*, 2:402, 473) suggests that Milton participated in military drill, drawing on a passage in *An Apology Against a Pamphlet* (*YP*, 1:886). This interpretation has been generally rejected, and with good reason. Years later, in *Defensio Secunda*, the poet remarked, "I did not avoid the toils and dangers of military service without rendering to my fellow citizens another kind of service that was much more useful and no less perilous" (*YP*, 4:552). He was defending himself against "the charge of timidity or cowardice" in *Regii Sanguinis Clamor*, where he was described as "weak," "bloodless," and "shrivelled" (*YP*, 4:1045). If he had performed any military service at all, we can be assured that he would have said so.

48. *The Early Lives of John Milton*, ed. Helen Darbishire, pp. 66–67.

1642 and another on a more joyful occasion when the Trained Bands turned out on 26 September 1643 to greet the regiments returning with Essex from the successful relief of Gloucester. There were probably others on critical occasions, such as the day Rupert's cavalry plundered Wycombe in June 1643, when, as Gardiner observes, "from all parts men ran hastily to their posts on the line of defence."[49] Aldersgate Street itself was a scene of activity. It was the designated "allarum place" for units of Wollaston's regiment, which formed "by Long Lane end," but a few steps from Milton's door;[50] and in the September 1643 muster it was the assembly point for the Hamlets Regiment.[51] It can only be assumed that the poet responded to these events with the same interest as any London citizen committed to the fortunes of Parliament.

History records at least one close association between Milton and the city Trained Bands, his friendship with John Hobson, whose wife, Lady Margaret Ley, was the subject of the poet's sonnet. Hobson was a neighbor in Aldersgate Street and an officer in the Westminster Regiment. He joined that unit and trained with it at the Artillery Garden in St. Martin's in the Fields rather than enlist in one of the city regiments, for reasons not difficult to determine. The officers of the city regiments were, almost to a man, chosen from the Honourable Artillery Company, and Hobson was not a member. Moreover, he was somewhat older than most officers, forty-five at the opening of the war, and already held the rank of captain in the Trained Bands of the Isle of Wight, his home before moving to London; and thus may not have been entirely welcome in the somewhat exclusive HAC. At any rate, by 1644 he had risen to the rank of lieutenant-colonel of the regiment and had served in a number of campaigns, chiefly with the army of Sir William Waller in the south. He was in the siege of Basing House

49 *Civil War*, 1:156.

50. "September 29, 1642. The Persons to whom the Militia of the Citie of London is Committed, for saftie of the said Citie, have thought fit, and hereby Declare." BM 669. f. 6. (79). The other John Milton was a captain in this unit. In March 1644 he was wounded and taken prisoner at the battle of Cheriton. See John Adair, *Cheriton, 1644: The Campaign and the Battle*, p. 194. One wonders if their paths ever crossed during such musters.

51. "The Manner of the March and Embattelling of the Trayned Bands and Auxiliaries of the City of London, Hamlets, Westminster men, and the Burrow of Southwarke, as it was appointed by the Honourable Committee of the Militia; and performed on Tuesday the 26. of September 1643. London Printed, 1643." BM 102. a. 14.

in November 1643, the battle of Alton the following month, and may well have been at Second Newbury in November 1644, where his colonel, Sir James Harrington, commanded the City Brigade. Milton obviously visited his home with some frequency, and one need not stretch the imagination to reconstruct the conversation on those occasions when his friend had freshly returned from the field. From men like Hobson, Milton kept abreast of the course of the war, the controversies of command, the state of the armies, the problems of supply, and the defeats or infrequent victories of the Parliamentary armies.[52]

Milton's practical experience with military units probably extended no further than that of an interested observer of the musters and drills that were an ever-present part of London life at the time. His house was, as has been noted, a few minutes from the Artillery Garden, where the Trained Bands practiced their marvelously complex maneuvers (the firing of the musket alone involved fifty-one separate and distinct commands). His familiarity with the drill is perhaps best reflected in an extended image from *The Tenure of Kings and Magistrates*, where he characterizes the ministers' rhetorical circumlocutions in these terms:

> For Divines, if ye observe them, have thir postures, and thir motions no less expertly, and with no less variety then they that practice feats in the Artillery-ground. Sometimes they seem furiously to march on, and presently march counter; by and by they stand, and then retreat; or if need be can face about, or wheele in a whole body, with that cunning and dexterity as is almost unperceavable; to winde themselves by shifting ground into places of more advantage. . . . At thir turnes and doublings no men readier; to the right, or to the left; for it is thir turnes which they serve cheifly.[53]

His familiarity with the Honourable Artillery Company can only be a matter of conjecture, the suggestion that he was a member having finally been laid to rest.[54] Something may be said for his association with members of the unit, however, as it was the heart and soul of the city's defenses and the Garden was the focus of its

52. David Masson, *The Quarrel between the Earl of Manchester and Oliver Cromwell* (1875), pp. 47–48; and John S. Smart, *The Sonnets of Milton*, pp. 159–61. Christopher Whichcott's regiment of "Green Auxiliaries" also served in the fall campaign of 1643. It was recruited around Cripplegate and may have had members of Milton's acquaintance (Adair, *Cheriton*, p. 27).

53. *YP*, 3:255.

54. See Fallon, "John Milton and the Honourable Artillery Company," pp. 49–51.

activities as well as "a prominent center of the secular activities of the Puritans," as Valerie Pearl remarks.[55] The HAC was composed of men of Milton's social class and political and religious persuasion; and among its members, listed in the *Vellum Book*, appear the names of many of his neighbors in Aldersgate Street.[56] Bread Street Ward, where Milton spent his youth and held property until after the Restoration, was a stronghold of Puritan sentiment, second only in importance perhaps to Coleman Street Ward, where the impassioned John Goodwin preached from the pulpit of St. Stephens. Bread Street was also the home of Sir John Venn, who as a younger contemporary of Milton's father and fellow parishioner at All Hallows Church was surely known to the family. Venn, a successful "silkman" by trade, joined the HAC in early 1614, was nominated for the position of captain-leader in 1631, appointed captain-serjant-major in 1636, and elected vice-president of the company in 1639. Milton would have seen little of Venn after his father moved from Bread Street, or indeed during the war, when from 1642 to 1645 Venn was governor of Windsor Castle, but it is through such men that the poet would have been familiar with the HAC from his youth.[57]

There is one further suggestion of a linkage between Milton and the HAC, which, since it bears directly on the poet's art, deserves consideration here. Many years ago, James Holly Hanford drew attention to Milton's knowledge of a book by his contemporary Robert Ward entitled *Animadversions of Warre*, citing an entry from the work in the *Commonplace Book*. Hanford suggested that Milton gained the familiarity with military formations he demonstrates in *Paradise Lost* from Ward's book; and he cited as evidence such passages as "Half wheeling to the Shield, half to the Spear" (4.785) and "th' Angelic Squadron bright / Turnd fierie

55. *Puritan Revolution*, p. 170.

56. This can be determined by comparing Raikes, *Vellum Book*, which is indexed, with T. C. Dale, *The Inhabitants of London in 1638. Edited from MS 272 in the Lambeth Palace Library*. A survey of St. Botolph Without Aldersgate, Milton's parish (pp. 201–6), reveals over fifty names that appear on both lists. There is certainly no assurance that identical names mean identical persons, but a generous percentage can be assumed. Unfortunately, the list for St. Giles Without Cripplegate (pp. 236–39), which occupied the east side of Aldersgate Street, includes only a few names, among them, however, the Earl of Bridgewater; but a comparable number would probably be found in that parish, which included the Artillery Garden within its boundaries, and to which Milton moved in 1645. All Hallows, Bread Street (p. 9) contains neither names nor residences.

57. "Venn, Sir John," *DNB* (1896). See also Pearl, *Puritan Revolution*, pp. 187–89.

red, sharpning in mooned hornes" (4.977–78), among others, all maneuvers that Ward describes as in common usage at the time.[58]

Another book of drill more widely used at the time, however, was *Militarie Discipline: or the yong artillery man*, by William Barriffe, who joined the HAC in 1635 and eventually rose to the rank of lieutenant-colonel in the Trained Bands before his death in the summer of 1643.[59] This work, which went through three editions during Barriffe's lifetime and three more by 1661, was a practical drill manual used extensively by both Puritan and Royalist armies in the war. Several factors suggest that Milton's surprisingly detailed knowledge of military exercises may have come, not from reading Ward, but from personal observation, with the aid perhaps of Barriffe's book. First, speaking realistically, anyone who has been called upon to actually read a manual of drill will agree that it does not lend itself to abstract contemplation. To study it without actual participation in or observation of the maneuvers described is an exercise in futility for even the most acute of minds. Aside from the fact that it makes the dullest reading imaginable, it is virtually unintelligible to those inexperienced in the formations. Since seventeenth-century movements were far more intricate and involved than any today, I believe that Milton had to see the exercises and study them at the time in order to be able to recall them, twenty years later, with the degree of accuracy that Hanford demonstrates; and it is not too fanciful to suggest that he did so with Barriffe's book in hand: Ward's work is a massive folio, fit only for the study table, while Barriffe's is a handbook of quarto size, designed to be carried and referred to by officers directing exercises in the field.

There are two other factors, of more literary interest, which tend to strengthen the suggestion that Milton knew and used *Mili-*

58. Hanford, "Art of War," pp. 192–95. The full title is *Animadversions of Warre; or, A Militarie Magazine of the Truest Rules, and Ablest Instructions, for the Managing of Warre*. In two Bookes. By Robert Ward, Gentleman and Commander. London, 1639. I have been unable to determine what he was "commander" of.

59. *Militarie Discipline: or the yong artillery man. Wherein is discoursed and showne the Postures both of Musket and Pike: the exactest way, etc. Together with the Motions which are to be used, in the exercising of a Foot-company. With divers and severall formes and figures of Battell; with their reducements; very necessary for all such as are studious in the Art Military*. London, Printed for Thomas Harper, for Ralph Mab, 1635. Guildhall Library, London, Mss. A. 9. 1. no. 23. There is a copy of the third edition of 1643 in the British Library, BM 717. g. 33. See Walker, *HAC*, p. 47.

tarie Discipline. The bulk of the phrases that Hanford finds in *Paradise Lost* come from those sections of Ward's book devoted to infantry drill, including references to such formations as the hollow and solid square, the "convex half-moone," and the "Horne-Battell." What has escaped notice, however, is that Ward, in a most flagrant example of seventeenth-century literary borrowing, lifted this entire section, somewhat condensed but virtually word for word and illustration for illustration, from *Militarie Discipline*, with only the briefest nod to the author.[60] Moreover, Ward condenses quite freely, omits useful illustrations, and often crams several chapters of Barriffe's careful descriptions into a few folio pages of small print without divisions, thus making the material more incomprehensible than ever. Ward is given to lengthy moral and philosophical discourses, such as in the section from which the *Commonplace Book* entry is copied, where the author is dealing rather tediously with the duties of soldiers. Milton is more likely to have consulted him for the theoretical discussions of war; he certainly would have been hard-pressed to master the military exercises from *Animadversions of Warre.*

One further note: in Milton's sonnet to Sir Henry Vane, the opening line reads, "Vane, young in yeares, but in sage counsell old," an address that has puzzled some, since Vane, thirty-nine at the time, was hardly a youth, indeed only four years younger than Milton.[61] In Barriffe's *Militarie Discipline* the initial pages are devoted to a group of dedicatory verses, obligatory, it would appear, for even drill manuals of the day, composed by his comrades-in-arms from the HAC. Among them is one signed "Amicus H. Pe-

60. Compare, for example, Barriffe, *Militarie Discipline*, chap. 10, with Ward, *Animadversions*, pp. 227–28; and Barriffe, chap. 31, with Ward, chap. 84. For illustrations, compare Barriffe, pp. 25–26, with Ward, p. 213; p. 27 with p. 214; p. 188 with p. 260; and p. 256 with p. 276. The designs are identical, except that where Barriffe uses *m* to represent "musketeer," Ward unaccountably has *s* (shooter?). On p. 259, Ward remarks cursorily, "I will follow Master Barriffe's directions, who hath excellently well described them, both by discourse and figure." Some of the dedicatory verses in the 1643 edition of Barriffe's book are a bit defensive about the borrowing. One includes the lines:

> A worthy Author hath referr'd to thee
> (In all that did concerne the Infantrie)
> Who knows it bootlesse, and a thing unfit,
> To write of that which thou before hadst writ. (n. pag.)

61. In the Trinity Manuscript, the title of the sonnet "To Sir Henry Vane the younger" has been scratched out. Vane was so called to distinguish him from his famous father, and it has also been suggested that the "young in years" is an echo of this custom. See Smart, *Sonnets*, p. 85.

tow," which opens: "Young and so old in Martiall Discipline? / Distrust will say, This work is none of thine." It is a theme repeated in a later verse: "Young though our Barriffe be, yet this his Book / Will speake him old, if well thereon you looke." The echo, of course, is unmistakable. There is no need, however, to stretch this chronicle of coincidence further. A conclusion drawn from such evidence could never go beyond the suggestion that Milton was familiar with the HAC, had acquaintances in its ranks, and, like many Londoners who were attracted to the Garden when the company was so important to the city, had probably watched its musters and parades with some interest.

Edward Phillips noted a further circumstance that associates Milton with the military at this stage of his life: "I am much mistaken, if there were not about this time a design in Agitation of making him Adjutant-General in Sir William Waller's army."[62] Parker suggests that either Samuel Hartlib or Hobson made the recommendation, though the latter seems a more reasonable source, since Hobson had campaigned with Waller and would have been a more likely man to advise him on military appointments. Phillips seems unsure, not concerning the "Agitation" itself, but about the time at which it occurred. He suggests that the "new modeling" of the army interrupted the appointment, which would indicate early 1645; but his uncertainty leaves open the possibility of an earlier date. It will be recalled that during the crisis in command of the summer of 1643, Waller was proposed as commander of two new armies. The plan was defeated by Pym's timely interference, but while it was under active consideration, Waller would have been thinking about selecting a personal staff composed completely of London citizens dedicated unreservedly to the overthrow of the King; perhaps Milton's name was put forward then. Regardless of when it occurred, the incident identifies Milton as a man known and respected in military circles in the city and further confirms his association with the war effort.

The influence of this experience on his art is indeed marked. Of course, the chief product of his pen during the first three years of the war was his Divorce Tracts, works singularly bare of martial imagery. While others may have found metaphors of battle highly suitable to the subject, Milton's brief experience with the marital state was probably not sufficient to suggest warfare to his imagina-

62. Darbishire, ed., *Early Lives*, p. 68.

tion as an appropriate parallel. Two other tracts, however, both better known and more widely admired, will attest to the increase in the frequency and vigor with which he used military imagery. *Of Education* and *Areopagitica* are both about battle, the first quite literally as an educational program designed in part to prepare young men for war, the second figuratively as a metaphor for the struggle between truth and error; both reflect the impact of the experience of London during those years on Milton's moral sense and on his creative imagination.

Well before he wrote these tracts, however, Milton gave us a glimpse of his response to war. In early November 1642 King Charles was marching on London, and all that stood between him and his palace at Westminster were some six thousand tired and dispirited veterans of Essex's army who had straggled back from Edgehill. To meet the challenge the city prepared for battle: shops were boarded over, barricades were raised, and the entire force of the London Trained Bands, some eighteen thousand strong, prepared to confront the Royalists at Turnham Green. Aside from their numbers, they cannot have been a very formidable sight. The six auxiliary regiments, their ranks filled chiefly with apprentices, had been organized only since September and must have presented a ragtag spectacle as they answered the muster on the night of 12 November. There were probably few in uniform and many without arms; but all, though short on training, were apparently long on spirit as they stumbled through the dark streets. Battle threatened, and the grim consequences of defeat had been brought home dramatically only hours before, when Rupert had crashed into Brentford, a few miles to the west, where he destroyed irrecoverably Denzil Holles's regiment of Londoners and put the town to the torch after fearful plunder. Was this to be the fate of London? Who could think else?

Milton did not march out with the Trained Bands, but he did record his reaction to the events in a sonnet; and into its lines he compressed his mixed feelings on this, his first encounter with war and the closest he would ever come to the "rough edge of battle."[63]

63. It is remarkable, given the circumstances at the time of its composition, that so many commentaries have detected a rather light-hearted tone in the poem. One will suffice as illustrative: Smart observes, "While suspense and anxiety prevailed around him in the city, Milton, with his inflexible composure, remained calm and detached, and converted the moment of peril into a theme for slightly playful verse" (*The Sonnets of Milton*, pp. 48–49). Others are cited in Fallon, "Milton's 'defenseless doors': The Limits of Irony."

Hanford has described Milton's tensions during the war as those of a man "condemned by the limitations of his own nature to be a spectator where he would be an actor, a man of peace where he wants to wield the sword, a praiser of deeds which he would fain be doing, an exhorter of others to leadership which he feels should be his own."[64] Never before can he have felt so urgently and so immediately the call to the active life; and for a man of his laborious dedication to the development of his art, it must have been a soul-searching experience when he realized that should he join in battle he might be cut off, like Edward King, before fruition, that his "thin spun life" might be split by a thrust of pike by some illiterate farm boy. Milton was thirty-three at the time, untroubled as yet by defect of eyesight, and apparently of sound health. He was certainly not sedentary in his habits; as he later remarked, "I was not ignorant of how to handle or unsheathe a sword, nor unpractised in using it each day. Girded with my sword, as I generally was, I thought myself equal to anyone, though he was far more sturdy, and I was fearless of any injury that one man could inflict on another."[65] As has been suggested, many of his friends must have drilled with the Trained Bands, and the call to action must have been strong indeed as he watched them form ranks in Aldersgate Street to march against the King. He was subject to the conflicting demands in any man whose city goes to war over issues that are close to him, whether freedom, religion, family, or mere survival.

Milton's sonnet "Captain or Colonel, or Knight in Arms" records his resolution of those demands. Years later, in *Defensio Secunda*, he defined that resolution in more direct terms: "I exchanged the toils of war, in which any stout trooper might outdo me, for those labours which I better understood. . . . I concluded that if God wished those men to achieve such noble deeds, he also wished that there be other men by whom these deeds, once done, might be worthily praised and extolled."[66] The relatively calm and objective tone of this report, written a full decade later, does not reflect the trial of the moment, when Milton characteristically turned to poetry to help shape his resolution. The sonnet is addressed to an unidentified soldier, one who carries the contemporary rank of "Captain or Colonel" or the more ancient title of

64. *John Milton, Englishman*, p. 184.
65. *YP*, 4:583.
66. *YP*, 4:553.

"Knight in Arms," a figure, in brief, who embodies the call to the active life in any age. Milton tells him how bards have traditionally served men-at-arms and reminds him of the respect great warriors have always had for the "Muses Bowre." This is not a judgment against war and violence, as some have suggested, but a simple statement of the role he has chosen to play in the conflict.[67] He will do the poet's work and bring praise not only on the soldier's prowess but also on his humanity, "such gentle acts as these." This indeed is the role he was to fulfill when in later years he praised Cromwell, Fairfax, and the New Model Army not only for their military victories but as frequently for their strong religious faith, mercy, and sober conduct, to spread their names "o're Lands and Seas."

Thus the soldier will bear arms, the poet will praise his valor and guide his humanity. Each will have his part; and if the poet here rejects the active military life, it seems unlikely that on the eve of Turnham Green he would speak with any disregard for the "Captain or Colonel" on either side, those whose arms he knows will ultimately decide the cause. There is none of this in the sonnet, at least. The soldier addressed is not charged with pettiness and insensitivity; he only needs reminding of what can be easily forgotten in the heat of battle. Indeed Milton compliments him by assuming that he will respond to a poem, citing those soldiers who have been aware of the higher value of beauty and learning. The stern Spartans, the classic personification of a warrior class, were moved by song; and the glorious Alexander knew that cities like burning Thebes would rise again, but that the house of art, once destroyed, was lost forever. Milton has made his choice and asks the soldier to respect it, reminding him of his most distinguished martial models.

Milton's tone can be seen in this light as one of directness and quiet resolve, of confidence in his own worth even though he has chosen not to bear arms. He will not be aloof from the war but very much a part of it, performing the traditional poet's role. There is composure in the lines but it arises from the confidence that he has found his place in the swelling events and not from some sense of superior detachment or amusement, as has been suggested. The poem does not reflect the conflicting emotions that

67. E. R. Gregory, "'Lift not thy spear against the Muses bowre': Essay in Historical Explication," p. 113. Gregory suggests that in the poem Milton rejects war as an appropriate subject for his art.

would have marked such a decision but is rather a simple statement, the choice having been made, of the relative value of the two callings, a judgment, he tells the soldier, which is honored in "What ever clime the Suns bright circle warms." Milton may well have been naive in these sentiments, as Nicolson and Hanford imply,[68] but at the time he knew little of war; and when it was finally thrust upon him, he turned instinctively to poetry and the language of learning, which to that point had been the only source for all he did know of it.

The years that followed Turnham Green dispelled much of that naivete; Milton's brief tract *Of Education* shows his growing awareness. This work, however, presents at first glance some puzzling contradictions. He proposes that the end of learning in general—and by *learning* we may assume both the slow growth of the individual mind over a lifetime of study and mankind's accumulation of knowledge through centuries of inquiry—is to "repair the ruins of our first parents by regaining to know God aright." At least one of the purposes of education, however—and by *education* we may assume the formal schooling of boys between the ages of "twelve and one and twenty"—is to prepare men to perform the offices of war.[69] To some minds these objectives are thoroughly incompatible; hence much of modern commentary on the tract will acknowledge with an embarrassed nod the military tone of the academy and quickly pass on to a more agreeable discussion of the humanistic value of his scholastic curriculum.[70] Another difficulty lies in the rigor of the student's day and the scope of his studies, and it is generally agreed that only a student body composed exclusively of young Miltons could survive such a program. How did his curriculum become so impossibly crowded, and how did it come to be directed toward such seemingly contradictory ends?

If the John Milton of 1638, quietly secluded at Horton, had been asked to describe the ideal academy, there is less likelihood that he would have advocated such an intense pursuit of the martial arts; he probably would have included little more than a daily exercise of swordsmanship and perhaps "the locks and gripes of

68. Nicolson, *Reader's Guide*, pp. 161–62; Hanford, *John Milton, Englishman*, p. 184.

69. *YP*, 2:366–67, 379.

70. Some avoid mentioning it altogether. See Edward Wagenknecht, *The Personality of Milton*, pp. 41–43.

wrastling, wherein English men were wont to excell."[71] There is nothing in his background or what we know of his own course of studies to suggest that he would perceive a sharp need for military training for the young gentlemen of England. The intellectual content of a 1638 curriculum would probably differ little from that proposed in 1644; in all likelihood the Horton scholar would have included the same practical activities proposed later, the observation of craftsmen and artisans at work and the riding out "with prudent and staid guides, to all the quarters of the land," for many educational reformers of the Renaissance, in their opposition to stuffy scholasticism, had been suggesting such practical measures for years—even Gargantua was schooled thus—but it is most unlikely that he would have had his students riding out in military formation for the purpose of "observing all places of strength."[72]

The crowded curriculum suggests that military training has been dumped on top of an already demanding program that Milton had evolved in theory and practice over the years. Without sacrificing any of his beloved classics, he simply added the course in military arts once he had become impressed by the need through observation of the ineptness of the Parliamentary commanders during the first two years of the Civil War. There is no need to pursue here all that Milton proposes; but some of the subjects seem more closely identified with the events of those years than others, and thus are especially relevant to our inquiry. His academy is small and the student body organized into military units, "to the convenience of a foot company, or interchangeably two troops of cavalry."[73] Milton proposes twice that his students should be skilled in the art of fortification, an emphasis suggested to him perhaps by the immense effort by Londoners to ring the city with entrenchments. His young scholar is to study "the institution of Physick" so that he may "save an Army by this frugall and expenceless meanes only; and not let the healthy and stout bodies of young men rot away under him for want of this discipline; which is a great pitty, and no lesse a shame to the commander."[74] This proposal calls to

71. *YP*, 2:409.

72. *YP*, 2:413. See Francois Rabelais, *Gargantua and Pantagruel: Selections*, p. 42. In "Prolusion III" the young Milton urges his fellow students to "seek out and explore the nature of all living creatures, and [study] the secret virtues of stones and herbs"; but he does not mention military training (*YP*, 1:246).

73. *YP*, 2:381.

74. *YP*, 2:393.

mind the sorry spectacle of Essex's army sitting outside London in the spring and summer of 1643, reduced by neglect, disease, and desertion to a pitifully ineffective remnant, defenseless against the attacks of Rupert. Accounts of the deplorable condition of the lord general's forces reached London and were in part responsible for the effort of the Committee for the General Rising to create a new army under Waller that summer.

By the time Milton's scholars graduate they will have "serv'd out the rudiments of their Souldiership in all the skill of embattailing, marching, encamping, fortifying, beseiging, and battering" so that "they may as it were out of a long warre come forth renowned and perfect Commanders in the service of their country." Milton is most perceptive in placing the blame for the host of ills common to the armies of the day squarely on the shoulders of the officers in command. His students, for example, would not, "if they were trusted with fair and hopefull armies, suffer them for want of just and wise discipline to shed away from about them like sick feathers, though they be never so oft suppli'd."[75] Desertion, not only of individuals but of whole units, was a serious problem in Parliamentary units, which soldiers would leave with impunity to join other armies where pay was more regular and supply more dependable. The Trained Bands of London, composed of artisans, tradesmen, and merchants who were required to neglect their livelihood while in the field, would frequently form ranks and march home in the midst of a campaign, leaving an exasperated general to carry on as best he could.[76] The practice made it extremely difficult for Essex and Waller, who depended on the Bands to swell their ranks, to plan and carry out any concerted plan of campaign; and it prevented them from assuming the strategic initiative in the war until the fall of 1644. Milton shrewdly observes that commanders trained from youth in the

75. *YP*, 2:411–12.

76. In November 1643, for example, Waller was forced to abandon the siege of Basing House when the Trained Bands deserted in a body, shouting as they left, "Home! Home!" (Gardiner, *Civil War*, 1:250–51). Waller had earlier persuaded them to stay at Alton only by pleading that they hadn't won anything yet and shouldn't go home until they had. For a contemporary account see *A True Relation of the Marchings of the Red Trained Bands of Westminster, the Green Auxiliaries of London, and the Yellow Auxiliaries of the Tower Hamlets, under the command of Sir William Waller, from Monday the 16. of Octob. to Wednesday the 20. of Decemb. 1643*. By Elias Archer Lieftenant to Captain William Archer. London, Printed for Edward Blackmore, dwelling at the Angel in Pauls-Churchyard, 1643. BM 101. b. 64.

arts of war and the obligations of leadership would be able to impose "just and wise discipline" to prevent the kind of decay that plagued the armies defending London in 1643.

Thus the course of the war shaped Milton's concept of an ideal academy. His perception of the inadequacies of the Parliamentary armies was incisive and his vision of exemplary commanders in some ways prophetic, for in the army of the Eastern Association was a body of men who, though for the most part unschooled in the liberal arts proposed for Milton's students, embodied the courage, skill, and discipline he perceived as so sorely lacking in the forces of which he had knowledge. A month after the publication of his tract, the "Ironsides" regiments of Oliver Cromwell carried the field at Marston Moor and revived the hopes for the cause of Parliament. Within months their example would inspire the New Model, the "Army of Saints" that would achieve the final victory.

Milton, then, gained some practical knowledge of military affairs during the early months of the war, but there are also indications that the experience began to exercise a strong influence on his creative imagination. It was commonplace, of course, in the sermons and religious literature of the seventeenth century for the spiritual struggle over the soul of man to be described in terms of armed conflict, as indeed it has been since. As William Haller observes, "The Puritan imagination saw the life of the spirit as pilgrimage and battle," wherein man "was a soldier who, having been pressed to serve under the banners of the spirit, must enact faithfully his part in the unceasing war of the spiritual against the carnal man"; thus pulpits rang with fiery images of the sword of righteousness and the shield of faith.[77] Milton's early works contain little of this martial metaphor, and when he does address himself to the subject he seems to prefer figures from ancient myth. In the poems on the Gunpowder Plot, which might be expected to suggest images of warfare, it is Pluto who instigates wars while his teeth grind "like the clash of arms and the blow of spear against spear"; but that is about all.[78] Comus is certainly no soldier, and the two brothers, though armed, strike no blows for righteousness and bungle the job anyway. "What, have you let the fals enchanter scape?" cries the exasperated Attendant Spirit, who must then call

77. *The Rise of Puritanism*, p. 142.
78. "In quintum Novembris," *CW*, 1:239, lines 38–39.

on a "gentle Nymph" to free the lady from the bonds of evil. In the antiprelatical tracts, as we have seen, martial imagery is scattered; while there is a reference to the "helmet of salvation,"[79] when Milton does discuss the struggle between the flesh and the spirit, as in *Of Reformation*, for example, it is seldom in terms of temporal warfare.[80]

By the fall of 1644, however, when Milton decided to voice his opposition to the Licensing Act, the war had sparked his imagination, and one can find in *Areopagitica* military images of a frequency and power quite new to his art. Indeed, it has been noted that apart from personifications they are the only figures at all developed in the work.[81] Censorship is a subject somewhat removed from the field of battle, certainly more remote than, let us say, the dire warnings of civil war in *Of Reformation*; and one might not expect that martial figures would present themselves to the imagination as appropriate to an appeal for freedom of the press. Yet they abound in *Areopagitica*, for Milton saw the issue as a part of the struggle between the truth and error, between good and evil, and he had come to see that spiritual confrontation in terms of armed conflict.

Central to Milton's thought was the belief that man can come to know and love good only through a knowledge of evil and that he can be truly virtuous only if faced with temptation. The knowledge of good and evil came "from out the rinde of one apple tasted," and the poet had no respect for those who shunned the struggle made tragically necessary by that act:

> He that can apprehend and consider vice with all her baits and seeming pleasures, and yet abstain, and yet distinguish, and yet prefer that which is truly better, he is the true warfaring Christian. I cannot praise a fugitive and cloister'd vertue, unexercis'd & unbreath'd, that never sallies out and sees her adversary.[82]

79. *An Apology Against a Pamphlet*, *YP*, 1:953.
80. *YP*, 1:519–22.
81. Alan F. Price, "Incidental Imagery in *Areopagitica*." Price observes that Milton's description of the struggle between truth and error in the work "reaches its fullest expression in the images derived from war. This is natural: there are classical and biblical precedents for seeing this conflict in terms of the clash of armies, and the Civil War, presumably, offered plenty of material for images of strife" (p. 217).
82. *YP*, 2:514–15. The textual question whether Milton is referring to a "wayfaring" or a "warfaring" Christian has been variously discussed. In *YP* Ernest Sirluck favors the military image. *CW* uses the pilgrimage figure (4:311) but suggests that the other is equally acceptable (4:367). The kinetic "warfaring" cer-

Under the influence of his troubled times, images of battle have now risen to the surface of his imagination. They occur to him with surprising frequency, not just for occasional emphasis or decoration, but as figures that embody the very core of his meaning. Censorship is his subject and, he warns, to impose it will only weaken the spirit. Licensing will only raise a fortress to protect the slack divine against the encroachment of fresh thought, for he will have

> Sermons ready printed and pil'd up, on every text that is not difficult, . . . so that penury he never need fear of Pulpit provision, having where so plenteously to refresh his magazin. But if his rear and flanks be not impal'd, if his back dore be not secur'd by the rigid licencer, but that a bold book may now and then issue forth, and give assault to some of his old collections in their trenches, it will concern him to keep waking, to stand in watch, to set good guards and sentinells about his receiv'd opinions, to walk the round and counter-round with his fellow inspectors, fearing lest any of his flock be seduc't.[83]

The censor blockades the mind and saps the strength of the warfaring Christian; as "if som enemy at sea should stop up all our hav'ns and ports, and creeks, it hinders and retards the importation of our richest Marchandize, Truth."[84]

Milton's martial images are now extended and complex, sustained over a number of involved sentences. One example will suffice to illustrate the sweep and vigor of his new-found art. Truth, he writes, is inherently strong, and the virtuous man need have no fear in the spiritual battle:

> The Temple of *Janus* with his two *controversal* faces might now not insignificantly be set open. And though all the windes of doctrin were let loose to play upon the earth, so Truth be in the field, we do injuriously by licencing and prohibiting to misdoubt her strength. Let her and Falshood grapple; who ever knew Truth put to the wors, in a free and open encounter. . . . When a man hath been labouring the hardest labour in the deep mines of knowledge, hath furnisht out his findings in all their equipage, drawn forth his reasons as it were a battell

---

tainly would seem to fit better the energetic tone of the whole metaphor. Also, one would like to agree with Edward Le Comte that Milton intended the more aggressive "seeks" of the Bohn Edition (2:68), rather than "sees," since it matches more closely the movement of the military image, "sallies." Le Comte bows to editorial rule, however, as must we (*Yet Once More*, p. 149).

83. *YP*, 2:546–47.

84. *YP*, 2:548.

> raung'd, scatter'd and defeated all objections in his way, calls out his adversary into the plain, offers him the advantage of wind and sun, if he please; only that he may try the matter by dint of argument, for his opponents to sculk, to lay ambushments, to keep a narrow bridge of licencing where the challenger should passe, though it be valour anough in shouldiership, is but weaknes and cowardise in the wars of Truth.[85]

In his exhortation, he urges his readers to "polish and brighten the armoury of Truth" and praises the people of London as especially selected "to begin some new and great period in his Church." The city is filled with gifted men, he writes, ably prepared for such a task:

> Behold now this vast City; a City of refuge, the mansion house of liberty, encompast and surrounded with his protection; the shop of warre hath not there more anvils and hammers waking, to fashion out the plates and instruments of armed Justice in defence of beleaguer'd Truth, then there be pens and heads there.[86]

Later, in a direct reference to the political and military situation in London during 1643, he praises a London that is "besieg'd and blockt about, her navigable river infested, inrodes and incursions round, defiance and battell oft rumor'd to be marching up ev'n to her walls, and suburb trenches," but which in spite of the danger is still alive with "disputing, reasoning, reading, inventing, discoursing."[87]

Thus the spiritual struggle between truth and error is part of the universal struggle between good and evil, which the Milton of Aldersgate Street had come to see more and more in terms of the clash of arms on the battlefields of man. The Trained Bands that marched by his door and the reports of battles raging about beleaguered London had brought home to him the stark reality of this harsh dimension of our human nature and had enriched both his view of life and the scope of his imagination. Hanford has suggested that Milton's practical experience with war had less influence on his martial imagery than did his classical reading.[88] Perhaps it would be more appropriate to say that the early years in London gave life and motion to the unquickened body of his stud-

85. *YP*, 2:561–62.
86. *YP*, 2:553–54.
87. *YP*, 2:556–57, as noted in 557n.
88. "Art of War," p. 220.

ies as he gained a deepening insight into the nature of war and those who fought it. The contrast is striking indeed between those static, ceremonial figures in his earlier works, which he drew from his cloistered studies, and the tragic, towering shape of Satan, when

> on the Beach
> Of that inflamed Sea, he stood and call'd
> His Legions. (*PL* 1.299–301)

III

The Army of Saints

After the Battle of Marston Moor in July 1644, the city of London was relieved of the sharp anxieties of earlier years. In the weeks following the battle, however, the divisions that had been festering within the Parliamentary forces finally came to a head. The crisis passed, but not before those armies had been completely restructured, enabling Parliament to place in the field for the spring campaign of 1645 a unit unique in English history—the New Model Army.

Frequently some individual, institution, or place comes to embody all that a nation or a people value in their moral and spiritual life. Such is Rome, Mecca, or Jerusalem today, such was Napoleon to the French, Lenin to the Russian Revolution, the Areopagus to ancient Greece, or the Senate to pre-Augustan Rome. In just this way, all that the English Puritan of the mid-1640s held dear in the way of political freedom and religious toleration came to be embodied, although not in a person or place, but, strangely, in a military organization, this extraordinary Army of Saints.[1] It was a devotion that manifested itself to a degree surpassing the normal tendency of a people at war to identify with their military forces, for it was born of a time when Western man marched righteously to battle under the banners of God.

Many more moderate adherents to the cause of Parliament, those whose political and religious orientation led to their identification as Presbyterians, lived to regret their support of that Army. But John Milton was not among them. Ten years after Marston Moor he wrote of the New Model that

> no one has ever raised a larger or better-disciplined army in a shorter space of time than did Cromwell, an army obedient to his command in all things, welcomed and cherished by their fellow-citizens, formidable

1. In these pages, the word *Puritan* identifies those who stood to the left of the Presbyterians on the question of religious freedom. It was so used by Milton himself, who in *The Tenure of Kings and Magistrates* made the distinction between the Presbyterians and those "branded with the name of Puritans and Nonconformists" (*YP*, 3:242). William Haller, in *Liberty and Reformation in the Puritan Revolution*, describes how distasteful and divergent the Presbyterian ideas of church-state control were to the "Puritan brotherhood" (p. 100).

> indeed to the enemy in the field, but wonderfully merciful to them once they had surrendered;[2]

and six months before the Restoration he would still characterize it as an army "renown'd for the civilest and best order'd in the World, and by us here at home, for the most conscientious."[3] The New Model, until its dissolution in 1660, was perhaps the single most important factor in the political and spiritual life of the English Republic. It had a profound effect on Milton's perception of war and the men who fought it. The army's uniqueness arose from two characteristics: once in the field it never lost a battle, and in time it became charged with a strong spiritual fervor and fierce commitment to the cause of religious toleration. It rose to dominance as a result of the religious and political divisions that tore at the nation during the latter half of the 1640s, and before the decade was out, it had come to symbolize much that history has since identified as the English Revolution. In our own age a sympathetic association between poet and soldier would border on anomaly, since the death of Kipling at any rate; hence any proposal that England's greatest poet was politically and ideologically in accord with the convictions of a military organization will take some looking into. In order to assess the influence of the New Model Army upon the imagination of John Milton, therefore, it will be necessary first to summarize briefly the events that led to its formation and brought it to prominence in English history.

To do so, we must go back a bit. Before his death in December 1643 John Pym had secured for Parliament a powerful ally—Scotland. The Scottish army that invaded England the following month was eventually to decide the war for Parliament, but the Scots had sold their allegiance at a price. In effect, they called upon England to abandon those principles of religious toleration so highly valued by more militant Puritans and to accept a Presbyterian political system resembling the one they had evolved from the teaching of John Knox. That system was based on a firm bond between church and state, and the Scots were determined that their powerful neighbor to the south should adopt a constitutional settlement sympathetic to their own. Thus, before a single Scottish soldier stepped on English soil, Parliament was forced to

2. In *Defensio Secunda*, *YP*, 4:668–69.
3. *YP*, 7:327.

endorse an agreement, the Solemn League and Covenant, which bound England to adopt Presbyterianism, a system and doctrine to which all Englishmen over the age of eighteen were obliged to pledge themselves. With the alliance came the Westminster Assembly of Divines, a gathering of distinguished English and Scottish clergy charged with the task of welding the religions of the two nations into an indissoluble union. Ironically, by their insistence upon such a church settlement, though motivated by equal measures of religious evangelism and political realism, the Scots unwittingly sowed the seeds not only for the dissolution of the Parliament they sought to strengthen but eventually for the subjection of Scotland itself.

The Scots proposed a church empowered to enforce discipline on all. A body of church elders was to set down a simple ritual and doctrine to be followed strictly by ministers and laity alike, and it was to dominate as well the secular life of the community. Church and state, in brief, were to be one, and the decisions of the elders in matters of religion and government were to be backed by a system of all-powerful church courts. The English Presbyterians did not embrace this strict plan of settlement with much enthusiasm; but they were not entirely unsympathetic to a design that seemed to preserve, in principle at least, the traditional relationship between church and state of the English Constitution and that promised to leave open the possibility of the King remaining as at least titular head of the church. The moderate party in Commons, with Denzil Holles as chief spokesman, held limited war aims, by no means revolutionary in nature. They simply wanted to come to an agreement with the King that, in Masson's words, "would permit English society to resume its course, with royalty under due Parliamentary check, and the Church reformed and popularized, but with other institutions disturbed as little as possible."[4] On the other hand, the small but energetic party of militant Puritans in Commons, which under the leadership of Sir Henry Vane came to be known as Independents to distinguish them from the majority Presbyterians, saw in these proposals the abandonment of their cherished dream of freedom of conscience. Such a settlement would change nothing, they felt, but only perpetuate a system in

4. *The Quarrel between the Earl of Manchester and Oliver Cromwell*, p. xxxvi. More recently, Robert Ashton, in *The English Civil War: Conservatism and Revolution*, confirms that the majority of MPs simply wanted to "restore the ancient harmony between Monarch and Parliament" (p. 130).

which, as Milton put it, "*New Presbyter* is but *Old Priest* writ Large." These differences, then, had important implications for the war, for since it appeared that the Presbyterians had "no thoughts or intentions to diminish His Majesty's just power and greatness,"[5] the Independents concluded that the religious freedom they so fervently desired could only be won by a crushing defeat of the King. In many ways the Independents were more acute in their evaluation of Charles, for history confirmed their belief that he would never accept what he considered an unnatural marriage of episcopacy and synod.

Thus, the political divisions in Parliament over the pursuit of the war became linked with the incendiary religious question; and the large uncommitted middle group of 1642–1643, through which Pym had controlled the body, became polarized after his death as its members split into a loose but discernible Presbyterian-Independent opposition. These groups bear little resemblance to modern political parties, however, for as Robert Ashton cautions, "the word 'party' is not here employed to describe a firm and cohesive organization with disciplined membership and consistent political behavior."[6] In a very general way it can be said that the Independents favored the total defeat of the King, some even

5. As specified in the Solemn League and Covenant, *The Constitutional Documents of the Puritan Revolution, 1625–1660*, ed. Samuel Rawson Gardiner, p. 269.

6. *English Civil War*, p. 194. In recent years a great deal of close and careful research into voting records and regional history has cast doubt on the assumptions of earlier historians like Gardiner and Firth that MPs fit into these convenient political classifications. J. H. Hexter, in "The Problem of the Presbyterian-Independents," questions whether the religious labels can be attached to political factions at all; and in *The Reign of King Pym* he identifies the "middle group" of 1642–1643. David Underdown in *Pride's Purge*, pp. 230–36, demonstrates that a number of Independents were barred from Commons in 1648 along with the Presbyterian majority. These historians cite numerous MPs whose voting records simply defy classification. Some, like modern senators, cast ballots on the basis of regional interests; others who remained firm in their convictions were simply overtaken by the sweep of revolutionary events, so that one day's radical, without changing his position, became the next day's conservative; still other more mercurial members underwent dramatic changes in their allegiance. Before the war, for example, Denzil Holles and Henry Marten were agreed in their opposition to the King, so much so that they were two of the five members that Charles sought to imprison on 4 January 1642. After the shooting started, however, Holles became the chief spokesman for the peace party and Marten the impassioned leader of the war party in Parliament. Indeed, some who supported Strafford in 1641 even survived Pride's Purge (Ashton, *English Civil War*, p. 141). This weight of scholarship makes it very difficult to present the type of summary essayed here. I can only hope that the labels employed do not stray too close to the precipice of oversimplification.

proposing the abolition of the monarchy so as to insure the separation of church and state, while the Presbyterians favored accommodation and a church-state settlement to be devised by the Westminster Assembly. On most issues the majority of Parliament supported the more moderate Presbyterian position, as indeed did the bulk of the people; but the most effective leadership in Commons came from the ranks of the militant Independents, in particular from Sir Henry Vane. The course of the war tended to strengthen their hand, for despite the intervention of Scotland, Parliament continued to suffer more defeats than victories during 1644. The Scots proved a disappointment. Their contribution to the one great victory of the year, Marston Moor, was limited; it took them nine months to reduce Newcastle; and their rear was in constant peril because of the startling series of successes in their homeland by the brilliant Earl of Montrose. Their failures embarrassed the Parliamentary Presbyterians and enhanced the authority of the Independents.

These political divisions soon made themselves felt in the ranks of the Parliamentary forces, where all the commanders of the major association armies (with the exception of Fairfax) and many of the lower-ranking officers were members of Parliament.[7] In the field, men of opposing political and religious convictions, sharply divided on the objectives of the war, were called upon to serve side by side. But these men, who faced each other in hostility at Westminster, could not be expected to bury their differences simply because they donned the same uniform and marched under the same banner; and the Parliamentary armies were soon filled with tensions that no military force can long endure.

An incident in the army of the Eastern Association during the fall of 1644 illustrates the effect of politics on a military unit. The Earl of Manchester, in command of the army, was a man of Presbyterian sympathies, who looked with horror on the growing sentiment for deposing the King.[8] Oliver Cromwell was the earl's lieutenant-general of horse and a man of militant Puritan sentiments, who had filled the ranks of his own regiments with soldiers similarly committed. Manchester's commander of foot, Major-

7. D. Brunton and D. H. Pennington, *The Members of the Long Parliament*, p. 22.

8. G. W. Prothero and E. M. Lloyd, "The First Civil War, 1642–7," in *The Cambridge Modern History*, 3 : 322.

General Lawrence Crawford, was of the same mind as his commander, a fine soldier but a Scot Presbyterian of the most narrow kind. Manchester's actions during the summer and fall of 1644 had convinced Cromwell, with some justification, that it was the "soft" attitude of such men toward the war that was the core of Parliament's troubles. There soon developed violent differences between Manchester's two subordinates, a feud finally so fierce that, under Cromwell's influence, two of Crawford's regiments refused to take orders from their commander. Cromwell appeared before Manchester threatening that his colonels would resign unless Crawford were dismissed; and Manchester, faced with a mutiny, was forced to travel to Westminster with Cromwell and Crawford to put the case before Parliament.[9]

Here then is the absurdity of a military commander compelled to take time out from his campaigns to conduct feuding subordinates to the legislature for arbitration. But Manchester's hands were tied. He could not dismiss Cromwell, which would have been the customary reaction to such a blatantly mutinous demand, and he did not want to dismiss the capable Crawford. The two figures represented the two parties in Parliament, and the rest of the army was similarly split. The commanding general could dismiss neither without causing a revolt in his army and bringing down upon his head the wrath of half of Parliament. The incident was smoothed over for the moment, but to no one's satisfaction; the animosities continued to smolder, finally flaming up again after the Second Battle of Newbury.

The divisions in Parliament and the army were further complicated by the composition of the committee appointed to conduct the war. It became apparent to even the most jealous of Parliamentarians that a legislative assembly of some two or three hundred men was not an appropriate organ to direct a military campaign and that the Committee of Safety they had appointed for that purpose had insufficient authority to do it properly. With the intervention of the Scots the problems of control became even more complex; it was evident that some body would have to be formed to coordinate the efforts of the two nations and their several armies. Early in 1644 Sir Henry Vane pushed through Parliament a bill creating a Committee of Both Kingdoms, which was charged

9. The incident is fully described in Masson, *Quarrel*.

to "advise, consult, order and direct, concerning the carrying on and managing of the war."[10] In effect, the committee was given executive authority in all matters pertaining to the conduct of the war. Parliament, though reluctant to surrender even this small measure of its prerogatives, was persuaded to do so by the obvious necessity of war and the political skill of Vane.

The prospective members of the committee, all men of Vane's choosing, were designated in the ordinance. The list included seven men from the House of Lords, fourteen from Commons, and four Scots; but it is the political orientation of the members that excites interest. Of the lords, six were Presbyterians, including Manchester, Waller, and Essex. Of the remaining fifteen English members, twelve were Independents or leaning in that direction, and in the entire body only four could be identified as what Wallace Notestein calls "thoroughgoing friends of peace."[11] Further, since many of the Presbyterian members were officers with the armies in the field, the committee that was to sit regularly at Westminster was to be a predominantly Independent body; and it was to be strongly influenced by Vane, himself the leading Independent.[12] In May 1644 he pushed through yet another ordinance appointing a second Committee of Both Kingdoms, with its membership unchanged but its powers much enhanced, to include "whatsoever may concern the peace of His Majesty's dominions."[13] It now had virtually the powers of an executive body, including the authority to treat with the King.

Here, then, was an executive group under the control of the minority party, charged with the responsibility to direct the armies of Parliament, which in turn were commanded by generals whose sympathies were with the majority party. Such a condition is unstable enough in itself, but when the incendiary ingredient of religion is added to the formula, a conflagration is almost inevitable. The spark was struck by the Earl of Manchester's brilliant lieutenant-general of horse, Oliver Cromwell.

10. "The Ordinance appointing the First Committee of Both Kindgoms," Gardiner, *Documents*, p. 272.

11. "The Establishment of the Committee of Both Kingdoms," p. 487.

12. James K. Hosmer, *The Life of Young Sir Henry Vane*, p. 203. Valerie Pearl questions whether the committee was dominated by antipeace members in "Oliver St. John and the 'Middle Group' in the Long Parliament, August 1643–May 1644," as does Mark A. Kishlansky, *The Rise of the New Model Army*, pp. 23–24 and note, pp. 295–96.

13. "The Ordinance appointing the Second Committee of Both Kingdoms," Gardiner, *Documents*, p. 274.

To understand how the New Model Army came to embody so much that Puritans like John Milton believed in, one cannot do better than to examine with some care the man who became both its spiritual exemplar and military leader. Oliver Cromwell was an intensely religious man. He had experienced early in his life a spiritual "conversion," which had been very personal and mystical in nature, much in the Calvinist tradition; and since he had found God in his own way, he believed that all men should be free to seek a like experience. He joined no formal church, for he looked upon such institutions as more of a hindrance than a help to salvation. In Maurice Ashley's words, "He did not want priest, ritual, or ceremony to intervene between him and his Maker."[14] These convictions, which prompted him to oppose Charles and inspired many men of like mind to serve under his banners, formed a basis for the sympathy that developed between the great statesman of the English Republic and the poet who towers over his age.

Cromwell looked upon the war as a religious crusade, and he was among the first to recognize the King's intransigence on the subject of his church. He realized early that, unless it was forced upon him, Charles would never permit the degree of toleration that English Puritans believed necessary to their salvation. When Cromwell joined in battle, all other issues were subordinate to the cause of religious freedom. As Masson puts it:

> In him there was not merely a predetermined judgement upon points in dispute, but one which he believed to be infallible, because communicated to his mind by the Spirit of God. Call it enthusiasm, cant, fanaticism, hypocrisy, or what you will. He saw God's Church defiled by hirelings. He witnessed how they strove to bring back within the sacred precincts the soul-destroying trumpery of rejected superstitions. Those who profaned God's Church could not be otherwise than enemies of the Lord of Hosts. To oppose them was the cause of God. It was in this cause, uniting the hero with the prophet, that he drew his sword; and whenever his efforts were triumphant, he devotedly believed the success to be a token of God's approval—the flashing of his sword to be the lightning of God's vengeance.[15]

This single-minded dedication was his source of strength in battle. He was never plagued with the doubts that sapped the energies of his fellow generals, of an overcautious Manchester, for example, who after Newbury was heard to say, "If we beat the King ninety

14. *The Greatness of Oliver Cromwell*, p. 49.
15. *Quarrel*, p. xxxiv.

and nine times, yet he is king still, and so will his posterity be after him; but if the King beat us once we shall all be hanged, and our posterity made slaves."[16] Cromwell's way was clear and his goal uncomplicated—crushing defeat of the Royalists—and all else must be laid aside until that goal had been attained.

Cromwell returned to Cambridge in the summer of 1642 to raise a force of cavalry. The modest troop of sixty men that fought under him at Edgehill grew eventually into the mighty "Ironsides," eleven hundred strong, that carried the field at Marston Moor. It was clear, however, that their strength was not so much in numbers as it was in the fighting qualities that Cromwell had inspired in them. In *Of Education*, we have seen how perceptive even an untrained civilian like John Milton was in judging the divided and inept leadership in the Parliamentary armies. Cromwell, of course, was even more conscious of these inadequacies, for he suffered their consequences directly in battle. At Edgehill he viewed with disgust the dispirited and undisciplined mobs on both sides and set out to fill his ranks with men of his own mind, who saw the war as he did and would apply themselves with the same fierce determination that was his nature. His contemporary Richard Baxter observed, "At his first entrance into the wars . . . he had special care to get religious men into his troop. These men were of greater understanding than common soldiers, and therefore more apprehensive of the importance and consequences of war." Cromwell enlisted "such men as had the fear of God before them and made some conscience of what they did";[17] and the Ironsides soon became an elite corps, sternly disciplined, fierce in battle, devoted to its commander, and filled with the same fervent religious spirit that was the source of his own strength. The Parliamentary cause, so shaken until then, revived with the news of Marston Moor and hailed this new leader and his regiments. Within a year Parliament was to reorganize its armies on this model, but not before new divisions and defeats. In the end it was Cromwell who defined the need and forced the issue.

It was at the Second Battle of Newbury in October 1644 that matters came to a head. Because of poor communications and Manchester's inaction, the King, trapped and outnumbered al-

16. As reported by Sir Arthur Hazelrig in Gardiner, *Civil War*, 2: 59.

17. In his *Reliquiae Baxterianae* (1696), cited in Charles Harding Firth, "The Raising of the Ironsides."

most two to one by the combined armies of Essex, Waller, and Manchester, managed to escape almost unscathed.[18] After a day of fierce but uncoordinated assaults, the Parliamentary armies rested during the night and awoke to find an empty field. Under cover of darkness the Royalists had simply packed up and marched off, completely undetected, toward Oxford. A part of the problem was the complex command relationships that were bound to develop when three independent army commanders attempted to operate under the direction of a Parliamentary committee, which added to the confusion by appointing to their council of war two civilian "observers" empowered with a veto power over tactical decisions. To further complicate matters, the titular commander-in-chief, Essex, was too ill to be present.[19] But Cromwell thought he saw more than just a cumbersome command structure in the lost opportunity. His first reaction to the fall campaigns and their disgraceful climax at Newbury was one of anger; and the full force of his rage fell on the man he considered responsible for the entire debacle, the Earl of Manchester. On 25 November, Cromwell appeared before the full House of Commons and delivered a scathing denunciation of the actions of his superior. He pointed to the earl as the one "most at fault for most of those miscarriages and the ill consequences." He charged that it was not just because Manchester was incompetent that the victory was lost; there were darker reasons: it was through his "backwardness to all action." And more damaging,

> that backwardness was not [merely] from dullness or indisposedness to engagement, but withal from some principle of unwillingness in his Lordship to have this warre prosecuted to a full victory, and a designe or desire to have it ended by accommodation [and that] on such termes to which it might be disadvantageous to bring the King too lowe.[20]

It was an accusation of treason. Commons hurriedly appointed a committee to investigate the charges and, finally propelled into action, with the same breath requested the Committee of Both Kingdoms "to consider a Frame or Model of the whole Militia, and present it to the House, as may put the forces into such posture as may be most advantageous for the service of the public."[21] Out of

18. According to Cromwell; see Masson, *Quarrel*, p. 85.
19. Gardiner, *Civil War*, 2:42–44.
20. Masson, *Quarrel*, pp. 78–79.
21. Ibid., p. lxvii.

this heated forge of political and religious antagonism was cast the New Model Army.

Thus men of different convictions, in the armies and the benches of Parliament, saw the war with different eyes. We cannot be sure how John Milton stood on these issues at the time, but we can safely assume that he gave them thought; for they were the subject of a heated public debate whose outcome would determine a cause to which he was profoundly committed. It is striking how often events in his great works hinge on just such issues: Moloch is for open war, Mammon advises peace, and Beëlzebub falls somewhere between. Abdiel argues it vain "Against th' Omnipotent to rise in Arms," but Satan replies that his cause is liberty and that the choice is between servility and freedom (*PL* 6.136, 169). God permits the war in Heaven, fulfilling "his great purpose" (*PL* 6.675) to glorify his Son through triumph in battle, the same Son who later comes to earth praising "deeds of peace" (*PR* 3.91). Adam turns in tears from a scene of armed conflict only to learn that peace corrupts no less than warfare wastes (*PL* 11.675, 784). Christ scorns the "cumbersome / Luggage of war" (*PR* 3.400–401) but Samson yearns for "combat to decide whose god is god" (*SA* 1176). These issues of peace and war, freedom and slavery, victory and defeat first touched John Milton's life in the streets and parlors of London; and the spectacle of honest men urging either side must have convinced him that such questions were not easily resolved.

The confrontation between Cromwell and Manchester precipitated two important pieces of legislation. The Self-Denying Ordinance required all members of Parliament to resign their military commissions. It was an obvious effort to rid the army of the political divisions of the legislature, but it was a drastic remedy indeed! Because they were MPs, almost every experienced major commander in the army, including Cromwell, would have to leave the field, in effect perilously purging the high command of a military force then in the midst of an active campaign. But the political consequences of the measure, though less obvious, were even more dramatic. All of the commanders who would be required to step down—Essex, Waller, Manchester, Warwick—were men of Presbyterian sentiments. Among the vigorous young officers who would replace them were many trained in the mold of Cromwell—Independents and Sectarians dedicated to the active pursuit of the war, the crushing defeat of the King, and a church settlement permitting a degree of toleration totally unacceptable to the bulk of Parliament.[22]

The New Model Ordinance followed closely. There were to be twenty-two thousand men organized into twelve regiments of foot, eleven regiments of horse, and a thousand dragoons. There was to be a single commander-in-chief, a single lieutenant-general in charge of horse, and a single major-general of foot.[23] Sir Thomas Fairfax, who was not an MP and had remained generally aloof from political controversy, was appointed commander-in-chief, with Phillip Skippon of the London Trained Bands to be major-general. The post of lieutenant-general was left significantly unfilled, however, pending the implementation of the Self-Denying Ordinance. After a short period of uncertainty Parliament recognized the folly of dismissing its finest soldier in the hour of its greatest need; Cromwell was exempted from its provisions and appointed lieutenant-general in time to participate in the decisive battle of Naseby.

But what kind of army was this which was to operate under a Committee of Both Kingdoms that Vane had packed with Independents? The young leaders who now assumed positions of authority in the army were certainly more capable military men than their predecessors, but the most prominent among them disagreed with Parliament on the key issue of religion. Even prior to the organization of the New Model, there had been some concern about the growth of Independency in the military; there had been little alarm, though, so long as the army commanders had been sound Presbyterians. Since the beginning of the war, these commanders had been supported by a group of army chaplains who were largely of the same faith, but the last of these, Edward Bowles, left the army shortly after Naseby. The men who replaced them were generally militant Independents like William Dell, John Saltmarsh, and Hugh Peters.[24] What had been in effect a Parliamentary commissariat had been replaced by men who came to look on Oliver Cromwell as a military and spiritual guide.

22. Gardiner, *Civil War*, 2:194.

23. Charles Harding Firth, *Cromwell's Army*, p. 33. The New Model was essentially a reorganization of the forces of Essex, Waller, and Manchester. It was at no time the only force that Parliament had in the field. In 1646, for example, Col. Edward Massey commanded an army in the west and Maj.-Gen. Sedenham Poynz another in the north (Ashton, *English Civil War*, p. 294).

24. Leo F. Solt, *Saints in Arms: Puritanism and Democracy in Cromwell's Army*, p. 9. See also *YP*, 3:12.

The Independents, though a minority in both army and Parliament, were the most able and active members of both bodies. They dominated Parliament on matters pertaining to the war, though in most other questions, particularly religion, the Presbyterians had a clear majority both in Commons and the country as a whole.[25] The Independents remained a minority in Parliament until Pride's Purge, but it was otherwise in the military, where, as Firth explains, "During the two years which followed the formation of the New Model this Independent minority obtained by degrees complete control of the army."[26] The religious ideas of Independency soon became those of the army, and a majority of the officers came to look upon the war as a crusade for toleration. Parliament had, in effect, given up control over those militant, psalm-singing ranks, leaving the way open, as William Haller observes, for "Cromwell and his associates in the army [to forge] the spiritual energies aroused by Puritanism into an instrument of decisive action in the State."[27]

A glance at the situation that prevailed at the end of hostilities will help explain how the New Model Army was propelled into political prominence in England. Following the defeat of his forces, Charles shrewdly surrendered, not to Parliamentary forces, but to the Scots, where he hoped to turn to his advantage what he perceived as distrust between the two nations. Further, the army of Scots, now with a Stuart king in their hands, refused to leave English soil. They insisted upon remaining until certain promised sums were forthcoming from Parliament, and their presence exerted a subtle pressure on the English to adopt a Presbyterian church settlement. This circumstance, plus an impending Irish campaign, persuaded Parliament to maintain the New Model Army at full strength for months after the fighting had ended.

During this inactive period the army became a slowly boiling cauldron of democratic ideas and diverse religious movements. Battle is a leveling experience. When a man has fought for his life aside another man, considerations that might otherwise divide them lose significance in the face of the more fundamental bonds that unite them. In the New Model, young men of good family fought side by side with draymen and cobblers, and in their campgrounds Anabaptist bedded down with Brownist, all bound by

25. Gardiner, *Civil War*, 2:2.
26. *Cromwell's Army*, p. 319.
27. *Liberty and Reformation*, p. 342.

one common experience—they were good soldiers who had shared hard campaigns together. With no marches to make and no battles to fight, the soldiers turned to religious discussions. Particularly among the officers, that portion of time and energy not devoted to the essential business of training was taken up with preaching or listening to one another on the question of salvation and the various paths thereto. Although there were many diverse ideas on the subject, that special brand of toleration common to men who have faced death together created among the soldiers a strong unanimity on at least one point: each man should be permitted to find God in his own way and not by direction of the state. The reports reaching London of this growing sentiment for toleration in the army were viewed with some alarm by the Presbyterian members of Parliament, who now that the war had ended were once more asserting their majority position. When the King's person had finally been secured and the Scot had withdrawn beyond the Tweed, they hastily turned their attention to the reduction of the army.

Machiavelli remarks on how frequently a free city, fearing the loss of its liberties, will make the error of "giving offence to citizens who should be rewarded, and the suspecting of citizens in whom confidence should be placed."[28] Something of this order occurred when the Presbyterian majority of Parliament set out to eliminate what they had come to perceive as an organized threat to their plans for the political and religious settlement of England. They took steps to disband the New Model Army summarily, stubbornly refusing to make provisions for pay, long in arrears, or the all-important amnesty for those acts of war for which individuals might be held accountable by civil courts. The soldiers of the army—in Parker's marvelously descriptive phrase, "the hard-fighting, zealous, Scripture-quoting, democratic, political-minded Englishmen who had won victories for Parliament"[29]—were stung with this demonstration of ingratitude; and fearful of retaliation for their religious views, they struck back. It may seem fatuous to suggest that the course of English history would have been changed if Parliament had scraped together a little money and, promising more, paid its soldiers a token sum with an appropriately high-sounding vote of thanks; but, had they done so in

28. *The Discourses of Niccollo Machiavelli*, trans. Leslie J. Waller, S.J., 1:279.
29. *Milton: A Biography*, 1:321.

March 1647, the English Republic might never have appeared on the stage of history.[30] By summer it was too late, for on 1 June, Cornet Joyce, with the approval of Cromwell, secured the army's artillery train at Oxford and two days later took the King himself into custody.

An army is an instrument of force that operates in many ways according to laws comparable to those governing the physical universe. Once committed to a course of action, it is extremely difficult to stop; it will pursue that course until it is slowed by attrition or confronted by another force of equal or superior strength. In securing the artillery train and the King, the army had committed an open act of hostility against Parliament, one from which there could be no turning back; and, as G. M. Young observes, in this "struggle between a drilled, determined, and self-conscious minority and a loose, slow, compromising organ which every Parliament is bound to be," there could be only one outcome.[31] By July the New Model Army was marching through the streets of London in a show of strength, and a year and a half later Pride's Purge left a Rump Parliament in which an Independent majority, supported by military force, could decree the trial of King Charles and establish the English Republic.

Considering the tradition against which the army hurled itself, however, it was only a matter of time before it would fall in turn. The political history of England over the next thirteen years is an account of one attempt after another to call together a Parliament acceptable to the army. Each attempt failed, as the New Model purged or disbanded one impotent Parliament after another, until in a final anarchic frenzy it returned, like a prodigal child, to its first parent and recalled the King. During these years the focus of political power in England lay in the ranks of the New Model; and those Englishmen who, like John Milton, believed in liberty of conscience looked to these soldiers as the guardians of their freedom to find God in their own way.

There are only brief glimpses of John Milton's response to the

30. Kishlansky, *The Rise of the New Model Army*, pp. 179–222. This is a valuable study of the relationship between the army and Parliament in 1645–1647. The author argues that the polarization of Parliament took place much later than has been thought and that it was not until 1647, when the army was politicized by the hostility of the Presbyterian Parliament, that it developed its radical ideological fervor. See also Ashton, *English Civil War*, pp. 294–95.

31. *Charles I and Cromwell, An Essay*, p. 104.

events of this half-decade. By 1645 the tide of battle had ebbed from the vicinity of London, which had entered a period of relative calm. The war went on, but in more distant fields, and the city could return to a more normal existence. News of victories still roused the citizens to celebration, to be sure, but the Trained Bands seldom answered alarm calls and, save for the army's show of force in 1647 and occupation of the city in December 1648, the march of troops was infrequently heard in the streets.[32] The year 1645 was an eventful one for Milton, however. His wife returned to him unexpectedly, to be followed by a horde of relatives, evicted from their lands in Oxford, and the little house at Aldersgate Street was soon bursting at the seams. The family moved to larger quarters in Barbican, where Milton became immersed in the problems of his expanded household. His "slow-endeavouring art" bore first fruit with the publication of *Poems of Mr. John Milton*; and he appears to have achieved some measure of fame by this time, though it was not because of his poetry, as he might have wished. *The Doctrine and Discipline of Divorce* went through a third and fourth edition that year and was receiving attention from a growing list of detractors. He published *Tetrachordon* and *Colasterion* in March to answer their charges and at about the same time began to consider writing a history of the British nation.

There is little from his pen to record his immediate response to events between the First Civil War and the establishment of the Republic. His attitude toward the Presbyterians is clearly expressed in his tailed sonnet "*On the new forcers of Conscience under the Long PARLIAMENT*," in which he assails the Westminster Assembly with savage wit; but one must look to his later works for evidence of his reaction to the many twists and turns of the revolution that led finally to the execution of Charles I. It would appear, from these works, that at some point he developed a decided distaste for London and its citizens. After the early months of the war, when Londoners were bound together by the common cause of keeping the King's armies from their streets, he must have become increasingly uncomfortable there. As Valerie Pearl observes, there was always a strong residual Royalist sentiment in the city, and the majority of Londoners were staunchly

32. The last major engagement in which the Trained Bands participated appears to have been the Second Battle of Newbury, 27 October 1644, where six regiments (Gardiner has five, *Civil War*, 2:43) served under Sir James Harrington in Manchester's army (Raikes, *History of the HAC*, 1:141).

Presbyterian in their allegiance.[33] Once the fighting had ended, that majority, like its counterpart in Parliament, began to make itself felt. In early 1647 Presbyterians gained control of the city government and the Trained Bands, dismissing such Independent commanders as Isaac Pennington and John Fowke. With the King defeated, they launched what was in effect a counterrevolution against the loose alliance of radical sectaries, Independent politicians, and religious tolerationists that had dominated the war effort. In May the First Presbyterian Synod convened and immediately drew up lists of heresies punishable by imprisonment or death, and the first three chapters of the oppressive Westminster *Confession of Faith* were passed by Parliament. Mobs thronged to Westminster demanding that the army be disbanded; and in July, as the New Model gradually approached London, the Presbyterians set about organizing their own army, structured about the Trained Bands, with which to repulse the anticipated attack.[34] In that same month, further mobs of Londoners literally invaded Parliament, demanding, to use Masson's summary, "strict observance of the Covenant, the defence of His Majesty's person and just power and greatness, the disbandment of the Army, the thorough settlement of Presbyterian Government, the suppression of Conventicles, and defiance to the crotchet of Toleration."[35] These counterrevolutionary forces of London, in brief, stood for just about everything that Milton deplored.

London, thus, was no longer for him the "City of refuge, the mansion house of liberty" that it had been in *Areopagitica*, but a stronghold of Presbyterian intolerance where, as he wrote in *Pro Populo Anglicano*, "hucksters and artisans together with the most partisan ministers" opposed "an army famous for its loyalty, moderation, and courage." It was a city from which "a most insolent band of striplings, apprentices from shops" marched on Parliament, forcing the government "by their shouting and threatening to decree whatever they please," as he observed in *Defensio*

33. *Puritan Revolution*, pp. 107–59; Ashton, *English Civil War*, p. 303.

34. Pearl, "London's Counter-Revolution." See also Underdown, *Pride's Purge*, pp. 69–83, and Ashton, *English Civil War*, pp. 291–304. All attest to the difficulty of distinguishing a Presbyterian from an Independent; but, having so cautioned, they continue to use these apparently indispensable labels, as must we. Pearl attributes the counterrevolution to what she identifies as a "High Presbyterian" party, in alliance with the Peace party and London Royalists.

35. *Life*, 3:549–50.

Secunda.[36] Indeed, his early admiration for the Trained Bands also seems to have worn thin. In *Eikonoklastes* he wrote glowingly of "our Train'd Bands, which are the trustiest and most proper strength of a free Nation"; but after thinking it over, he qualified the remark in the 1650 edition by specifying that it applied only to a "Nation not at warr within it self."[37] Presbyterian London was no place for John Milton, which may help explain why he put more distance between himself and its mobs and synods, moving in the fall of 1647 to the quieter and more congenial district of High Holborn. Before that move, however, he probably had his first look at the army that was to play such an important part in his life. On 7 August 1647, the New Model marched through London. According to a Royalist sympathizer, their disciplined ranks impressed all with "the perfect order kept, and the abstinence from every act, word, or gesture, that could give offence";[38] and we can feel sure that Milton stood to watch the famous units pass, there to catch a glimpse of Fairfax, Cromwell, Skippon, Fleetwood, Lambert, and many others with whom he was later to associate in the councils of the English Republic.

But the wars and tumults seemed never to end. In 1648 there were Royalist uprisings in Kent, Essex, and Wales; there were more unruly mobs in London; and the Second Civil War ensued. Responding to this turbulence, Milton in a sonnet to Fairfax addressed himself for the first time directly to the New Model Army. He praises the lord general's firmness at Colchester but despairs that all that expense of blood and treasure has produced so little; it has certainly not brought peace, "For what can Warr, but endless warr still breed." One can detect in the lines a certain impatience, even frustration, with developments as he exhorts Fairfax to a "nobler task," ridding England of fraud and avarice. Of course, to a militant Puritan in the summer of 1648 it was a devious and tyrannical King, a Presbyterian Parliament, the treacherous Scots, and the shrill, intolerant London mob that were responsible for the continuing "Violence" and "Rapine" in the land; and though Milton, given the limitations of the sonnet form, is

36. *YP*, 4:511, 665.

37. *YP*, 3:448. Milton, however, always supported the rights of citizens to bear arms, as a safeguard against tyranny. See *The Readie and Easie Way*, *YP*, 7:435, 461.

38. Masson, *Life*, 3:554.

necessarily vague about what specifically is to be done, it is quite clear that he looks to the army to do it. What the soldiers did, of course, but a few months later, was occupy London, purge Parliament, and cut the King's head off. This may not have been what Milton had in mind at the time, but shortly thereafter he was to praise all three acts unreservedly.

The language of the sonnet is indeed harsh. Though he singles out Royalist rebellions and "the fals North" for condemnation, the references to "Public Faith" and "Public Fraud" indicate that he finds the real cause for the troubles much closer to home. He expresses his mind more plainly but with equal vehemence in his digression to *The History of Britain*, written but a few months earlier though not published at the time. There he attacks the members of the Long Parliament for their treachery and oppression, for "Foul and Horrid Deeds committed daily," and for fomenting "those Troubles and Combustions in the Land." He excoriates the Presbyterian divines as "Time-servers, Covetous, Illiterate Persecutors," seeking to set up "a Spiritual Tyranny by a Secular Power." Later in the digression he regrets that Britain is "fruitful enough of Men stout and courageous in War [but] not over-fertile of Men able to govern justly and prudently in Peace." Englishmen, he continues, are "Valiant indeed, and prosperous to win a field; but to know the end and Reason of winning, unjudicious and unwise"; hence "their Victories prove as fruitless, as their losses dangerous."[39] As the Fairfax sonnet implies, Milton can find no institution in the land capable of restoring peace and freedom to England except the New Model Army, for he exhorts its commander-in-chief to secure the fruits of his soldiers' victories, else "In vain doth Valour bleed."[40]

On 6 December 1648, the army committed a direct, physical act of aggression against the Parliament of England. Under the direction of a council of officers, whose guiding spirit was Henry

39. *YP*, 5:442–50.

40. Some have discovered in this sonnet, and in the two addressed to Cromwell and Vane, evidence of Milton's rejection of the military. Michael Wilding, for example, in "The Last of the Epics," discovers in its lines "an incipient distaste for war and military methods" (pp. 119–20), which, he suggests, evolved into the pacifism of *Paradise Lost*. Milton may well have been war weary but he was certainly aware that the troubles were being perpetuated by Royalist uprisings and Presbyterian mobs; and he was asking the commander-in-chief of the army to bring order out of the chaos. He did not make the mistake of many who confuse cause with agent and insist on blaming the war on the army. To Milton, the New Model was the solution, not the problem.

Ireton, Col. Thomas Pride barred the doors of the House of Commons to those members, most of them Presbyterians, who opposed the army's intention to bring King Charles to justice.[41] Cromwell and Fairfax were not personally involved in the decision, but they quickly voiced their approval, Cromwell with perhaps more enthusiasm than his superior. Milton was called upon to defend Pride's Purge frequently during his service in public office, and he performed the duty with eloquence. In *Pro Populo Anglicano*, for example, after reviewing the negotiations of the Treaty of Newport, in which Parliament and the King had come to an agreement totally unacceptable to the army, Milton comments:

> That part of the House, therefore, which was uncorrupted [i.e., the Independents] on seeing themselves and the commonwealth betrayed sought the aid of the army, which was ever brave and loyal to the state. In this affair my belief is, though I hesitate to express it, that our troops were wiser than our legislators, and saved the commonwealth by arms when the others had nearly destroyed it by their votes.[42]

The army, then, finally seized the power of government, initiating a military regime in England that Milton was to defend with his great wealth of learning and eloquence, his "noble task" of which all Europe would talk "from side to side."

* * *

Thus the soldiers of the New Model Army came to represent much that the poet valued in the religious and political life of the country. But what of Milton's muse? During this period, of course, he wrote largely with his "left Hand," and an assessment of the full effect of these events upon his art must await an examination of the major poems; but one work at least, *The History of Britain*, gives some indication that the victories of this Army of Saints, victories not only in the field of battle over the enemies of England but also in the streets of London and the halls of Parliament over the enemies of God, had stirred his imagination with the desire to write on a martial theme.

The young Milton had nourished an ambition to sing of "Arthur,

41. See Underdown, *Pride's Purge*, pp. 230–36, and Hexter, "Presbyterian-Independents," p. 31. Both discuss the difficulty of attaching party labels to the members excluded or admitted.

42. *YP*, 4:332–33. See also *Observations Upon the Articles of Peace*, *YP*, 3:327–28; and *Defensio Secunda*, *YP*, 4:665–66. In the latter Milton incorrectly attributes the purge to Cromwell.

who set wars in train even 'neath the earth, to tell of the high-hearted heroes bound together as comrades at the peerless table."[43] Early in the 1640s, however, he abandoned this design to write in the classical tradition of the martial hero; and it was suggested earlier in these pages that he did so because he found the time not ripe and his art not ready for such an effort.[44] It is ironic that Milton should have rejected the British theme just when he did, for England stood at the threshold of events that offered ample inspiration for such a work. In 1644 the stage was set for the appearance of a warrior figure equal in grandeur to any Achilles or Aeneas. Cromwell's Ironsides revived the image of a warlike English race, and the New Model Army was to become the embodiment of militant Puritanism, invincible in the wars of truth, surpassing every standard of virtue and courage that legend had attributed to early British arms. Marston Moor, Naseby, the revolt of the army, Cromwell's fury at Drogheda, his mercy after Worcester—these are the stuff of epic. Milton lived through it all, watched the regiments march to battle, shared the depression of defeat and the exhilaration of victory, and later sat at council with the victors. By the early 1650s the time was indeed right, the epic matter was there, and moreover the poet himself was ready.[45]

Much of his *History* attests to his evolving skill with martial narrative. The first full-fledged battle account, that of Caesar's invasion of England, contains many of the elements of epic wars: the landing of the ships, a "sudden tempest," the setting of ambush, stately speeches like that of the noble Caractacas,[46] scenes of general combat, and numerous passages describing individual valor. Two of the latter will give some flavor of the poet's ripening art: there is an account of the Roman standard bearer who while

> yet in the Gallies, first beseeching his gods, said thus alowd, *leap down Souldiers, unless ye mean to betray your Ensigne; I for my part will perform what I ow to the Commonwealth and my General.* This utter'd, over-board he leaps, and with his Eagle feircely advanc'd runs upon the Enemy; the rest hartning one another not to admit the dishonour of so nigh loosing thir cheif Standard, follow him resolutely;

43. *CW*, 1:293.
44. See pp. 37–40 above.
45. John Shawcross, "Survey," p. 343, has Milton beginning the *History* in 1647 or 1648. French Fogel, *YP*, 5:xxxix, suggests that he might have started as early as 1645.
46. *YP*, 5:72.

and another of "Scaeva a Roman Souldier," who,

> having press'd too farr among the *Britans*, and besett round, after incredible valour shewn, single against a multitude, swom back safe to his General; and in the place that rung with his praises, earnestly besought pardon for his rash adventure against Discipline.[47]

Though these accounts of battle may not have as yet the full epic ring, they are skillful works of imaginative description, evidence of Milton's growing mastery of the art of martial narrative.

But Milton did not return to that early design for his epic poem, a decision since applauded by centuries of readers of *Paradise Lost*; and the reasons may be found, once again, both in the nature of his studies and in the chronicle of his days. Milton's early expressions of enthusiasm for the Arthurian legend are rather charming; they have a delightful air of naiveté about them, suggesting a youthful awe at the exploits of those "high-hearted heroes." Or at least so they sound to more worldly modern ears, and it is generally agreed today that his turning from the theme is a sign of artistic and intellectual growth. Milton himself confirms this judgment to some degree in *An Apology Against a Pamphlet* of 1642, where he writes, almost nostalgically, of the wanderings of his "younger feet":

> I betook me among those lofty Fables and Romances, which recount in solemne canto's the deeds of Knighthood founded by our victorious Kings; & from hence had in renowne over all Christendome. There I read it in the oath of every Knight, that he should defend to the expence of his best blood, or of his life, if it so befell him, the honour and chastity of Virgin or Matron. From whence even then I learnt what a noble vertue chastity sure must be, to the defence of which so many worthies by such a deare adventure of themselves had sworne.[48]

The studies of his "riper years" took him to Plato and Xenophon, as he tells us; and eventually he was to focus the cold, hard light of history on the Arthurian legend and conclude that it was simply not true. The first accounts, he discovered, were written by those who were "blind, astonish'd, and strook with superstition as with a Planet; in one word, Monks," hence totally unreliable, and he came to question "whether ever any such reign'd in *Britain*." Perhaps, also, he had read of the resourceful Benedictines of Glaston-

47. *YP*, 5:45–46.
48. *YP*, 1:890–91.

bury, who announced in 1191 that they had found the bones of Arthur and Guinevere, thus enhancing immensely the appeal of their abbey as a place of pilgrimage.

Milton's studies, therefore, had convinced him that Arthur was "more renown'd in Songs and Romances, then in true stories";[49] but the experience of the early 1640s persuaded him in yet another way that those legends were not "true." In those years Milton viewed the grim face of war and emerged with the realization that the fabled "heroes of the table" were but pale figures of the fancy, unworthy of his art. They presented a highly idealized and totally unrealistic picture of both love and war. The young scholar had pored over works of courtly love and chivalric heroes, "those lofty Fables and Romances" recounting "deeds of Knighthood," and he was taken by their imaginative sweep and charm; but they were, of course, a literary fiction, at a distant remove from life, and their essential falseness was severely underscored by the tragic reality of Milton's own time. The idealized image of love was probably shattered in the summer of 1642, when his wife of a month rode off to Oxford, there to remain for three years; his vision of war was altered drastically by the months of despair and military defeat that followed. Lord Essex was no Arthur, and the ragged remnants of his dispirited army, straggling back to London in defeat, bore no resemblance to the knights-errant who rode out in search of the Grail. War, he found, was blood and iron; it was sorrow, disease, hunger, mutilation, and undignified death. Warriors were not a band of brave brothers united under the Cross, sacrificing their lives for virtue in the name of God, "bound together as comrades at the peerless table," but a group of wrangling generals, each blindly jealous of his preference, directed by a Parliament of contentious men squabbling endlessly over money while their soldiers wasted away from neglect. War was the problems of supply; it was taxes, requisitions, fearful alarms; it was marching out at dawn to stand for weeks in cold trenches, bored and listless. There were few heroes in those early years, before the New Model Army took the field. The soldiers of the Trained Bands trooped out worrying about their shops while their generals sipped wine and maneuvered for privilege. The contrast between the real and the imagined worlds was too blatant, too stark, to sustain for long the gleam of Prince Arthur's armor, which in

49. *YP*, 5:127–28, 164, 156.

Spenser's lines glittered "Like glauncing light of Phoebus brightest ray" (*The Faerie Queene*, 1.7.29). That gleam, corroded by the grim reality of war, dimmed in the imagination of the poet.

Further, if, as has been suggested, the prewar British soldier provided little inspiration for epic song, in quite another way the New Model trooper was equally inappropriate as a subject for celebration in a poem based on the Arthurian legend. The epic singer is at once poet, priest, and vessel of history. In shaping a tale of ancient heroes, he pictures a moral guide for men and women of his own time. Achilles and Hector were models for the contentious Greeks who attended Homer's song; and Virgil, in praising the Trojans of Aeneas, was celebrating the legions of Caesar. If the appearance of the New Model had stimulated Milton to praise the British Mars in epic song, his heroes would have been patterned on men who filled the ranks of that army. But Sir Lancelot bore little resemblance to Henry Ireton, and the Round Table's aristocratic knight-errant was a far cry from the Ironsides's "plain russet-coated captain" or its God-fearing draymen and cobblers. The two images clash so sharply that the New Model Army simply could not be praised in terms of the chivalric tradition; it would have been aesthetically indecorous and ideologically contradictory to celebrate the achievements of Cromwell with a poem about Arthur. It is true that both marched under the banner of God, both brought peace to a strife-torn kingdom, and both presided over councils devoted to Christian principles; but Arthur was, after all, a king, who, in the legend at least, ruled a priest-ridden court that subscribed to an archaic chivalrous code requiring unquestioned loyalty to the monarch and devotion to the church. His legend, moreover, had been adopted by the enemy; it had become, as E. M. W. Tillyard remarks, "a Royalist affair."[50] The New Model Army became for Milton a symbol of religious principles that were fundamentally at odds with these medieval allegiances. Its regiments were "gathered churches" where men came together to seek God, each as his individual conscience guided him. Its soldiers had joined the ranks to rid themselves of the yoke of kingship and the oppression of clerics who sought to force upon them the word and ritual of the one true way. If Milton had wanted to celebrate the Army of Saints, it would have been with a poem that praised not only its victories but also the pre-

50. "Milton and the Epics," p. 193.

cious freedom of conscience that it embodied. Arthur was simply not an appropriate vehicle for such a work. By 1648, at any rate, Milton's enthusiasm for the kings of his native land, indeed for kings of any land, had cooled considerably; and he had no interest in perpetuating the superstitious myths of the medieval church.

Milton was still confronted with the problem of what to do with all that material, the fruit of long hours of study and planning. He had given the project for a "British Troy" a great deal of time and thought, at one point jotting down a long list of subjects he considered appropriate to such a work, including the observation that "A Heroicall Poem may be founded somwhere in Alfreds reigne. especially at his issuing out of Edelingsey on the Danes. whose actions are wel like those of Ulysses."[51] Further, as has been noted, by 1647 England had produced an army whose deeds were most apt for epic song, and the poet, inspired by their victories, must have felt a rekindling of his youthful ambition to compose on a martial theme. But it was not to be; for at some point, seated at his desk in Aldersgate Street or Barbican, surveying that wealth of material, he decided to write a history instead.

James Holly Hanford has characterized *The History of Britain* "as a commutation of Milton's earlier projects for a drama or an epic on a British legendary theme";[52] indeed, the pages of that work ring with battle and abound in martial heroes. Aside from the extended passages on Brutus and Caesar, they trace, among others, the campaigns of Seutonius, who defeated Boadicea, and of Julius Agricola, including a detailed narrative of the battle of Mons Gropius. The reader finds that, save for the story of Leir, these narratives offer the only relief from the dreary recital of successive chiefs and kings that makes up the bulk of the early chapters. If one reads the opening pages of the work with Hanford's thought in mind, it is possible to catch a glimpse of what the discarded project might have been, for here are passages that would have adorned a poem composed in the epic tradition. We find Brutus, the grandson of Aeneas, destined before his birth to "be the death of both his Parents," banished to Greece when the prediction proves true. There he "so thrives in vertue and in Arms, as renders him belov'd to Kings, and great Captains above all the

51. *CW*, 18:241–45. There is no mention of Arthur in the list. By the time Milton began to search seriously for a subject, he had apparently abandoned the Arthuriad.

52. *Handbook*, p. 115. Tillyard agrees in *Milton*, p. 174.

Youth of that Land." Here are sieges, ambushes, battles, and the trick of Anacletus, which is worthy of Odysseus. There is poetry, too—Milton's translation of Diana's oracle:

> Brutus *far to the West, in th' Ocean wide*
> *Beyond the Realm of* Gaul, *a Land there lies,*
> *Sea-girt it lies, where Giants dwelt of old,*
> *Now void, it fitts thy people; thether bend*
> *Thy course, there shalt thou find a lasting seat,*
> *There to thy Sons another* Troy *shall rise,*
> *And* Kings *be born of thee, whose dredded might*
> *Shall aw the World, and Conquer Nations bold.*

There follows an odyssey "past the *Herculean Pillars*," further battles in Aquitania, and the founding of Tours, until finally, Aeneas-like, Brutus comes to his destined England, where he subdues the Giants in war and heroic games.[53]

Epic stuff indeed, though the inclusion of the legend of Brutus may seem something of a contradiction for a historian who had rejected Arthur as "more renown'd in Songs and Romances, then in true stories." Milton appears a bit uneasy about the inclusion himself, for he defends it at some length, citing the practice of ancient authors, Geoffrey of Monmouth in particular, as precedent. The historian may properly include such legends, he argues, since "oft-times relations heertofore accounted fabulous have bin after found to contain in them footsteps, and reliques of somthing true." Hence, in this tale of Brutus he is willing to include anything "so far as keeps alooff from impossible and absurd, . . . as the due and proper subject of Story"; and he apparently considered a magician's prediction and an oracle of Diana acceptably "alooff."[54]

It is perhaps sufficient to say that Milton opened *The History of Britain* with the myth of Brutus simply because he wanted to. Inspired by a heroic time, he wrote of an ancient hero in a history, where it seemed to him that myth had a place, though he apparently felt that one must select one's myth with care. Brutus was safe, perhaps because his legend was of a time before the church had enthralled the souls of men and thus might hold some lessons for us—but Arthur was not similarly safe. It does seem curious, however, that Milton would feel justified in mixing legend with

53. *YP*, 5:8–17.
54. *YP*, 5:3, 9.

history, which one would expect to be a reasonably accurate account of events, and yet reject myth as inappropriate for an epic poem, particularly when his classic models held no such reservations—surely the gods battling on the plains of Troy, the marvelous voyage of Odysseus, and the adventures of Aeneas owed little to rigorous documentation. In this apparent contradiction may well be seen Milton's judgment of the relative value of the two genres. Historians were given to errors, distortions, and partisan accounts. In his polemics of the 1650s, Milton was to use history as a pliable weapon, priding himself that he could turn the very facts cited in the attacks on the Republic into shafts against his opponents, who then lay "prostrate, smitten by their own missiles."[55] For him, history was an uncertain art and the epic poet must seek surer guides; his words must be in all things true. Thus, in his search for a subject, Milton turned from the dubious accounts of medieval monks to the pages of Holy Scripture, the word of God and the vessel of all truth.

Milton was not to celebrate the deeds of the New Model Army until he took up his pen as secretary for foreign languages to the English Republic's Council of State, but its victories seem to have reawakened in him for a time the desire to compose on the theme of a British Troy. In a sudden burst of creative energy, he poured all those years of study and thought into the pages of a history of warriors and their wars; and in so doing he set himself to school in the ancient art of martial narrative. Though he would never record the temporal triumphs of the Army of Saints in epic song, he would later recall their banners and anthems to figure the struggles of the spirit in lines that reflect the full flowering of that art:

now storming furie rose,
And clamour such as heard in Heav'n till now
Was never, Arms on Armour clashing bray'd
Horrible discord, and the madding Wheeles
Of brazen Chariots rag'd; dire was the noise
Of conflict; over head the dismal hiss
Of fiery Darts in flaming volies flew,
And flying vaulted either Host with fire.
So under fierie Cope together rush'd
Both Battels maine, with ruinous assault

55. *YP*, 4:399.

> And inextinguishable rage; all Heav'n
> Resounded, and had Earth bin then, all Earth
> Had to her Center shook. (*PL* 6.207–19)

But England's wars were not at an end. The Army of Saints had further battles to fight and victories to win, and further years of triumph and sorrow awaited Milton before the experience of these times was to bear full fruit in his art.

IV

Mr. Secretary Milton

From early youth I eagerly pursued studies which impelled me to celebrate, if not perform, the loftiest actions.—*Pro Populo Anglicano Defensio*

Shortly after two o'clock in the afternoon of 30 January 1649, on a scaffold built for the purpose outside Inigo Jones's splendid Banqueting Hall in Westminster, Charles I lost his head. The fall of the axe ushered in the eleven years of the English Republic, a period of political and constitutional experiment that was to have a profound influence on the evolution of the democratic system of government. The headsman also severed England's traditional executive authority from the body politic of the nation and presented the new government with the immediate problem of what to put in its place. The makers of the Revolution wrestled with this problem for the entire period of the Republic, unsuccessfully it would seem, since in the end England called back a king to resume his ancient role. For all but a few months of these eleven years John Milton was a servant of the various executive bodies that presided over the English government, and his experience of war during the period came as a consequence of that service. This experience was, however, very different from that of the previous decade, when as a concerned citizen of London he watched the flow of troops through the city streets and followed the news of victories and defeats on English battlefields. As secretary for foreign tongues to the Council of State he served a body that made the crucial decisions concerning the wars, that determined when they would begin and when they would end, that directed campaigns, raised funds, debated strategy, and shaped alliances upon which success or failure depended. There is no evidence that he had a voice in these decisions—he was valued more for his immense learning, his skill with languages, and the power of his pen—but he watched and listened as the makers of the Revolution determined the course that his nation would take in the affairs of Europe, then divided painfully between hostile Catholic and Protestant powers. Here he encountered warfare in new and larger dimensions. He had grown accustomed to the news of Roundhead and Royalist clashing among the familiar downs and pastures of Surrey or Kent; but English arms soon reached from Baltic shores to Caribbean beaches, and Milton wrote letters that followed them to strange and distant addresses—the Bey of Algiers, the Governor of Tetuan, and the Emperor of all Russia.

All was not calm at home, of course, but after 1651 the conflicts were those of the council chamber rather than the battlefield, and those soldiers who had dealt so resolutely with crises in military command were now confronted with the far more complex question of constitutional control. It was a basic tenet of the English Revolution that all authority in the state rested ultimately with the people, who expressed themselves through the voice of their elected Parliament. The executive power of the king, according to this theory, was only delegated to him in a social contract that could be nullified by the people once he showed himself a tyrant. In the years between the death of Charles I and the restoration of his son, the English Republic went through a series of constitutional crises, precipitated by efforts to adapt that high theory to the realities of seventeenth-century political life. In discussions of these experiments with executive authority, the eleven years of the Republic are generally divided into three periods. During the four years of the Commonwealth, 1649–1653, executive power resided in the Council of State, a body of forty-one men elected annually by Parliament, largely from its own ranks. During the Protectorate period, 1653–1659, authority was delegated to Oliver Cromwell and, for a short time, to his son, Richard. In the final year of the Republic, aptly called the Anarchy, the executive authority was assumed by a succession of bodies, some at times sitting simultaneously, contending for power.

A paucity of evidence hinders any precise definition of the status of Mr. Secretary Milton in these governments;[1] but it is clear that throughout the various transitions he was always the servant of the executive authority of the state, and an examination of

1. Recent critical comment has sought to diminish the scope of Milton's position in government, especially in the distasteful Protectorate. Parker, in *Milton: A Biography*, for example, identifies him as "little more than a translator and interpreter for monolingual bosses" (2:945). Austin Woolrych, in "Milton and Cromwell: 'A Short but Scandalous Night of Interruption'?" observes that by "the autumn of 1651, Milton was all but totally blind, and his official tasks had thinned to a trickle" (p. 188), a judgment which a brief glance at the Mylius papers will serve to correct (*YP*, 4:828–51).

those institutions may cast some light on the scope of his position.[2] The Commonwealth Council of State was an unwieldy and inefficient body that did most of its work through assorted committees, some standing, some ad hoc. That it was able to accomplish as much as it did is a tribute to the sacrifice and dedication of its members, who sat at least once daily for six and sometimes seven days a week. Though only some twenty members attended with any regularity, those who did put in a very full day, rising early to transact business before the meeting of Parliament, where most of them had seats, in addition to conducting committee meetings, hearings, audiences, and negotiations, as well as preparing the elaborately worded correspondence of seventeenth-century diplomacy. Government was a cumbersome process where issues had to be debated in council and then again in Parliament, often by the same men. The Rump was extremely sensitive of its prerogatives. Having done away with the monarchy, the members jealously guarded against an undue assumption of authority by any single individual. The first Council of State was directed to rotate the presidency monthly, and Parliament relented only when John Bradshaw refused to lend his considerable prestige to the body unless he were installed permanently in that position. Bradshaw sat as president of the council until December 1651, when at Parliament's renewed insistence the office began once more to be rotated among the members.

Barely a month after its first meeting, John Milton was called to serve the council "especially in connection with foreign affairs," as he put it later.[3] As secretary for foreign languages, he was responsible for correspondence between the council and foreign states; but since contact with European powers was somewhat limited during the uncertain early days of the revolutionary government, he was called upon to act in a variety of other capacities, among them licenser, translator, interpreter, secretary to committees, investigator, censor, and, probably the most time-consuming of all his tasks, political polemicist. In his faithful performance of these functions he became, in Don M. Wolfe's words, "a prompt, resourceful coworker in the immense variety of duties imposed

2. The material that follows is a much condensed summary of a more detailed study of the subject: Fallon, "Filling the Gaps: New Perspectives on Mr. Secretary Milton."

3. *YP*, 4:628.

upon the Council by the daily issues faced by the new republic."[4] He attended meetings of the Council of State where issues of war and peace were discussed,[5] took part in diplomatic negotiations, and assisted at audiences for foreign envoys, at the same time that he was preparing the lengthy *Articles of Peace* and composing *Eikonoklastes* and *Pro Populo Anglicano Defensio*. With the final fading of his eyesight in early 1652 he was forced to accept a less active role but apparently continued to perform many of the same duties. In March of that year the elderly Georg Weckherlin, who had been Latin secretary to Charles I, was engaged, it would seem, as an assistant to Milton.[6] When the old man died in February 1653, Milton wrote to Bradshaw recommending Andrew Marvell as his replacement, if "ye Councell shall thinke yt I shall need any assistant in ye performance of my place."[7] Whatever Milton's position was "in connection with foreign affairs," it had diminished considerably in importance by that time, for the council saw no need to replace Weckherlin, and Marvell had to wait four more years for an appointment. John Thurloe, who had been engaged a year earlier as secretary to the council and to the important Committee for Trade and Foreign Affairs, was becoming increasingly influential in government and had probably assumed most of Milton's duties, as well as a host of others.

On 20 April 1653, Cromwell dissolved the Rump and its Council of State. After several months of further experiments with at least the outward forms of republican government, he finally accepted the position of Lord Protector under a constitution, *The Instrument of Government*, which entrusted to him many of the executive powers that the Rump had been so careful to deny any single person. He revived a number of the institutions of the monarchy, including the offices of exchequer and secretary of state, and, as if to symbolize his new status, moved his family from the cramped confines of the old Westminster Palace on the west side of

4. *YP*, 4:144.

5. The Mylius papers alone reflect his attendance at council on twelve separate occasions from 16 October 1651 to 2 March 1652 (*YP*, 4:828–51).

6. Weckherlin was engaged as "assistant secretary for the Committee for Foreign affairs." Thurloe assumed duties as secretary to that body in May, but until then Milton was the only permanent member of the secretariat charged with responsibility for foreign affairs. See Fallon, "Mr. Secretary Milton," pp. 173–75.

7. *YP*, 4:860. In a letter of June 1654, Marvell addressed Milton as "Secretarye for the forrain affairs" (*YP*, 4:863).

King Street to the more spacious royal apartments, which had stood vacant since Charles I had left them in 1642. Cromwell became king in all but name, and the diminished size and importance of the Council of State emphasized this concentration of executive authority in his person. It was a smaller body under the Protectorate, sixteen in number, the majority of them military men who sat at Cromwell's pleasure, not as before by Parliamentary election, and it eventually became identified as the Lord Protector's "Privy Council." Cromwell assumed many of the functions of the monarch, the most important of which was the conduct of foreign affairs; and John Thurloe, appointed secretary of state, became his principal operative in that area. Thurloe headed an office that included the Latin secretaries, no longer identified as servants of the council, and he eventually drew under his control all of the functions of government that dealt with foreign powers, including a widespread intelligence system and the office of postmaster-general, which gave him access to the mails. These changes marked a decided shift toward conservative institutions after a republican experiment with the diffusion of executive powers, which had proven singularly ineffective in the seventeenth-century political environment.

In the final months of his fading eyesight, Milton had moved from the cramped and unhealthy quarters the council had provided him in Scotland Yard to a more spacious and pleasant house in Petty France, where he was in fact no further from the centers of government than he had been in his official residence.[8] He continued to perform what duties his infirmity permitted, and there is nothing to indicate that he was any less concerned or less well informed about the affairs of his country than he had been during the years of his more active participation. He retained his position as secretary for foreign languages and composed or translated an increasing number of state letters for the government, though there is no evidence that he was called upon for any services other than that correspondence. In his official status, it would appear, he acted under the direction of John Thurloe and thus became a part of the official circle that answered directly to the Protector.[9] His

8. The council and its committees conducted most of their business in old Westminster Palace on the west side of King Street, the site occupied today largely by the Treasury building. Milton's house was a short distance west of the Palace along modern Birdcage Walk. See Parker, *Milton: A Biography*, 2:999.

9. Fallon, "Mr. Secretary Milton," pp. 184–87. Milton's reply to Peter Heim-

defense of the Republic had made him an international figure with a reputation for learning and eloquence, which he enhanced with the publication of the *Defensio Secunda* and *Pro Se Defensio*, neither of which, unlike his earlier tracts, seems to have been commissioned by the government.[10]

Upon Cromwell's death in September 1658, his son, Richard, assumed the position of Lord Protector; but he lasted only nine short months. Richard lacked the skill and towering prestige of his father, and during his brief tenure political and religious forces that had been kept in check began to surface, bursting forth in the spring of 1659 to precipitate a period of political anarchy ending in the restoration of the monarchy. In April the army ended the Protectorate and the following month recalled the Rump Parliament, but the animosity between the soldiers and MPs was so deep-rooted that the two bodies were soon at each other's throats. In a little over a year four different Parliaments sat at Westminster, interrupted by three military coups (including Monk's assumption of authority in February 1660); and at least six separate bodies assumed the mantle of executive authority at one time or another.

Milton maintained his position as secretary for foreign languages for most of this period. He wrote a number of letters for Richard, and two more for the restored Rump in May; but though he was still on the payroll in October, he was probably little employed by a government too torn by internal strife to concern itself much with foreign affairs. After a long silence, he took up his pen as a private citizen to address himself once more to the problems of his day, this time directing his words to the English people rather than the international audience that had occupied his official attention as Latin secretary. He published two parts of a long

---

bach on 18 December 1657 is frequently cited as evidence of his isolation from public affairs (Hill, *Milton*, p. 191). Heimbach had written seeking Milton's aid in securing a position as secretary to the new minister from Holland, George Downing. Milton replied that he was unable to provide such help, pleading that his "influential friends were few" and that he was "nearly always at home." It cannot escape notice, however, that Milton was singularly well informed about the embassy for one supposedly so cut off from events. He knew that the position had already been filled and was even able to give accurate information as to the schedule of the party. Indeed, he had prepared Downing's credentials, dated only the day before (*YP*, 5:816). French suggests, accurately I think, that the pleading of lack of influence was probably a polite way of putting the young man off (*Life Records*, 4:189).

10. In *Pro Se Defensio* Milton says that he wrote *Defensio Secunda* "Because I was so ordered" (*YP*, 4:767), but there is no mention of the matter in the Order Books of the Council of State. It is possible that Thurloe may have commissioned the defense, but there is no record of such an order.

argument on religious freedom: *A Treatise of Civil Power in Ecclesiastical Causes* in April 1659, addressed to Richard's Parliament, and *The Likeliest Means to Remove Hirelings out of the Church* in August, this time to the restored Rump. The following spring he published *The Readie and Easie Way to establish a Free Commonwealth*, a utopian scheme designed among other things to reconcile the feuding Parliament and army, and his last word before the Restoration, *Brief Notes on a Late Sermon*. During the last years of the Republic, with his defense of the Revolution behind him and his official duties much diminished, he devoted his time to the composition of *De Doctrina Christiana* and, it is generally agreed, began *Paradise Lost*, though these projects probably received little attention during that final time of troubles.[11]

Two features of this eventful decade of Milton's public service bear directly on the subject of our study and deserve special attention as forceful influences on his creative imagination. Of primary importance is the fact that the English Republic was almost constantly at war. The Council of State had hardly convened before it was confronted with the problem of Ireland. One of Milton's first assignments was to prepare the text of the *Articles of Peace* negotiated in January 1649 between the Royalist Earl of Ormond and the Irish rebels and to write his *Observations* condemning the treaty. Cromwell left for Ireland with an army in July, but not before he and Fairfax had been forced to subdue an incipient Leveller mutiny in the army. The war in Ireland, conducted, as Milton later wrote, "in full accordance with the will of God,"[12] lasted the better part of a year. Cromwell's return to London in May 1650 was brief, however, for within a month he was leading the New Model north to Scotland, where Parliament's former ally had embraced the young Charles II and was threatening invasion. There, as Milton put it, "in about one year [Cromwell] completely subdued and added to the wealth of England that realm which all our kings for eight hundred years had been unable to master."[13]

England's domestic conflicts ended at Worcester, where in September 1651 Cromwell completely routed a Scottish army led by Charles II; but in less than a year the country was engaged in a protracted naval war with the Dutch, which dragged on until the middle of 1654. Milton was involved in the abortive negotiations

11. Shawcross, "Survey of Prose," pp. 367–68.
12. *YP*, 4:458.
13. *YP*, 4:670.

that preceded the Anglo-Dutch War, though because of his blindness his duties probably went no further than the preparation and translation of documents.[14] Hard upon this conflict came Cromwell's ambitious Western Design, which involved the dispatch of a large force to the Caribbean; and in the fall of 1655 there followed a treaty with France, which precipitated war with Spain, lasting until the Treaty of the Pyrenees in 1659. The Spanish war was primarily a naval action, but it did include the landing of an English expeditionary force in Flanders in 1658. Milton was called upon to prepare correspondence concerning the culminating action of that campaign, the capture of Dunkirk by an Anglo-French army and the city's immediate transfer to English control.[15] The next year brought the Anarchy, with its incessant military activity and the threat of civil war. Thus, the drums were seldom silent for the Republic; indeed, England was to engage in yet two more wars with the Dutch before Milton's death. This spectacle of global warfare provided the backdrop for the stage that Milton filled with rival armies of warrior-angels locked in cosmic conflict.

During the 1650s the soldiers of the New Model Army did not restrict their activities to the battlefield. Its officers were among the more active architects of the English Republic, and the militant minority that formed the various governments of that republican experiment held power only through the support of a politically oriented standing army.[16] When that army opposed the government, as in 1653 and 1659, it fell; when the army was virtually demobilized, as in 1660, the Republic itself fell. Though it had no more battles to fight after Worcester, the New Model was

14. Roger Williams spoke of teaching Dutch to Milton at about this time. It may well have been the poet's responsibility for the documents used in the exchange that excited his interest in the language. See Parker, *Milton: A Biography*, 2:1008.

15. *YP*, 5, State Papers 148, 149, and 150.

16. *Calendar of State Papers, Domestic Series, Commonwealth*, ed. Mary Anne Everett Green, 1:lxxiv. This is a summary of the records of attendance, including late and early arrivals, at meetings of the Council of State during the first year of the Commonwealth, meticulously kept by the council's secretary, Gualter Frost, Sr. Though there were 41 members elected, attendance was irregular during the first twelve months when members sat on an average of only 33% of the time, or about 13 members per meeting. The record of the 12 military members was notably better than that of the balance of the body. During the critical first months of the Republic, for example, before the army rebellion of May required many of the officers to take to the field, Cromwell attended 74% of the meetings, Jones 67%, Stapley 57%, Constable 54%, Ludlow 54%, Wauton 45%, and Fairfax 40%. There were exceptions, of course; Skippon, who was regularly elected to the council, took little interest in the proceedings.

maintained at near full strength, an alert and highly professional force never far from the consciousness of those who exercised power in England. Its officers sat in Parliament and the Council of State, close to the ear of Cromwell, who deferred to them in many critical decisions, among them his rejection of the crown. They were highly visible, especially after 1655, when the kingdom was divided into eleven districts and each placed under the administrative control of a major-general of the army, a most unfortunate experiment in military government. Indeed, it was not until 1660, when the Rump succeeded in dismantling and demoralizing the army and dispersing it to distant corners of the country, that the Royalists began to entertain realistic hopes of restoring the monarchy.

In trying to understand Milton's attitude toward these wars and soldiers of the English Republic, the scholar is somewhat handicapped, for aside from the veiled allusion of his later poetry, Milton had little or nothing to say about the entire period of the Protectorate. In the *Defensio Secunda* he praises Cromwell for assuming power, but his survey of the history of his time ends there. Thus all we have are opinions on the Commonwealth period and the brief interval of the Barebones Parliament, which he dismisses with a scornful phrase: "The elected members came together. They did nothing."[17] Further, most of these opinions are expressed in highly partisan tracts intended for an international audience, and it is surely possible that his admiration for Cromwell and the New Model may have been more qualified than those tracts reflect.

Given this paucity of evidence, it has been customary for scholars to infer his attitude toward events by extrapolating opinions from his other works and applying them to the matter in question; and this is certainly a useful device under the circumstances. In doing so, however, one must be cautious to avoid attributing to him views that would seem to contradict what he actually did say. Admittedly, the encomia in defense of the Republic are somewhat exaggerated, but they cannot therefore be dismissed as mere exercises in rhetoric, a mature display of skills developed in his schoolboy prolusions. He may not have said all that he thought, but it can surely be assumed that he was sincere in what he did say; and no nice analysis of tone or language, or resort to the open-ended

17. *YP*, 4:671.

possibilities of irony, should be permitted to persuade us that he meant the opposite of what he said. We are not at liberty, for example, to suggest that he disapproved of the dissolution of the Rump in 1653, since he stated rather unequivocally that he applauded the act.

In considering events about which Milton provides no expressed opinion, it is a natural temptation for the fond scholar to attribute to his favorite figure sentiments very close to his own. A modern, liberally oriented student of literature, devoted to individualism and freedom of inquiry, can happily embrace Milton's passion for liberty of conscience; but he may have difficulty accepting the poet's loyalty to a military dictatorship and may, therefore, search among his words for sentiments that would seem to qualify that loyalty. Unfortunately, Milton is not much help. It is entirely possible that he regretted Cromwell's foreign adventures in the Caribbean and on the Continent, preferring that the nation's energies be directed to the resolution of domestic problems—but he nowhere says so. One might assume that he found the rule of the major-generals distasteful—but he nowhere says so. A close reading of Michael's revelations in books 11 and 12 of *Paradise Lost* may persuade one that Milton became disenchanted with the Protectorate; but such an interpretation must be balanced against the fact that he continued to serve his government faithfully; and if the policies of that regime did displease him, unfortunately again, he nowhere says so. There are so many things we might wish he had said. It is possible, for example, to read in the lines of *Paradise Lost*, so rich in allusion, latinate double meanings, and subtle tones, an antimilitarist persuasion; but to conclude that the Milton of 1648, of 1653, or of 1660 was therefore opposed to the military or single-mindedly set against war and violence, no matter how admirable such sentiments, is to fly in the face of historical context and his own written words. As a political polemicist, he may well have exaggerated his admiration for the soldiers of the New Model Army, but aside from his distress over the coups of 1659, he penned nothing but praise for them.

After the founding of the Republic, Milton's expression of approval of the Army of Saints continues undiminished, but it is more frequently associated with praise for its lord general. His first public reference to Oliver Cromwell is in *Observations on the Articles of Peace*, where the poet cites his "eminent and remarkable Deeds" in contrast to Ormond's lackluster military achievements.[18] In *Pro Populo Anglicano* he again praises Cromwell's victories over the "villainous and savage scum of Ireland," which, as Wolfe notes, must have included the brutal sack of Drogheda and Wexford.[19] Indeed, in the almost two hundred pages of the work, Cromwell is the only member of the Puritan cause singled out by name. In the *Defensio Secunda* Milton devotes twenty pages to the Lord Protector, interrupted only by a brief aside on Fairfax—over ten percent of the entire tract! In this work Milton fulfills most dramatically the role he had proposed for himself in his sonnet "Captain or Colonel, or Knight in Arms," one which he redefines early in the text: "And so I concluded that if God wished those men to achieve such noble deeds, He also wished that there be other men by whom those deeds, once done, might be worthily praised and extolled, and that truth defended by arms be also defended by reason."[20]

Thus Milton commends Cromwell's piety, modesty, and self-control; he acclaims his qualities of leadership and his ability to attract devout men to the ranks of his regiments; he lauds his bravery and recites the list of his victories; he applauds the dismissal of the Rump, a body of men whom he condemns as more attentive to their private interests than to the welfare of the state; and he glorifies the assumption of power by the Lord Protector: "Cromwell, we are deserted! You alone remain." Milton addresses him as the "liberator of your country, the author of liberty, and likewise its guardian and savior," one who has "outstripped not only the achievements of our kings, but even the legends of our heroes."

Rather heady stuff, admittedly, but even accepting but half the praise, it is difficult to dismiss the impression of strong approval and admiration. It has been suggested that in the next few pages of the tract there appears a tone of disapproval, or of warning. Milton cautions Cromwell against the tainting influence of pomp and power and urges him to continue the struggle in the cause of liberty. The best way to avoid the corrupt influence of privilege, Milton advises, is to admit "those men whom you first cherished as comrades in your toils and dangers to the first share of your counsels." After two more pages of eulogy, he names those "comrades"—Fleetwood, Lambert, Desborough, Whalley, Overton—in all twelve, eight of them officers in the New Model Army. These are the men who, he is confident, will counsel Cromwell to pro-

18. *YP*, 3:312. 19. *YP*, 4:323, 458n. 20. *YP*, 4:553.

mote freedom of worship, simplify the laws, educate the young, eliminate censorship, and be open to the free expression of conscience.[21] Only one with the acuity of hindsight could read into these pages an implied criticism of Cromwell and the Protectorate. The Lord Protector surely did not live up to all of Milton's hopes, particularly his fond desire that the civil power would "leave the church to the church," but it cannot therefore be concluded that Milton washed his hands of the whole regime.

This paean to the Lord Protector has the same rhetorical structure as a number of Milton's public addresses—a praise of former deeds, a note of caution or reminder of issues at hand, and an exhortation to future greatness. It is the same message to be found in his sonnet to Fairfax of 1648 and in those written to Cromwell and Sir Henry Vane some four years later. These three works are occasionally cited as evidence of Milton's antiwar sentiments, reflecting, in the words of one commentary, "an incipient distaste for war and military methods."[22] Such readings suggest that the octaves and sestets of the poems present, respectively, the alternatives of war and peace to the men addressed, and that Milton is urging them to reject one and embrace the other. The Fairfax sonnet can hardly support such an interpretation, as we have seen—Milton is urging the commander-in-chief to make use of the army, not turn from it—and the two later poems are equally as difficult to fit into the antimilitary mode. When Milton composed the sonnet to Cromwell in the spring of 1652, there were no wars to be rejected; England had been at peace since Worcester. When he wrote to Vane a few months later, the English fleet in the Downs had only just been badly mauled in what was seen as a treacherous sneak attack by the Dutch; and Milton was not one to propose that they turn the other cheek. He is praising Vane's handling of the devious Dutch, his ability "to unfold / The drift of hollow states hard to be spelld" and his skill in advising "how warr may best, upheld, / Move by her two maine nerves, Iron & Gold."[23] Actually, Milton's mind is not on the issue of war versus peace,

21. *YP*, 4:662–78.

22. Wilding, "The Last of the Epics," p. 119.

23. Masson, *Life*, 4:372–73. Masson suggests that Van Tromp's attack on Blake was an accident, but to the English it seemed a treacherous and unprovoked act of war, the final in a series of indignities they had suffered at the hands of the Dutch, beginning with the hostile reception of the Strickland—St. John mission of early 1651 and the assassination of Isaac Dorislaus in the Hague that May (ibid., 4:49, 275–78).

which seems to preoccupy the attention of so many twentieth-century commentators. His concern is religious freedom, as it so often is, and the threat that the Parliament's newly appointed Committee for the Propagation of the Gospel may be preparing to impose restrictions on liberty of conscience. He is asking the two men to take notice, reminding Cromwell that "peace hath her victories / No less renownd then warr" and Vane that he is admired for his knowledge of "Both spirituall powre & civill, what each meanes." Cromwell is then urged to act with the same resolve he displayed on the battlefield "to save free Conscience" from those who would seek to enslave it, and Vane is reminded more subtly that he is the "eldest son" of Religion.

Milton is not making distinctions or defining choices. In these sonnets he is pointing out to the two men that the opportunities of peace are theirs *as a consequence of* their triumph in war, not as an alternative to it. With the King beheaded, the Irish and Scots subdued, and Charles II chased from the land, it is time to reap the benefits of all that effort. It is the same thought he expressed in *Pro Populo Anglicano* concerning the situation in the summer of 1647, when Parliament acted to insure that the king would not "pluck the sweet fruit of victory from our army,"[24] and again in 1648, when he urged Fairfax to a "nobler task," lest valor bleed in vain. The movement of these poems is temporal, not discriminating. The octaves look to the past, praising Cromwell for his military prowess and Vane for his political skills. The sestets look to the future, the one exhorting the soldier not to flag in his efforts, for "much remaines" to be done, the other, more obliquely, reminding the statesman of the cause for which these wars had been fought. Milton is cautioning his countrymen that, having won the war, they must take care not to lose the peace.

Though, as has been noted, there is little evidence to go on, it would be unreasonable to assume that Milton approved of everything that Cromwell and the New Model Army did. If Christopher Hill is correct and the poet identified himself ideologically with the extreme sectarians, then he may have had some reservations about the suppression of the Diggers and Levellers in the spring of 1649.[25] It is difficult to imagine him warming to the rule of the major-generals, no matter how dangerous the threat of Royalist

24. *YP*, 4:510.
25. *English Revolution*, p. 170.

plots at the time; and he was to be disappointed in his hopes that the Protectorate government would succeed in separating church and state.[26] He disapproved of the manner in which the army dismissed Richard's Protectorate Parliament in April 1659, though he can have had no regrets about the dissolution of a Presbyterian body that had ordered the hated Solemn League and Covenant read in every church; and he found Lambert's coup of October fraught with peril.

It will be of value to examine these latter events with some attention, because many scholars have found in Milton's tracts during the Anarchy evidence that he repudiated Cromwell, rejected the government he had served as Latin secretary, and turned his back on the army that supported it.[27] Frustrated by Milton's si-

26. A letter to Milton from Moses Wall, dated 26 May 1659 (*YP*, 7:510–13), is occasionally cited as an indication of the poet's disenchantment with the Protectorate. As evidence, however, it is highly questionable. Milton had sent Wall a copy of *A Treatise of Civil Power* with a letter enclosed, which has not been recovered, and the commentary attempts to reconstruct the substance of that letter from Wall's reply. In the process, many of Wall's views are attributed to Milton and there is further confusion when Wall's response to the book is misinterpreted as a reply to the letter. Wall remarks that he "was uncertain whether yor Relation to the Court (though I think a Commonwealth was more friendly to you than a Court), had not clouded yor former Light; but *yor last Book* resolved that Doubt" (italics mine). The parenthetical remark clearly represents Wall's response to the book and is thus highly subjective, as there is nothing in *A Treatise of Civil Power* to substantiate conjecture about Milton's political preferences. The work deals with the church-state issue, and though Milton was disappointed with the Protectorate's inaction in the matter, he certainly does not criticize the regime in its pages, quite reasonably, since he is addressing the book to the Protectorate Parliament. The only reference *to Milton's letter* is Wall's comment that the poet had complained "of the Non-progresency of the nation, and of its retrograde Motion of late, in Liberty and Spiritual Truths"; and it is surely possible that in the letter Milton had voiced his dissatisfaction with the Presbyterian-leaning Parliament's recent order reasserting the Solemn League and Covenant. Taking this comment as his cue, Wall launches into a highly charged diatribe against the entire Protectorate, blaming all of England's problems on those who "watched or Saviors Sepulchre to keep him from rising," in brief, the military. *These are Wall's views, however, not Milton's*; and any conclusions about Milton's sentiments drawn from this reply to his unrecovered letter must be open to serious question. Christopher Hill cites Wall's words in his argument that Milton held antimilitary views and wished to disassociate himself from the Protectorate (*English Revolution*, pp. 192, 201, 202, 214). Hill errs at one point (p. 191) by quoting from Milton's *A Letter to a Friend*, written five months later, as if it were a reply to Wall. The "Friend" has not been clearly identified but internal evidence precludes the assumption that he was Wall.

27. Hill suggests that he praised the Rump in 1659, "and so by implication" criticized Cromwell (*English Revolution*, p. 197). Austin Woolrych proposes that the tracts of 1659 represent a "complete rejection of the Protectorate" ("Milton and Cromwell," p. 185). See also Barbara Lewalski, "Milton: Political Beliefs and Polemical Methods, 1659–1660," p. 192; Don M. Wolfe, *Milton in the Pu-*

lence on the Protectorate, scholars have looked ahead for clues to the final days of the Interregnum, when for a brief time he wrote once more with his left hand to cry out a warning and counsel against despair in a period of political disorder. They find evidence for his rejection of the Protectorate in his disapproval of the army's actions during those days and in his often-repeated warning, in both published and unpublished works, about the dangers of government by a "single person."[28]

Perhaps a brief glance at the salient events of that final year will serve to place Milton's words in context. In April 1659 four thousand troops of the New Model, since Cromwell's death under the nominal command of his son-in-law, Major-General Charles Fleetwood, marshaled in St. James Park and forced the dissolution of Richard Cromwell's Parliament, in effect bringing the Protectorate to a close. The following month, at the urging of the younger officers and men of the army, Fleetwood recalled the members of the Rump whom Cromwell had dismissed six years earlier. That body was no sooner seated than it began to remodel the army. The memory of 1653 still rankled in the minds of MPs, who sought to draw the teeth of the New Model by systematically cashiering the Cromwellian officers in its ranks, those who unfortunately constituted the backbone of its effectiveness. By October over 160 officers had been decommissioned, and by the following February half the officers of the army had either been dismissed or transferred to remote posts.[29] General George Monk, in distant Scotland, was able to resist the worst effects of this campaign and, having conducted his own remodeling, emerged with a cohesive force entirely loyal to him.

This slow emasculation of the army was interrupted on 1 August, when Sir George Booth led an ill-timed and poorly organized Royalist uprising, which General John Lambert quelled at Winnington

---

ritan Revolution, p. 290; and Merritt Y. Hughes, *Ten Perspectives on Milton*, pp. 267–68.

28. For a more thorough discussion of the issues see Fallon, "Milton in the Anarchy, 1659–1660: A Question of Consistency." In the process of condensing the material, I have reluctantly omitted the interesting controversy over the "short but scandalous night of interruption" from the preface to *The Likeliest Means* (pp. 131–34). In brief, I agree with Masson that the "interruption" was the two-week interval between the dismissal of the Protectorate Parliament and the recall of the Rump (*Life*, 5:607). For alternative explanations, see Woolrych, "Milton and Cromwell," pp. 185–218, and William B. Hunter, Jr., "Milton and Richard Cromwell."

29. Godfrey Davies, *The Restoration of Charles II, 1658–1660*, p. 261.

Bridge some three weeks later. Parliament, initially generous in its praise, grew increasingly uneasy at the presence of such a large body of troops in the field, and in acting to protect itself only succeeded in angering the army. Lambert marched on Westminster and dissolved the Rump on 13 October. A Committee of Safety assumed executive authority, but on the issue of Parliament the military split into two factions. Monk in Scotland, the army in Ireland, and the fleet declared openly for the Rump, while the forces around London supported Fleetwood and Lambert. Pressure mounted until on 24 December the committee was forced to reseat the Rump. That body rapidly became unpopular, however, and by the end of January 1660 the government was virtually powerless, leaving Monk, who had managed to remain relatively untouched by events, as the only credible political or military figure in England. On 3 February he marched an army of five thousand men into what had by then become a political vacuum. He occupied London, much to the relief of Parliament and the distracted citizens of the city, and in so doing became the most powerful figure in England. On 21 February, he reseated those members of Parliament who had been secluded in Pride's Purge, some eleven years prior, in effect paving the way for the Restoration. Monk quickly dissolved that body once it had provided for new elections. The Convention Parliament met on 1 May and seven days later declared Charles II king.

Such a brief summary cannot hope to develop the many complex issues involved; but it does highlight the single most important political factor that led to the downfall of the Republic—the open struggle between the army and Parliament, each blindly striking out at the other, both apparently oblivious to the fact that their survival depended upon the union of their efforts. Lambert's coup was the last, desperate effort of the New Model Army, by then much weakened and demoralized by the Rump's remodeling, to prevail as a force in the government. The failure of that effort left the Republic without support and created a power vacuum into which rushed long-dormant forces, propelling the country toward the Restoration. The spectacle of the two chief props of the Republic destroying one another compelled Milton to interrupt his work on *Paradise Lost* and turn his attention to the question of a constitutional settlement, which must have been far from his mind at the time. It has been suggested that in his Anarchy tracts Milton finally repudiated the Army of Saints that he had admired and extolled so eloquently in earlier days. I would argue that this was not his intent or his effect, and that he was, rather, struggling to evolve a political settlement that would reconcile the two feuding bodies and save the Republic.

Milton's response to the crisis is recorded in five documents, constituting a political testament of no small importance: *A Letter to a Friend*, dated 20 October 1659, written after a visit from an unnamed acquaintance who had given him an account of Lambert's coup; *Proposalls of Certaine Expedients for the Preventing of Civill War*, written sometime between that date and the reseating of the Rump in late December; *The Readie and Easie Way to Establish a Free Commonwealth*, published in February 1660, with a second edition appearing in April; *The Present Means, and brief Delineation of a Free Commonwealth*, written to General Monk in late February 1660; and *Brief Notes Upon a Late Sermon*, a reply to Dr. Matthew Griffith, published in April. These works do not by any means represent a carefully thought-out corpus of political thought. Milton, "the practical politician, close to events," as Barbara Lewalski puts it, was responding to the various phases of the crisis; and his central concern throughout was to rescue the Puritan cause from the threat of restored monarchy.[30] He was improvising, reacting to the swift decline of order, searching for ways to reconcile Parliament and the army, ultimately devising a utopian scheme that he thought would make possible their living with one another.

Lambert's coup shocked Milton. In *A Letter to a Friend* he records his immediate response to the event and begins to sketch out a constitutional design intended to heal the breach between the two bodies. It "amazes" him, he says, that the army should dissolve Parliament. It is an act other nations will look upon as "most illegal and scandalous, I fear me barbarous." But there is a distinct note of tension in his remarks, as if he cannot believe what he has heard, or doesn't want to. His criticism is heavily tempered with qualifications: "I presume not to give my Censure on this Action, not knowing, as yet I do not, the bottom of it. I speak only what it appears to us without doors, till better cause be declar'd." His chief concern is the reputation of the army: "Other Nations will judg to the sad dishonour of that Army, lately so renown'd for the civilest and best order'd in the World, and by us here at home, for

30. "Political Beliefs," p. 197.

the most conscientious." There must be some other explanation: "For, neither do I speak this in reproach to the Army, but as jealous of thir Honour, inciting them to manifest and publish, with all speed, some better cause of these thir late Actions, than hath hitherto appear'd."

He nowhere proposes that the powers and prerogatives of the army should be curtailed. On the contrary, he accepts the suggestion that the Rump may have been "well dissolv'd, as not complying fully to grant Liberty of Conscience," as he had urged at such length in his tracts earlier in the year. It is not his purpose here to take sides, however; he is searching for a formula for reconciliation. Since it was the Rump's campaign to cashier officers and the army's retaliation in October that had precipitated the crisis, he hopes to defuse the situation by proposing that both officers and members of his legislature be granted life tenure, and that they declare "a mutual League and Oath, private or publick, not to desert one another till Death." While this expedient may at first glance appear somewhat visionary, even naive, it must be remembered that Milton is writing in haste, feeling his way in an unfamiliar task, the structuring of a utopian government. He is sketching out alternatives, which will have to be reconsidered when leisure permits: either recall the Rump or leave it "well dissolv'd," establish "an Annual Democracy, or a perpetual Aristocracy"—he is unsure as yet which would be best. He draws on both his wealth of learning and his decade of experience in government to find a way out. In some matters he is clearly resolved, however: the army "cannot discharge at once both Military and Civil Affairs" and so must create "a Senate, or General Council of State" to govern the land; it matters not which so long as its members agree to two conditions, "full liberty of conscience, and the abjuracion of Monarchy." But something must be done quickly, he tells his friend, for they stand in "the hazard of our Safety from our common Enemy, gaping at present to devour us."[31]

Within days the country stood on the brink of civil war, with half the army supporting the Committee of Safety and the other half, joined by the fleet, demanding the recall of the Rump; and hostile regiments of the once-proud Saints faced each other across the Tweed.[32] In December Milton wrote some more carefully con-

31. *YP*, 7:324–33.

32. Davies, *The Restoration*, p. 172. From late November until the end of December, Lambert, with a force of perhaps twelve thousand men, faced Monk's

sidered recommendations, a ten-point program aptly entitled *Proposalls of Certaine Expedients for the Preventing of Civill War.* The army's Committee of Safety is to continue its vigilance against enemies at home and abroad; but, he has decided, the Rump must be reseated, once more to "sitt indissolubly," its members assured life tenure, as are the chief officers of the army. Its name is to be changed to "a Grand or Supreme Counsell" and all concerned bound once more by an oath to support liberty of conscience and oppose "a single person & house of Lords." He is filling in the gaps of his design by now, though still somewhat sketchily, with proposals for elections, local government, and the judiciary.[33]

But events were moving too swiftly. The Rump was recalled and did little except complete its work of dismantling the army, losing all credit in the eyes of the people. Monk occupied London, restored the secluded members, demanded new elections, and finally dissolved the famous Long Parliament for good, while Royalists' cries for the return of the king rose to a crescendo. Against this background, with the Republic crumbling about him, Milton continued with a single-minded intensity to define his vision of a free commonwealth, and in late February *The Readie and Easie Way* appeared in print. In April, while members of the Convention Parliament were making their way to Westminster and Charles II sat at Breda awaiting the propitious moment to embark, the poet brought out a second edition of this fiery warning against the evils of kingship. This puzzles most. Milton was politically aware; he must have known it was all over, that he could change nothing, that he already walked in the shadow of the gallows—and yet he insisted on that last, defiant denunciation of monarchy, a second edition, as if the first were not enough. *Paradise Lost* was but a brilliant fragment at the time, and as a consequence of that final, desperate cry, "*O earth, earth, earth*!" it might have come down to us as yet another of those unrealized masterpieces of the language. What could have possessed him? Was it a "magnificently courageous gesture," as Christopher Hill suggests;[34] or was it the last, quixotic unfurling of a doomed banner on that shattered battlefield of the wars of truth; or was it simply an act of helpless anger,

army of two-thirds that number. Lambert's army dissolved with the restoration of the Rump, and Monk began his march to London on 1 January without opposition.

33. *YP*, 7:336–39.

34. *English Revolution*, p. 199.

a blind Lear raging against the elements, "then let fall / Your horrible pleasure; here I stand"?

We shall never know; our interest in this complex and provocative document is more prosaic in nature, a concern with its definition of the relationship between the military and the civil government and the identity of that ominous "single person." The reseating of the Rump in December had proved a disappointment; and since the reconstituted Long Parliament was unlikely to be sympathetic to any design for the continuation of the Republic, Milton now proposes elections in which a carefully controlled constituency will choose members of a "supreme Senate," who will sit perpetually. It has been suggested that Milton's preference for such a body arose from his mistrust of the English people, his growing conviction that they had not achieved a level of spiritual maturity that would warrant self-government. He was very likely further influenced by the immediate necessity to assure any English legislator security in office, a conviction born of the experience of recent events; and he may have been reaching back for a model to the more stable years of the Protectorate, when Cromwell's Council of State sat as just such a body. In any event, he proposes no limitations on the authority or independence of the army; indeed, he clearly indicates that he depends on the military, as he always has, to safeguard the commonwealth against tyranny from within and without. He anticipates that the major objection to his constitutional design will be the fear that the senate will wield too much power, and he is careful to assure his readers that this will not be the case so long as the army is there to check its aspirations:

> Neither do I think a perpetual Senat, especially chosen and entrusted by the people, much in this land to be feard, where the well-affected either in a standing armie, or in a setled militia have thir arms in thir own hands.[35]

He repeats the assurance later in the tract:

> And when our forces by sea and land, either of a faithful Armie or a setl'd Militia, in our own hands to the firm establishing of a free Commonwealth . . . what can a perpetual senat have then wherin to grow corrupt, wherin to encroach upon us or usurp; or if they do, wherin to be formidable?[36]

35. *YP*, 7:435.
36. *YP*, 7:461.

Milton is silent on the question of who is to control the armed forces if the Grand Council does not. In what seems a contradictory statement, he proposes elsewhere in the tract that the Grand Council "have the forces by sea and land committed to them for preservation of the common peace and libertie."[37] I can only suggest that he conceived of the army as a separate entity in the commonwealth, to be kept from the control of the Grand Council during time of peace, thus serving as a deterrent to that body's aspirations for power, but to be "committed to them" during time of national emergency. Some hint of his intention can be found in *The Present Means*, in which Milton is attempting to persuade Monk to adopt the program. The Grand Council, he tells the general, will "dispose of Forces, both by Sea and Land," but no one need fear its power because the council will direct the military only "under the conduct of your Excellency."[38] So there will be some person in control of these forces, one powerful enough to maintain them as an authority distinct from his perpetual senate, presiding over them independently in time of peace and commanding them under its direction during time of war. Milton's meaning is not clear; he was probably not sure of it himself. One cannot escape the conclusion, however, that throughout the tract his chief concern is to limit the power of the senate, *not* the military.

It has been widely suggested that Milton's warning against government by a "single person" in these tracts constitutes a repudiation of Cromwell and the entire Protectorate regime.[39] The phrase began to appear in the literature of the period with some frequency after the army had dismissed Richard Cromwell's Parliament in April 1659, when the anti-Cromwellian forces were strong in the restored Rump and that body proposed an oath for

37. *YP*, 7:432–33.

38. *YP*, 7:394. Hill's suggestion that Milton was concerned with how "military intervention [was] to be prevented" (*English Revolution*, p. 200) needs reexamination in this light. I can find nothing in the tract to substantiate his assertion that the militia "would guard against the influence of the army at the center" (p. 201).

39. Austin Woolrych, in "Milton and Cromwell," p. 212, finds the poet reacting "against a whole regime rather than a single personality." A. S. P. Woodhouse, in *The Heavenly Muse: A Preface to Milton*, ed. Hugh MacCallum, pp. 115–16, states that in his final tracts Milton is opposed to "any form of single person rule—such as the Protectorate." More recently, Mary Ann Radzinowicz suggests in *Milton's Mind*, p. 146, that in *The Readie and Easie Way* he "declines to continue an implicit endorsement of rule by a single person." See also Arthur E. Barker, *Milton and the Puritan Dilemma, 1641–1660*, pp. 261, 263.

members of its Council of State to support the Commonwealth "as it is declared by Parliament without a single person kingship or house of peers."[40] There is no doubt as to what the Rump meant in May 1659, but to suggest that Milton shared these views in February 1660 is to rip these words out of historical context and to identify him with one of the many divisive factions whose existence he deplored. It should be observed that at no time in his writing does he use the full wording, "single person kingship or house of peers"; it is everywhere abbreviated to "single person or house of peers," or a similar expression. I would suggest that he edited the phrase in this way because he considered the full wording tautological, for in his own mind the "single person" was always identified with "kingship."

During the anarchic months that followed Lambert's coup, Milton's chief concern was the threat of a restored monarchy. In *A Letter to a Friend* he defines the oath to be required of members of Parliament, "Liberty of conscience to all professing Scripture to be the rule of their faith & worship; And the Abjuracion of a single person." A few lines later, in almost the same breath as it were, he restates the provisions of the oath in more specific terms, "liberty of conscience, & the abjuracion of Monarchy." There is no mistaking his meaning. In the letter he urges a strong union between the army and the proposed Grand Council, and warns that if the army does not accept the agreement, "be confident there is a single Person underneath." He repeats the warning later: unless his proposals are accepted, "we instantly ruine; or at best become the servants of one or other single person, the secret author & fomenter of all these disturbances."[41] Masson suggests that the "single person" in this case is Lambert, but this seems unlikely.[42] Lambert was far from being "underneath" anything, and there was certainly nothing "secret" about marching four thousand troops to the gates of Whitehall and locking the Rump out of Parliament House. Nor is Milton raising the ghost of Oliver Cromwell; the phrase refers to the King, as it always does. Milton may well be accused of seeing a Royalist under every bush, but there is ample justification for his suspicions, with Booth's rebellion fresh in his memory and the sentiment for Charles growing at every hand. It is

40. Davies, *The Restoration*, p. 102, quoting the Council Register of 25 May.
41. *YP*, 7:330–32.
42. *Life*, 5:619.

the anarchy, the "Disturbances," which are making England ripe for Restoration, and Milton may be forgiven for assuming that there is a mind behind it all.

The phrase "single person" appears frequently in *The Readie and Easie Way*, but given the circumstances under which the tract was written, the danger posed by the deterioration of both army and Parliament, the increasingly open expression of Royalist sentiment, and the rampant rumors of invasion by Charles II, it is difficult to imagine Milton occupying his thoughts with the long-since-expired Protectorate. It is even more difficult to imagine him at that time condemning a regime that at the height of its power would have crushed any Royalist threat with a word. Milton is looking to the uncertain future, not the dead past, and warning against the consequences of restoration, an event he believes would sweep the whole experiment into the dustbin of history—the Commonwealth, the Protectorate, liberty of conscience, freedom of worship, the English Republic itself—and replace it all with the despised monarch and his stable of bishops. This was surely not an occasion to contemplate at leisure the inadequacies of the Protectorate, whatever he may have thought them to be. It is difficult, again, to read *The Readie and Easie Way* without recognizing it as a warning against monarchy. It is subtitled "The inconveniences and dangers of readmitting kingship in this nation," and the words *king*, *kingship*, and *monarch* dot its pages as unmistakable landmarks of his meaning, appearing in almost every paragraph. The "single person" he warns against is not the long-dead Lord Protector, but the very-much-alive Charles II, waiting at Breda for the word to embark. Only by wrenching the phrase entirely out of historical context could one interpret it as a repudiation of Cromwell.

In *The Readie and Easie Way*, as in *A Letter to a Friend*, the words *king* and *single person* are so frequently juxtaposed as to leave little question of his meaning:

> And do they among them who are so forward to bring in the single person, think to be by him trusted or long regarded? So trusted they shall be and so regarded, as by kings are wont reconcil'd enemies.

He goes on to warn the army that they will be disbanded without pay and prosecuted for their acts in arms if kingship returns, the people that they will be deprived of liberty of conscience if kingship returns, the tradesmen that their commerce will languish if kingship returns, and the educators that their academies will fade, for "Monarchs will never permitt" the people to flourish.[43] In the winter and spring of 1660, John Milton feared but one "single person," Charles II. Indeed, as we have seen, he urged Monk to assume dictatorial power in February; and in his *Brief Notes on a Sermon*, which appeared at the end of April, he ventured that the English people would do well to choose "out of our own number one who hath best aided the people, and best merited against tyrannie, the space of a raign or two we may chance to live happily anough, or tolerably,"[44] rather than submit to the yoke of kingship. It is not too much to say that Milton would have welcomed such a figure, one who with one bold stroke could have united the feuding army and Parliament against the Royalist threat, in much the same manner as the army's action in 1648 had united the two by purging Parliament of elements opposed to the prosecution of Charles I. Monk might well have filled such a role in 1660, but as it turned out, he had other things in mind. That Milton misjudged him may be forgiven, for "Silent Old George" kept his purposes very close, an enigma to all.

This is surely not to imply that Milton considered a military dictatorship to be an appropriate form of government for England or any other country. There is no such suggestion in anything we have from his pen. But, as Michael Fixler writes of the Milton of the *Defensio Secunda*, "Indeed, he had long before justified temporary dictatorship with the example of the first Brutus who after expelling the Tarquins from Rome 'was for a time forc't to be as it were a King himself, till matters were set in order, as in a free Commonwealth.'"[45] What was true in 1654 was true in 1660. There is no inconsistency here. If a new Cromwell had appeared in that twilight of the English Republic to lead the Army of Saints against the threat poised across the Channel, who can doubt that Milton would have embraced him as warmly as he had the Lord Protector six years earlier? Milton was true to his guides from first to last, to "the cause of true and substantial liberty, which must be sought, not without, but within,"[46] and to the Republic, which for him was the last, best hope of those who sought the freedom to pursue that inner liberty. He was loyal to that cause and the army

43. *YP*, 7:453–60.
44. *YP*, 7:482.
45. *Milton and the Kingdoms of God*, p. 183.
46. *YP*, 4:624.

that embodied it to the end; indeed, he almost gave his life for it.

These "ten or twelve years prosperous warr and contestation with tyrannie,"[47] as Milton characterizes the period of his public service in *The Readie and Easie Way*, left a strong impression on his imagination; but the full measure of that influence is to be found in the great poems to come rather than in the works of those years. Most of Milton's energies were expended on tracts that allowed little scope for a soaring fancy, since the various works in defense of the Republic, and of himself, required more rational talents. Though rather liberally sprinkled with the rhetoric of invective, they are essentially exercises of close logic based on a thorough research of facts. He attacked the bishops, the monarchy, the Presbyterians, the Irish, and his various opponents by arguing semantics, twisting citations, challenging facts, and marshalling evidence in lengthy exchanges that called upon the subtle skill of the debater and scholar rather than the art of the poet. An epic tone may occasionally be heard in his praise for the defenders of the Republic, as in the eulogy to Cromwell in *Defensio Secunda*; but the exaggerations of these passages strike the ear more as the epideictic display of the orator than as the music of the bard. Indeed, it seems as if the imagination is given full sway only when Milton is insulting Salmasius or abusing More, where the wealth of invective may well rival Shakespeare's. The sheer inventiveness of epithet looks ahead to the descriptions of Satan and his "horrid crew."

In defending the Republic, Milton had to justify civil war and a military regime; thus his tracts included pages describing campaigns and battles, from the lengthy chapter on Hull and the Hothams in *Eikonoklastes* to the brief mention of Overton's role at Marston Moor in *Defensio Secunda*.[48] In *Eikonoklastes* he gives an account of the civil wars, and in *Pro Populo Anglicano* he goes over much of the same ground, advancing the narrative to include the Irish campaign. In *Defensio Secunda* he praises Cromwell's conduct of the war in Scotland, which ended at Worcester; he touches on the Strickland–St. John mission to Holland in early 1651, the failure of which inflamed the English and led to the

47. *YP*, 7:428.

48. George Michael Whiting, in *Milton's Literary Milieu*, p. 343, lists the many contemporary sources Milton consulted for *Eikonoklastes*, chief among them Thomas May's *History of the Parliament of England* (1647).

Dutch War; and, as we have seen, he pursues events down to the dissolution of the Rump and the establishment of the Protectorate. But the chronicling of military and political events is one thing, and the imaginative conception of fictional figures quite another; the first is the art of the historian, the second of the poet and novelist, though the distinction seems to have become somewhat obscured in modern practice. In fact, Milton is singularly spare in his use of martial imagery—a sonnet to Cromwell, a scattering of metaphors, none of them extended except perhaps for the drill image in *The Tenure of Kings and Magistrates* or the figure that opens his reply to More's *Supplementum*, plus an occasional adjective to underscore a point—so that nowhere does one find tropes with the force and frequency of those in *Areopagitica*, for example. Perhaps Milton felt that the narrative of military events was quite enough and that any further embroidering of the prose with martial figures would be overdoing it.

One metaphor appears with sufficient frequency to deserve mention, however, especially since it throws some light on Milton's perception of his place in events. He was fond of casting himself in a military role. In *Pro Populo Anglicano* he scorns Salmasius: "I shall confound and crush him as he struggles and scrapes his strength together, once I have formed my battle line of Luthers, Zwinglis, Calvins, Bucers, Martyrs, and Paraeuses"; and he prides himself that his opponent "has been long laid prostrate, smitten by his own missiles."[49] In *Defensio Secunda* he reviews the encounter with his former adversary: "When he with insults was attacking us and our battle array, and our leaders looked first of all to me, I met him in single combat and plunged into his reviling throat this pen, the weapon of his own choice"; but, he concludes, now that "he is dead, I think my war is over."[50] He ends his defense once more on a martial note: "I have not borne arms for liberty merely on my own doorstep, but have also wielded them far afield . . . to the supreme glory of my countrymen and as an example to posterity."[51] As it turns out, his battles were not over, and at the opening of *Pro Se Defensio* he complains that though his country is now at peace and "the fury and violence of the enemy have left off their raging; for me, as it appears, for me alone it remains to fight the rest of this war." Later in the same paragraph he compares himself in a

49. *YP*, 4:396–99. 50. *YP*, 4:556–59. 51. *YP*, 4:684–85.

brief simile to "a good general [who] fulfills the office of a good general against any kind of enemy whatever,"[52] in interesting contrast to his youthful nephew, John Phillips, who in his earlier *Responsio* had compared himself to "Roman recruits of old."[53] In the reply to More's *Supplementum*, Milton opens with an extended metaphor chiding his opponent for refusing "to resolve the contest in a single battle [and] enrolling in France a fresh army against me," one which was even then "approaching in a mighty band with the standards of war."[54]

These images underline Milton's oft-repeated claim that the role he had chosen to play in the Revolution was as important and perilous as that of any soldier in the field. To him this was much more than a fanciful notion or an elegant reflection of the long literary tradition of the relationship between knight and bard. He is not posturing when he writes in his sonnet to Cyriack Skinner that he is content to have lost his eyesight "overply'd / In libertyes defence, my noble task," but is instead voicing what is for him a moral certainty. History was to endorse his perception of the dangers of his role. Many a New Model general was to survive the Restoration with small discomfort. George Monk, for example, who as late as February 1660 had declared himself the champion of the Rump and loyal guardian of the Republic, was awarded the title Duke of Albemarle for his part in the Restoration and installed in spacious state apartments at Westminster while Milton languished in prison, fearing for his life.

It is not surprising to find Milton figuring himself as a soldier (or a general) in the wars of truth. He was witness to two decades of almost incessant military activity in England, a worldly conflict that mirrored the vast spiritual struggle between Christ and anti-Christ. For a time he had rejoiced in the victories of the God-fearing soldiers of the Army of Saints; and when that army, its battles over, prevailed as the bulwark of the Republic with its generals in the seats of government, charting the course of the Revolution, he quite naturally identified himself with them and, in his imaginative perception of the part he played in events, figured his confrontations with Salmasius and More as but an extension of their wars.

By drawing on the evidence of this historical chronicle and ex-

52. *YP*, 4:698–700. 53. *YP*, 4:891. 54. *YP*, 4:797.

amining the words with which Milton reflected his response to events, it is perhaps possible to judge what he thought of war and warriors in general. It is, I think, too much to say that he had a "philosophy of war," for we do not have from his pen any carefully thought-out exposition on the subject. The appearance of such a clear statement would certainly be welcome, but in its absence it has become customary to cite his later works as evidence and, reading backward, to extrapolate opinions he may have entertained in earlier years. Thus, if Satan demonstrates certain Cromwellian features, it has been assumed that Milton thought the Lord Protector evil; or if Michael shows Adam "The Brazen Throat of War," with all of its devastation, cruelty, and false glory, then it has been concluded that Milton "hated war" and deplored the conflicts of his own time. It would seem wiser to pause at this point and attempt to assess, from the evidence of his life and writings prior to the Restoration, when his great works were taking shape in his mind, the impression that the figure of the soldier had made on the imagination of the poet. Thus informed, we may be in a better position to evaluate the role that the figure plays in his art.

When examining the life and thought of a long-dead artist, the scholar's perspective is necessarily colored by the values of his own age. Western society has survived two devastating world conflicts and a host of smaller ones in little over half a century, and we now live under the threat of a war whose tragic proportions defy the imagination. As a consequence, a substantial segment of the intellectual community has come to view war, or even the thought of war, as intolerable, and to consider a military presence in society as distasteful and ultimately dangerous. For some, opposition to warfare is a profound moral and emotional commitment, so personal and strong that its blinding light does not always permit the exercise of that essential objectivity the scholar customarily brings to more academic matters; and it is natural for him to be drawn to a poet's lines that seem sympathetic to his own most deeply felt convictions. Indeed, so commonplace is it today to attribute pacifist sentiments to Milton that it is almost obligatory to give at least a passing nod to that position, whatever the text. In her study of the *Commonplace Book*, for example, Ruth Mohl finds it necessary to open a chapter on the political index with the observation "Surely no one ever detested war more than did

Milton" before addressing herself to a series of entries on the subject that say nothing of the kind.[55]

No matter how dearly modern advocates of peace may wish that Milton felt revulsion toward war and violence, the only sensible attitude, in their view, of an enlightened man toward the subject, his opinions on such matters must be examined with that same quality of disinterestedness that one brings to a study of his theology or his aesthetics; and one must take care not to attribute to a citizen of the seventeenth century a sensibility entirely alien to that age. Despite the devastation of the Thirty Years War, there was no surge of popular demand for an end to warfare and a reduction of armaments, for though voices were raised to deplore the destructive consequences of battle, it was generally accepted, sometimes with stoic resignation, that war was a tragic but unavoidable feature of the human condition. Renaissance scholars and statesmen spared little thought on theories about ending war; their chief concern was how to wage it efficiently, successfully, and *justly*. Sir Thomas More's Utopians "hate and detest war as a thing manifestly brutal," but they take up arms at the slightest provocation and feel fully justified in doing so for such causes as the productive use of idle land and incidents "when booty is taken from their friends."[56]

To attribute pacifist sentiments to English Puritans seems even more of an anachronism, unless one thinks of certain Quietist sects or of the docile Diggers. The image of the warfaring Christian was a Puritan commonplace. From any Puritan pulpit, one could hear the spiritual struggle defined in martial terms—the shield of faith, the sword of justice, the wars of truth—for in the century that inherited the painful legacy of the Reformation, armies marched from one end of Europe to the other, all in the name of God. The aspirations of devout Protestants to attain an eternal, as well as a temporal, kingdom were often embodied in the figure of the soldier, first in the armies of Gustavus Adolphus and then, for the English, in the ranks of the New Model Army. For Puritans, the religious wars that tore at the fabric of Western civilization in the first half of the seventeenth century were but another chapter in the cosmic struggle between the forces of good and evil,

55. *John Milton and His Commonplace Book*, p. 250.
56. *Utopia*, trans. H. V. S. Ogden, p. 63.

a confrontation in which it was man's fate to play a key role. While that struggle prevails, "Meek-ey'd Peace" will descend to earth only when a God is born or comes to rule again.

War was not unkind to John Milton, at least after the first years of division and dislocation. Military victories swept out the bishops, restored his wife to him (though this may have seemed a mixed blessing), dislodged the Presbyterians, eliminated a tyrannical monarch, and brought into power a regime that, for a time at least, gave promise of insuring the liberty of conscience that was his fondest dream; and he gained an international reputation by defending that government. The greatest disappointment of his mature life, after the failure of his eyesight, was the Restoration, and the King returned precisely because no war was fought. It was an act of peace, which Englishmen hoped would end conflict and reconcile divided factions. It was successful because there was no battle. Can it be doubted that Milton would have welcomed the appearance of an Army of Saints to block the triumphal return of Charles to London? Would he not have seen the resultant bloodshed as a sign of Providence that his freedom-loving countrymen had come to their senses and rejected the "captain back for *Egypt*"?

This is not to imply that Milton "loved war." It simply means that he thought it necessary and just at times for a people to go to war in their own and their "children's defence against a tyrant or an enemy alike."[57] For him, man's bellicose nature was a tragic consequence of the Fall; but he also believed that God, who brings good out of evil with cosmic inevitability, can use that flaw to enhance his own glory and advance the cause of freedom for the human race.

Milton did not, however, picture a God who intervened directly on the earthly battleground; he was never attracted by the medieval belief in "trial by combat," a fight to determine the will of God.[58] It smacked too much of a false chivalric code, perhaps, the throwing down of gages with Bolingbrokes and Mowbrays riding into the lists to decide who is lying. Cromwell was fond of attributing his victories to God, as well he might, since he never suf-

57. *YP*, 4:390.

58. See, for example, Dante's *De Monarchia*, trans. Herbert W. Schneider. He expresses the commonly held belief that there are "Contests for deciding God's judgment" (p. 40), which can be "sought out by gathering the powers of mind and body in a mutual test of strength. Such a clash is usually called a duel" (p. 44).

fered defeat; but Milton had his doubts. In the *Commonplace Book* he finds that duels are "not certain in deciding the truth,"[59] and in *Eikonoklastes* he is scornful of the Royalist claim that Hotham lost his head because the Almighty was avenging his initial disloyalty to the King at Hull, calling the notion one of those "petty glosses and conceits on the high and secret judgements of God . . . so like the quibbl's of a Court Sermon."[60] Milton's essential Arminianism applies to the battleground as it does to other areas of life where man must bear the responsibility for his own defeats and victories. It is up to him to grasp "Justice, the Sword of God" if he would prevail in his temporal battles, even as the "helmet of salvation" will protect him in the wars of the spirit.

God need not intervene, after all, since he had set down very explicit guides to regulate man in his conduct, including that in war. In *De Doctrina Christiana* Milton cites Scripture on how one is obliged to act in battle. None should enter into armed conflict without careful consideration; but once hostilities begin, the battle should be waged with skill and knowledge—in brief, professionally. Soldiers should act with holiness and moderation; but whatever restraints these conditions imply are lifted when confronted by a cruel enemy, who then "should not be spared." A godly army should not trust in its own strength, "but in God alone." Spoil should be distributed "equally and fairly," which in seventeenth-century terms translates into regular pay for the soldiers. Finally, he quotes St. John to warn against "unjust plunder and rapine." When conducted in this manner, war is justifiable, no "less lawful now than it was in the time of the Jews."[61]

Milton addresses himself frequently to the causes of war and makes a reasonably explicit distinction between just and unjust conflicts. The most reprehensible are those in which a king attacks his own people, for that is a violation of a sacred bond between them. In such an event, the people are obliged to defend themselves, since "the Law of civil defensive warr differs nothing from the Law of forren hostility." Actually, Milton sees little difference between offensive and defensive war, a rock upon which many a disarmament conference has floundered; and he even seems to condone preemptive attack: "defence in Warr equally offends, and most prudently before hand."[62] The most admirable of wars, as he

59. *YP*, 1:374–75. 60. *YP*, 3:428–30. 61. *YP*, 6:802–4.
62. *YP*, 3:214–15, 230.

never tires of saying, are those in which a people take up arms to oppose tyranny from within or without. It is as just for the English to oppose their own tyrannical king as it is to defend themselves against an invasion by the king of Spain.[63] He quotes St. Paul and in a long passage from *Pro Populo Anglicano* cites a host of other sources from Scripture and the church fathers to demonstrate that the "Christians warred on tyrants [and] used arms in their own defence" in the past and hence are justified in doing so again. For Milton, indeed, inaction in the face of tyranny is sinful; and he extols those nations that, like the Samnites, rebelled because to them "peace with slavery was worse than war with freedom."[64] In brief, there were some conflicts he approved of, and some he did not.

Admittedly, political tracts written in defense of a war are not the most reliable sources to consult in defining the author's attitude toward soldiers. Such works are anything but disinterested in tone and content, but certainly a great deal can be seen in the fact that Milton's prose contains frequent and sometimes lengthy references to what he thought admirable and what not admirable in a soldier. The passages reveal, in brief, opinions that might be expected of any thoroughly partisan citizen of a nation at war. He disparaged the qualities of his enemies and praised those of his own armed forces, much as any American in World War II scorned what he came to see as the ruthlessly regimented, jackbooted automatons of the German armies and loved the image of his own devil-may-care GI, who managed to maintain his individuality in the face of all efforts to reduce him to discipline and obedience, and who because of his clear-eyed dedication and self-reliance got the job done somehow in spite of the system. Neither of these perceptions was entirely accurate, of course, for many of the Germans were highly resourceful and Americans equally professional—nor were Milton's characterizations uniformly reliable. But something may be seen in the particular qualities he chose to praise or condemn; and in that praise, at least, we may observe just how far he was from the sentiments of modern pacifists, who seem to perceive anyone in a peaked hat and a buttoned tunic as a threat to humanity.

As we have seen, when confronted with the reality of war in

63. *YP*, 3:214.
64. *YP*, 4:413–18, 390.

1642, Milton quickly revised his attitude toward the chivalric hero, who, if he ever existed, remained alive only as a literary fiction. The "knight in arms" bore no resemblance to the soldiers he saw about him, and he rejected that figure as a mere fable, particularly in the long passage on the Arthurian legend in *The History of Britain*.[65] Moreover, he looked upon the ostentatious piety of the chivalric knight as a fabrication of mercenary monks, and upon his ancient code as a false front concealing corruption, cowardice, and barbarism. The figure of Harapha best illustrates all that Milton came to scorn in that tradition. He sees the Cavaliers in this light, the "dissolute Sword-men" who, he charges, are more often drunk than sober. With Machiavelli, he disapproves of the common practice of buying the service of mercenary armies, while at the same time insisting on regular pay for loyal troops. He is particularly bitter in his condemnation of the "hireling Army of Scots."[66]

In his exaggerated praise of Cromwell and the New Model Army, Milton shows what he values in a soldier. He admires in the lord general "his devotion to the Puritan religion and his upright life"; he is first "victor over himself," from which flows his ability to discipline others; and he is, by virtue of these qualities, successful.[67] As for the soldiers, they are well disciplined and obedient to their commander. They are brave, sober, and devout, using their leisure "in the search for truth [and] in careful reading of sacred Scripture." "Formidable indeed to the enemy in the field," they are merciful to their foe once he has surrendered; and in contrast to the violence of the Royalists in "their drunkenness, impiety, and lust," the New Model trooper is "mild and innocent of all offence, . . . a bulwark to all good men, a terror to the wicked, and in fact an inspiration to all virtue and piety."[68] In these rather extravagant terms, Milton tells us that there are some soldiers he likes, and some he does not.

Thus Milton on wars and warriors in the 1650s. It may be said in summary that he approved of wars fought by the right people, in the right manner, and for the right cause; further, it is evident that his definition of *right* could be very broad indeed, embracing everything from the defense of London to the sack of Drogheda. It is possible, of course, that he changed his mind as a result of the

65. *YP*, 5:165–71. 66. *YP*, 3:531, 545. 67. *YP*, 4:667–68.
68. *YP*, 4:648, 669.

Restoration; but there are no indications that he attached any blame for the failure of the Revolution to the military. Indeed, as late as February 1660, when the New Model had ceased to be a force in the country as a result of the Rump's persistent remodeling, Milton advised Monk to assume power, supported by the small but "faithful Veteran Army" he had marched down from Scotland. As we have seen, he also proposed in his constitutional scheme that the army should provide a counterweight in the government to discourage any tyrannical aspirations of the supreme senate. The closing pages of *The Readie and Easie Way* reflect his disappointment, not with the military, but with the English people as a whole for their love of luxury, their rottenness "in religion and all civil prudence," and for their rejection of the leaders of "the good Old Cause."[69]

In earlier pages I offered as a premise of the experiential method the principle that opinions arrived at through long experience will prevail and impressions stamped upon the imagination will remain unaltered unless subsequent events work some change in the conscious or unconscious perception of them. We have examined the image of the soldier as it took shape in the imagination of John Milton through twenty years of England's wars and a decade of his association with the leaders of the Revolution; and we may conclude, in accord with this principle, that since there is no evidence he had any further contact with military figures after the Restoration—nor can one conceive of any reason why he should have—therefore his perception of that figure would have changed very little, if at all, during the years that he was composing his great poems. The figure may have dimmed somewhat in his imagination—*Of True Religion, Heresie, Schism, and Toleration*, published in 1673, is all but free of military imagery—but when he conceived those massive scenes of warrior angels locked in cosmic conflict, it was with the admired figures of the New Model trooper and his triumphant generals still vivid in his memory.

69. *YP*, 7:461–63. It is fruitless to speculate about what Milton meant by "the good Old Cause." It was a phrase much bandied about at the time and, as Godfrey Davies says, "Who could define it, when Levellers, Fifth Monarchy men, grandees, and subordinate officers—to name a few of the groups within the Republican fold—all had different notions?" (*The Restoration*, p. 154). I would only suggest that he saw the cause as religious freedom; and if the phrase had any political implications, they referred to the rejection of the monarchy, as in his moving *vale*.

V

The Creative Process

Who would claim that things which are analogous must correspond to each other in every respect?—*De Doctrina Christiana*

For a poet who declared himself "Not sedulous by Nature to indite / Warrs" (*PL* 9.27–28), John Milton certainly did a great deal of it. *Paradise Lost* offers the visual imagination a stage crowded with uniforms. Over half the lines in the first six books describe military ceremonies, conferences, confrontations, or battle; and though there is less in the balance of the poem, Michael, as the commander of a military mission, is continually under arms during his visit to Eden, and his revelations include graphic descriptions of warfare.

Indeed, a glance at Heaven and Hell will discover both portrayed at one time or another as nations in arms. Prior to the war God summons his angels, who appear

> Under thir Hierarchs in orders bright
> Ten thousand thousand Ensignes high advanc'd,
> Standards, and Gonfalons twixt Van and Reare
> Streame in the Aire. (5.587–90)

As night falls, "Th' Angelic throng / Disperst in Bands and Files thir Camp extend" while Satan dislodges "With all his Legions" on a "flying march" (5.650–51, 669, 688); and we may safely assume that his were not the only angels organized that day as a military unit. Indeed, when Abdiel returns the next morning, he finds "all the Plain / Coverd with thick embatteld Squadrons bright" (6.15–16). Following his fall from Heaven, Satan arouses his forces from off the "fiery Gulf" and organizes what is essentially an armed camp. He directs his troops to reform into their units and march in review. He then delivers a stirring, militant speech, which ends in a vow that "Warr then, Warr / Open or understood must be resolv'd" (1.661–62). In dramatic response his followers "fierce with grasped Arms / Clash'd on thir sounding Shields the din of war, / Hurling defiance toward the Vault of Heav'n" (1.667–69).

After the expulsion of the rebel angels, Heaven presents the picture of a secure and peaceful kingdom where the "Powers of Heav'n" resume their role as proper angels, equipped with harps and halos rather than swords and helmets. Hostilities do not cease, however, for though Heaven itself is safe from incursion, a new arena of battle develops beyond those "ever-during Gates." Chaos becomes a cosmic no-man's-land where angels venture forth only in military formation, armed to the teeth. At the Creation of the world the Son himself does not appear in martial guise but there is, it would appear, need for escort. He leaves Heaven attended by "Chariots wing'd / From the Armoury of God" (7.199–200) and Raphael is sent with a force "Squar'd in full Legion" (8.232) to guard the gates of Hell.

Milton "indited" wars with sufficient frequency to cast doubt on the oft-repeated suggestion that the invocation to book 9 reflects antiwar sentiments.[1] He is writing there about poets, of course, expressing his disregard for those whose "onely Argument" is battle and whose art is confined to dissecting "With long and tedious havoc fabl'd Knights / In Battles feign'd." He mocks their descriptions of "tilting Furniture, emblazon'd Shields, . . . [and] tinsel Trappings" as little more than "The skill of Artifice or Office mean"; and he is clearly directing his scorn on those who have written about wars, not those who have fought them. In effect, he is distancing himself from his literary antecedents, who wrote of little else, to make a case for his "higher Argument" as one "Not less but more Heroic" than the themes of Homer and Virgil. In lines that define a poetic intent, not a moral judgment, Milton, never modest, proposes to outdo them all with "answerable style," reminding his readers of the promise in the opening lines of book 1 that his song would "soar / Above th' *Aonian* Mount, while it pursues / Things unattempted yet in Prose or Rhime" (1.14–16).

Thus Milton rejected warfare as an unfit "Subject for Heroic Song," but military imagery so pervades his great works that one may well wonder what it is doing there. If warfare is not the "Subject" of his epics, as he tells us, why is there so much of it and what is its function in his lines?

The balance of this study will essay a reading of that function, but to do so properly will require consideration of the closely re-

1. Mohl, *John Milton and His Commonplace Book*, p. 251; Wagenknecht, *The Personality of Milton*, pp. 52, 93; Revard, "Heroic Warfare," p. 121.

lated political and diplomatic imagery as well. During the civil wars, political divisions were frequently precipitated by questions of peace and war, and in the England of the 1650s, as in many nations of our own time, an army with its colonels and generals in seats of power was the most important political force in the country. Diplomats of the day dedicated much of their energy and eloquence to shaping and settling wars, forging alliances, and expanding commerce through the exercise of military power. During Cromwell's ascendency he was continually preoccupied with such matters as the Protestant League, the Dutch War, the Western Design, the Spanish War, and of course the persistent Royalist threat. Milton's experience as a public servant, one employed "especially in connection with foreign affairs," was, as we have seen, shaped by these events, subsequently coloring his vision of the role of the military in both his life and art. For example, "The Stygian Council" in Pandemonium is a deliberative body debating the question of peace or war. Further, in his encounters with Chaos, Adam, and Christ, Satan is often cast in the role of a diplomat with devious designs for political or military alliances.

The influence of contemporary events on Milton's works was both general and specific; where particular passages suggest parallels between life and art, the similarities will be discussed in terms appropriate to any analysis of influence, be it literature, iconography, the Bible, or the stage. To develop some understanding of the function of military and political imagery in Milton's works, however, will require a consideration of all that imagery; such an inquiry cannot limit itself solely to those figures for which one can find parallels among the historical events described in earlier chapters. The war in Heaven would seem to owe more to the poet's library than to his experience in the world, but it can hardly be ignored in a study of the function of such imagery in his works as a whole.

The more general and pervasive, if less specific, influence of Milton's experience with warfare and warriors is particularly germane to a consideration of function. We live in an age when few praise war or acts of martial valor. Our era is unique in that regard and so may well represent an especially enlightened interval in the unhappy chronicle of contentious man. In such a moral and intellectual climate a scholar may find it difficult to comprehend why anyone would write about warfare for a reason other than to deplore it—one simply assumes that military imagery cannot be other than antimilitary. Our survey of Milton's early life and works, however, has revealed a man of a very different mind. He was not opposed to war; indeed he praised extravagantly the soldiers of the New Model Army and thought of himself as especially chosen to celebrate their victories. In works composed to and about military leaders his chief concern was that, their battles won, they would fail to reap the harvest of those triumphs, else "In vain doth Valour bleed." It is possible, of course, that in his closest counsels he expressed sentiments of a very different order, or that the Restoration somehow shocked him into an attitude toward warfare and the military more sympathetic with twentieth-century thought; but in the absence of evidence to this effect, that reading of his mind is at best conjectural, at worst wishful thinking.

This survey of Milton's life and early works must therefore raise doubts concerning modern interpretations of the function of his martial imagery: Why would he write an antiwar poem? Why would the educator whose ideal academy is designed to prepare young men for the duties of peace and war, the historian who wrote glowing accounts of the exploits of Caesar and Julius Agricola, the apologist for civil war who praised the military unreservedly, the political theorist who confirmed "a faithful Armie" as a bulwark against tyranny—why would such a man compose works that criticize the military, parody warfare, and scorn heroic values? Such readings are so out of keeping with what is known of John Milton that the circumspect scholar will feel obliged to consider alternative explanations for the function of that imagery.

In brief, the central thesis of this study is that Milton employed military and political imagery in his works to define evil, more specifically to characterize it in all its complexity, to demonstrate the disobedience that gives rise to it and the obedience that is the only sure protection against its fatal appeal, and to dramatize its consequences for man. *Paradise Lost* is both a promise and a warning. Evil will eventually be defeated, we are assured, in God's good time; but in the interim Satan rules, exercising immense power over the affairs of men. When the citizen of any age thinks of power, he imagines it most vividly in terms of the assertion of military and political authority, of armies sweeping all before them and charismatic leaders rallying a people to a cause. Other images come to mind, of course—physical strength, money, size, natural disasters—but the most forceful are scenes of battle where blood and iron crush a foe or the acts of emperors who seal with a word the fate of nations. Satan is an accomplished political and military leader, devious, courageous, eloquent, and highly successful. He is also the embodiment of evil; but if in defining the nature of evil Milton frequently calls upon images of warfare and politics, it is not because he looked upon the soldier and the senator as evil in themselves, but again because such figures are common symbols of power. It will be seen, then, that a knowledge of Milton's experience with warfare and politics can be of value in an appreciation of his art. He lived through wars, in defeat and victory, and sat by the seats of power in the English government, experiences that fed his imagination and gave substance to his studies; and he drew on that time to add vitality and authority to his warning.

The creative process is a mystery and, as Jung observed, will probably always remain a mystery. The reader must analyze it after the fact, once the iambs are lined up on the page and the poet has all but forgotten how they got there. If asked, he will mumble something about inspiration or the compulsive need to write and then perhaps favor his questioner with irrelevancies about diet, hours per day at the task, revision techniques, or the encouragement of a revered master.[2] The scholar searches out sources, influences, and analogues to discover how a poet hit upon a certain form, tone, structure, or music in the lines. Confronted with effect, he puzzles over cause; but the magic moment between may well "forever elude the human understanding."[3] Analysis of the creative act is troublesome enough when it deals with the effect of poet upon poet, artist upon artist, but when one presumes to discuss the influence upon a work of something that is not itself the product of another creative imagination, in the present case the experiences of the artist's life, the difficulties mount.

Given the complexities of the inquiry, it seems wise to begin with specifics, to examine the lines first before advancing some general assumptions about the process whereby experience is transfigured by the poet's imagination into art. The present chapter will deal with two images, one military, the other political, which in their

2. For example, in *The Creative Experience*, editors Stanley Rosner and Lawrence E. Apt report on interviews with a variety of creative minds. Discussion of the creative process is limited to such matters as mood when at work, the source of ideas, and problem-solving and revision techniques.

3. C. G. Jung, "Psychology and Literature," in *Modern Man in Search of a Soul*, p. 153.

structure and detail seem to echo events of Milton's own time. The first of these is certainly the most pervasive military image of his works: the cosmic struggle between the forces of good and evil for control of the universe and possession of man's immortal soul.[4] Life for Milton, as for anyone, involved a series of choices; but in the dangerous and divisive seventeenth century those decisions were more than commonly difficult. He himself was called upon to choose between a clerical or secular profession, Amaryllis or "the thankless Muse," King or Parliament, eyesight or service, Parliament or Cromwell, submission or defiance; and each choice entailed painful consequences for life and fortune. His options, moreover, were shaped by larger forces unleashed in that turbulent age; none could be isolated from the great schism in Western society kindled at Wittenburg in 1517, which burst into devastating conflagration at Prague a century later. All choices were essentially moral; the Puritan felt the clash of contraries in his spirit and saw that same conflict played out on the battlefields of Europe where Christ and anti-Christ struggled for supremacy. There was a war on, within his breast, in shattered Germany, and eventually for the Englishman, upon his own downs and pastures. For the Puritan, these separate conflicts were all one, each reflecting a grander, cosmic struggle between the forces of good and evil that had been going on since the beginning of time, a struggle in which he was marked to play a central role. No act was without significance; each weighed in the fateful balance. The pull of contraries within his conscience mirrored the clash of armies in battle; Marston Moor was fought for his immortal soul and the victory gained only because he had lived his life so as to be worthy of it.[5]

Temporal battle is but a shadow of that cosmic conflict; it is the shape of the struggle as it is played out in the affairs of men. "Dream not," says Michael to Adam of the encounter between

4. C. M. Bowra, *From Virgil to Milton*, p. 212: "The conflict which begins in Eden and ends only with the end of the world takes place in man because God and Satan contend for him. Our human condition is thus the battlefield of supernatural powers whose nature is hard to express in any language and whose character seems almost inconceivable in the narrative of an epic." See also Lawrence W. Hyman, *The Quarrel Within: Art and Morality in Milton's Poetry*, p. 43; Whiting, *Milton's Literary Milieu*, p. 232; and J. H. Adamson, "The War in Heaven: Milton's Version of the Merkabah," p. 702.

5. As Cromwell wrote after the battle, "Truly England and the Church of God both had a great favour from the Lord. It had all the evidence of an absolute victory obtained by the Lord's blessing upon the godly party principally." Wilbur Cortez Abbott, *The Writings and Speeches of Oliver Cromwell*, 2:287.

Christ and Satan, "As of a Duel, or the local wounds / Of head or heel" (12.386–87); and Raphael's account of the war in Heaven is but "lik'ning spiritual to corporal forms" (5.573). But Milton is writing for men, not angels, and thus he defines the spiritual struggle in the traditional form of temporal warfare. Men's wars can assume many shapes, and in his poetic representation of that struggle Milton had a wealth of alternatives to choose from—a nation gobbling up a smaller neighbor, colonial conquest, the surge of empire, revolution—and his own times and studies would have provided numerous models for each. He chose two: first, he described the initial clash between good and evil as a civil war in which forces of comparable strength and armament meet on the field of battle; and second, the ensuing campaigns take on a very different shape, that of two large and powerful nations contending for control of a smaller and relatively weak territory. We will examine the latter image here, leaving that first battle to a chapter of its own.

Eden is just such a small and helpless state, a prize for competing powers. Once created it has all the appearance of a frontier post or colony of Heaven, where Adam acts somewhat in the fashion of a governor-general or vice-regent. Satan sees him thus; God made man, he says, and "for him built / Magnificent this World, and Earth his seat, / Him Lord pronounc'd" (9.152–54). Raphael defines Adam's role in much the same terms. Man is to subdue the earth and "throughout Dominion hold" (7.532) over all its creatures. God looks upon the world as "Th' addition of his Empire" (7.555), with Adam as a trusted subordinate whom the Father has made "chief / Of all his works" (7.515–16).

Control of the world is to remain in dispute, however, for by divine ruling Satan is free to act outside the walls of Heaven. When he refers to the world, it is in terms of conquest. It is a place, he tells his followers, where "may lye expos'd / The utmost border of his Kingdom, left / To their defence who hold it" (2.360–62); and when he gazes on the pleasures of Eden, he speaks of "conquering this new World" (4.391). Prelapsarian man is not left unprotected, however, for this outpost of Heaven is guarded by armed sentries. Gabriel, "Chief of th' Angelic Guards," sits outside Eden with his troop of the "Youth of Heav'n" equipped with "Celestial Armourie, Shields, Helmes, and Speares" (4.549–53). Under their watchful vigilance there is easy access between Heaven and earth. Uriel is unarmed and Raphael makes the trip without incident, passing by the sentinels' "glittering tents" on his way to Eden. Satan at this stage of the hostilities must come in disguise, a spy intruding on enemy land; and only when he is discovered does he assume his accustomed warrior posture, springing up

> As when a spark
> Lights on a heap of nitrous Powder, laid
> Fit for the Tun som Magazin to store
> Against a rumord Warr. (4.814–17)

He threatens battle: "on his Crest / Sat horror Plum'd; nor wanted in his graspe / What seemd both Spear and Shield" (4.988–90). God's scales presage his defeat in such a clash, however, and from this Satan learns that he must resort to covert guile to conquer "this new World."

During Milton's period of public service England was involved in a Continental war that in its broad design resembles this imaginative spectacle of two large powers contending for control of a small territory belonging to one of them. In 1655 Cromwell committed England for a brief time to what was actually a century-long struggle between two great powers, France and Spain, for control of the hereditary Hapsburg possessions in the rich provinces of Flanders known as the Spanish Netherlands, an area roughly included in the borders of modern Belgium. By the end of the Thirty Years War in 1648, Spain had lost its position as the undisputed major power of Europe. She had been forced to recognize the independence of the United Netherlands but had been able to retain control of the Spanish Netherlands. France, growing in power even as Spain was declining, was reluctant to give up whatever claim she had to those provinces and so persisted during the 1650s in efforts to secure them. England entered the war after a long period of diplomatic maneuvering, during which both Cardinal Mazarin of France and Philip IV of Spain actively courted an English alliance. In the end Cromwell threw in his lot with the French. The terms of the alliance included a secret agreement that Charles II was to be denied his political haven in France and that certain towns on the coast of Flanders were to be given to England upon their capture from Spain. The English agreed in turn to deploy their fleet against Spain itself and to land an army in Flanders to assist the French. Cromwell's strategy in the war was to concentrate energies in the Netherlands while Admiral Blake skirted the Spanish coast, interrupting the flow of gold from the New World and preventing the intrusion of enemy forces by sea. The enterprise met with considerable success, for Blake kept the Spanish fleet from taking any part in the fighting in Flanders.[6] Charles and his itinerant court were forced to seek refuge first in Germany and then in Spanish territory, and after the Battle of the Dunes, Cromwell gained control of Dunkirk, thus reestablishing an English presence on the Continent for the first time since Mary Tudor had surrendered Calais a hundred years earlier.

It is difficult to say how much Milton actually knew of the Spanish War. The blind poet was surely not as active in government as he had been earlier, but in his capacity as secretary for foreign languages he continued to be responsible for the preparation and translation of numerous letters and documents. He was a respected member of the Cromwell administration, his home in Petty-France but a short walk from Whitehall, and during the years when the alliance was being debated and the war fought, it can surely be assumed that he was as interested as any public official in its outcome and would have kept abreast of events through his social and official contacts in government circles.[7] He was decidedly involved in one of the climactic events of the war. In May–July 1658, he was called upon to prepare thirteen letters in the short period of six weeks, including ten to France alone.[8] The numbers are somewhat deceptive, since the protocol of the time required that any letter to Louis XIV have a companion to Mazarin, but seven of these letters mention Dunkirk and the last four concern the surrender of that city and its immediate assignment to England.[9]

The real and the imagined conflicts have similarities extending well beyond the broad pattern of events to include some of the details of the wars. For example, in the epics both Satan and God engage in diplomatic maneuvering of the type that preceded the

6. Charles H. Firth, *The Last Years of the Protectorate, 1656–1658*, 2:182. Blake's mission was in some ways similar to Raphael's during the days of Creation when he was sent to preclude any "eruption bold" which might have interrupted the divine work. Indeed, at one critical point in the campaign the presence of the English fleet in the Bay of Biscay prevented the dispatch of Spanish reinforcements from the port of San Sebastian to the Netherlands.

7. See Fallon, "Filling the Gaps," p. 190 and note 91.

8. *YP*, 5:823–46; State Letters 146–51 and 154–57.

9. Some scholars have suggested that Cromwell's Spanish Declaration of 26 October 1655, in which he announced his opposition to Spain, may also be Miltonic. John T. Shawcross, in "A Survey of Milton's Prose Works," p. 363, finds the ascription to Milton "noteworthy." *YP*, 5:711–12, rejects the document.

Spanish War. Prior to the Fall, Satan needs assistance on his cosmic voyage, and in the process of enlisting aid runs the gamut of diplomatic posturing, from his effort to bully Sin and Death into opening the gates of Hell to his subservient fawning before Uriel, whom he praises with the flowery hyperbole of a seventeenth-century courtier. One of his most effective performances is in the court of Chaos, where he finds that monarch unhappy about the recent incursions on his realm, territorial encroachments, he complains to Satan, that are

> Weakning the Scepter of old *Night*: first Hell
> Your dungeon stretching far and wide beneath;
> Now lately Heaven and Earth, another World. (2.1002–4)

Satan, the skilled diplomat, asks assistance in finding that world. Disguising his full intent, he promises that if successful he will seek to return that usurped region to Chaos, who can then "once more / Erect the Standard there of *ancient Night*" (2.985–86). All Satan wants really, he says, is revenge; he has no territorial ambitions.

Similarly, Raphael's role may be seen as that of an envoy from a great power. His diplomatic mission is to convince Adam of the benefits of his continued allegiance to his God and to inform him of the dangers inherent in defection of any kind. For a time, he tells Adam, the world is to be like some territorial possession of Heaven that may eventually achieve the status of statehood. Men will live on earth

> till by degrees of merit rais'd
> They open to themselves at length the way
> Up hither, under long obedience tri'd,
> And Earth be chang'd to Heav'n, & Heav'n to Earth,
> One Kingdom, Joy and Union without end, (7.157–61)

but only "if ye be found obedient" (5.501). Should Adam choose to violate the terms of his allegiance, however, the consequences are clear. Raphael's account of the defeat of Satan is a vivid lesson for any statesman pondering alternative alliances.

In *Paradise Regained* the imagery of contending nations persists, binding the two works with a pattern of events that identifies them as parts of a single vision. As a consequence of the Fall, Satan and his demons firmly possess the world and comfortably enjoy "this fair Empire won of Earth and Air" (1.63). The grand councils are no longer held in Pandemonium "but in mid air"

(1.39), and it is here that Satan gathers his followers to discuss what appears to be a threat to their control. His talk is all of conquest and dominion, of

> How many Ages, as the years of men,
> This Universe we have possest, and rul'd
> In manner at our will th' affairs of Earth. (1.48–50)

His position is comparable to that of a distraught Philip IV confronted with the French threat to the hereditary Hapsburg possessions in the Spanish Netherlands. Satan continues in this vein during the second council held in "the middle Region of thick Air" (2.117), where he reports that

> an Enemy
> Is ris'n to invade us, who no less
> Threat'ns then our expulsion down to Hell. (2.126–28)

Once more, we hear almost the same words from the mouth of God, who boasts of his Son as a man who will resist all of Satan's forces and eventually

> drive him back to Hell,
> Winning by Conquest what the first man lost
> By fallacy surpriz'd. (1.153–55)

But first Christ must be exercised in the wilderness, where he will

> lay down the rudiments
> Of his great warfare, e're I send him forth
> To conquer Sin and Death the two grand foes. (1.157–59)

Christ's exercise is an encounter with Satan, who appears in the guise of a skilled diplomat offering aid, concealing designs, and misrepresenting his position, as he did with Chaos in *Paradise Lost.*[10] When Satan falls from the temple's pinnacle, the angelic hosts descend to succor Christ; and in this, their only visit to earth in the poem, they carry out the imagery established in *Paradise Lost.* It is a military formation:

> strait a fiery Globe
> Of Angels on full sail of wing flew nigh,
> Who on their plumy Vans receiv'd him soft. (4.581–83)[11]

10. Satan as diplomat will be discussed in more depth in Chapter VI.
11. See Hughes, *Complete Poems*, p. 528n, where he identifies "Globe" as a "circular phalanx of troops," and p. 244n, where he refers to *OED* (8).

And when the choirs raise their voices, it is to sing of victories, the first in Heaven and now this, in which Christ has "regain'd lost Paradise, / And frustrated the conquest fraudulent" (4.608–9). He is the "heir of both worlds, / Queller of Satan" (4.633–34).

Of particular interest is the appearance in the poems of the image of a foothold, or bridgehead. One of the fruits of the Spanish War was the English acquisition of Dunkirk. This "footing in the continent," as it was called, was to be a "sally-port by which his Highness may advantageously sally forth upon his enemies," a base of operations, in Thurloe's words, "which might be made use of to the overthrow of France."[12] In *Paradise Lost*, the rebel angels, deliberating in Hell, speak of the world using just such terms. It is an outpost of Heaven which, once occupied, may even be used as a bridgehead for further operations to regain their "ancient seat." Beëlzebub offers promise that from there

> with neighbouring Arms
> And opportune excursion we may chance
> Re-enter Heav'n. (2.395–97)

The bridging of Chaos after the fall is, of course, a visual realization of this language, establishing the world as a literal "bridgehead."

God and Satan, as we have seen, often use similar language to define their relationship with man; and in depicting the war Milton frequently employs the same military image on both sides. The foothold is no exception. After the Fall God instructs Michael to return to earth and reoccupy Eden so as to deny access to "all my Trees" (11.124) to the forces of evil and the progeny of Adam. Milton enriches the biblical source by designating Michael as commander and emphasizing the military nature of the mission; thus, he both heightens the impression that the angels are entering a hostile environment and adapts the incident to fit the larger image of cosmic conflict.[13] Michael comes with a "Cohort bright / Of watchful Cherubim" (11.127–28) and he wears a "militarie Vest of purple" over his "lucid Armes" while "by his side / As in a glistering *Zodiac* hung the Sword, / Satans dire dread, and in his hand the Spear" (11.240–48). Their mission is to establish a "Cherubic watch, and of a Sword the flame / Wide waving, all approach farr

12. Firth, *Last Years*, 2:218.
13. Gen. 3:24.

off to fright" (11.120–21). The archangel obeys, ordering "his Powers to seise / Possession of the Garden" (11.221–22), thus creating a heavenly foothold in the Satan-infested world.

After the war in Heaven there are no more pitched battles in the cosmic conflict, but there are further victories and defeats. Milton continues to use the language of conquest, as we have seen, but in the absence of military confrontation he turns to the imagery of international diplomacy to define the changing fortunes of the two powers. The two pivotal events in the history of man, which alter both his role in the war and the relative strength of the antagonists, are his fall from innocence in the Garden and his redemption through the ministry of Jesus Christ. In his epics, Milton describes these two turning points in terms of the shifting balance of power among nations.

The middle of the seventeenth century presented a vivid model for such a shift. Until the Treaty of Westphalia in 1648, Spain had been considered the strongest power in Europe, but once its weaknesses were unmasked, that nation entered a period of sharp decline during which the powers of Europe scrambled for pieces of its crumbling empire. The United Netherlands sat confidently behind its dikes and built a fleet that made it the strongest naval and commercial power in the Western world.[14] France began a policy of territorial expansion that was eventually to unite all of Europe against her, and for a short time ambitious princes found that they could not ignore the rising star of Cromwell's England.

Shifts in the balance of power among nations are marked by many seemingly unrelated and inexplicable changes in official policy, whose significance skilled diplomats are quick to read. Old enemies are embraced and recent allies spurned, ambassadors are recalled and state visits cancelled, letters are exchanged, the wording of which is carefully analyzed, fleets are moved and tariffs raised—all outward manifestations, the "body language" of international affairs, reflecting changing alliances and shifts of power. When Catholic France signed a commercial treaty with militantly Protestant England in 1656, Cromwell dismissed the Spanish ambassador, Cardenas, and warmly greeted Mazarin's envoy, Bordeaux. Earlier, Charles II had been denied his sanctuary in France, where he had been a welcome guest for some years. Any

14. Charles Woolsey Cole, *Colbert and a Century of French Mercantilism*, p. 343. Colbert estimated that by 1665, Dutch vessels were carrying three-fourths of the trade of Europe.

alert statesman would conclude that if Cromwell had the power to force Charles to quit Paris and seek haven in Cologne, he could do much more. When England gained possession of a few square miles of Flemish coast in 1658, this small victory had repercussions that went far beyond the actual value of the place. Cromwell was hailed as the arbiter of Europe with, in Thurloe's words, "the keys of the continent at his girdle,"[15] praise which is not as excessive as it first sounds, for such small conquests are often the prelude to larger events.[16]

Milton describes the consequences of the Fall of man in terms of just such a shift in the balance of power. As a result of this small act of eating, it appears, to Satan at least, that God "hath giv'n up / Both his beloved Man and all his World" (10.488–89). And so it would seem, for the act is followed by a series of events, each minor in itself, whose sum is the inescapable conclusion that Adam's world has passed under the hegemony of the forces of evil. Sin mysteriously senses "new strength" as a result of the distant victory, and "Dominion giv'n me large / Beyond this Deep" (10.243–45). The bridge over the turmoil of Chaos symbolizes this authority, even as Cromwell's power reached across the stormy Channel after the occupation of Dunkirk. It creates, in Satan's words, "one Realm / Hell and this World, one Realm, one Continent" (10.391–92), invalidating forever God's offer of "one Kingdom, Joy and Union without end." Satan is now so powerful that he has no further need of old allies. He passes over his bridge, paying no heed to Chaos, who is raging against broken promises:

> on either side
> Disparted *Chaos* over built exclaimd,
> And with rebounding surge the barrs assaild,
> That scorn'd his indignation. (10.415–18)

In Pandemonium Satan tells of his conquest and urges his followers to "possess, / As Lords, a spacious World" (10.466–67), concluding with the triumphal words, "What remains, ye Gods, / But up and enter now into full bliss" (10.502–3).

The actions of Heaven reflect this same shift. God withdraws Gabriel and the angelic guards, an outward sign showing as tangi-

15. Firth, *Last Years*, 2:218.

16. A year earlier, Cromwell had been negotiating with the King of Sweden for control of yet another foothold on the Continent, the Duchy of Bremen. Ibid., 2:27n, 226.

bly as the withdrawal of Charles II from France or Cardenas from England that there has been a change in the subtle and hidden chemistry of the balance of power. Earth holds dangers now, and it is the mighty Michael who returns to occupy Eden, not with Gabriel's beardless "youth of Heav'n" but with his

> choice of flaming Warriours, least the Fiend
> Or in behalf of Man, or to invade
> Vacant possession som new trouble raise. (11.101–3)

"In behalf of Man" is surely interesting. God emphasizes the fact that man is no longer under his dominion, that it is Satan now who acts in the name of his new subject. Adam is diminished. No longer lord of an outpost of Heaven, protected by celestial guards, he and Eve are banished into a world where Satan rules. Subduing the earth seems beyond him now. The ground is cursed and man will eat only in the sweat of his face. He will end his days as dust, reduced to the element he was destined to rule.

In *Paradise Regained* there is another subtle shift in the cosmic balance of power, defined chiefly in terms of man's new role in the war. Christ is a pattern for the triumph of man, and the political and military imagery is particularly effective here, as it places the inner struggle in the perspective of the world. Michael had told Adam that Christ, when he came, would arm man "With spiritual Armour, able to resist / *Satans* assaults, and quench his fierie darts" (*PL* 12.491–92). Christ, as man, provides an example for the race, showing them that they need no longer be subject to the tyrant. The world is like a long-oppressed nation that, newly armed with hope, can rise and strike back at the occupying power; and Adam's progeny are now strong enough to reject the despotic commands of the usurper to "fall down, / And worship me" or "Cast thy self down" (*PR* 4.166–67, 555). Thrice-armed by Christ's ministry, man can now enter the lists on his own behalf; and though Satan is still powerful, his rule over the conquered territory need no longer go unchallenged.[17] As God predicted even before the Fall,

17. Edward Langton, *Satan, A Portrait: A Study of the Character of Satan Through All the Ages*, p. 86: "Before Satan was bound, and his power curbed by the triumph of Christ and the influence of the Gospels, the empire which the Devil and demons exercised on earth was much greater than now." Milton is more specific in the Nativity Ode: Satan "In straiter limits bound, / Not half so far casts his usurped sway" (lines 169–70).

Upheld by me, yet once more he shall stand
On even ground against his mortal foe,
By me upheld. (*PL* 3.178–80)

It is a role such as that which England anticipated the Flemish would assume, inspired by the presence and example of the English army in Dunkirk. Cromwell's French ambassador, William Lockhart, for example, expressed the hope that "many of the people of Flanders and those parts kept under [by] Spanish severity might declare themselves Protestant, and several of the great towns be induced to throw [off] the Spanish yoke."[18]

In tracing these parallels between experience and art, it is important to recognize the limitations of the process. Pushed too far, the analogies will only lead the reader into perplexities and contradictions. If, for example, the French effort to wrest control of Flanders from Spain is accepted as comparable to Satan's effort to win control of the world from God, one could conclude that Milton associated France with Hell and Spain with Heaven. The success of the two efforts would only seem to confirm the identification, for God surrenders the world to Satan in much the same way that Spain surrendered portions of Flanders to France at the Peace of the Pyrenees in 1659. But given Milton's attitude toward Catholic Spain, the bulwark of the anti-Christ, the author and fomenter of popish plots, and England's ancient enemy on the seas, is it possible that he could have considered that country analogous to Heaven? Moreover, England was allied with France during the war. Since the analogy seems to identify France with Hell, are we therefore to conclude that Milton perceived of the Protectorate government as an ally of the Devil?

The two images of the foothold are equally troublesome, for they would appear to contradict one another. In the first, Satan describes Adam's world as a bridgehead to be used for further incursions into Heaven. In the second, after the Fall, God reoccupies Eden, securing a foothold in Satan's world. The latter, postlapsarian image provides a more satisfactory correspondence with the historical event, the return of the armies of Protestant England to reoccupy a part of its former territory in Catholic Flanders; for Cromwell here is more appropriately comparable to God, England to Heaven, Spain to Hell, and Flanders to the fallen world,

18. Firth, *Last Years*, 2:219.

identifications with which one would assume Milton to have been more comfortable. The two images are, however, the same—a foothold. Can the reader reject the former analogy and accept the latter simply because one happens to conflict with our understanding of Milton's sympathies and the other does not?

Reason dictates that we need reject neither. The issue arises only when the analogy is pushed too far. *Paradise Lost* is not a poem about Spain or France or Dunkirk; nor is it a thinly disguised commentary on England's part in the Spanish War. It is a poem about, among other things, the power of evil; and if Milton finds in one of the wars of his own day a general pattern of events that strikes his imagination as appropriate to the depiction of a cosmic struggle in which he seeks to particularize and illustrate demonic power, this does not mean that he is passing judgment on the parties engaged in that war. It is quite possible that when Milton was sketching out his own epic conflict, he had in mind a war of which he had read rather than one of which he had personal knowledge, perhaps Tasso's treatment of the long struggle between the Moslem and Christian worlds for control of the Holy Land, or Polybius's account of the wars between Carthage and Rome for possession of Sicily. He may have discovered in Procopius a graphic example of a foothold in the Greek Exarchate at Ravenna during the fifth and sixth centuries.[19] History, like art, has a way of repeating itself; thus it should not be surprising that the European conflict of the 1650s assumed those same ancient patterns.

Of this possibility two things may be said. First, the fact that there is a perfectly reasonable historical or literary source for the image in no way weakens the case for an experiential source. The two are not exclusive; if literature reflects life, then one can expect to find in life a confirmation of the truths of literature. Second, any responsible scholar who observes the parallels between Milton's imaginative conflict and a literary or historical account would be most reluctant to draw from the analogy inferences concerning Milton's judgment on those ancient combatants. He disliked Turks, to be sure, but he had no more regard for medieval Crusaders who blindly answered the call of Rome or for the chivalric zeal that inspired them; and no one would presume to con-

19. Milton knew these ancient historians, of course. He quotes Polybius (*YP*, 1:599; 4:439) and cites Procopius twice in the *Commonplace Book* (*YP*, 1:416, 488) and elsewhere.

clude from such slight evidence as Milton's reading of Polybius how he felt about the Punic Wars. The circumspect scholar will exercise restraint in pursuing an analogy between a poetic image and a literary source to its logical conclusions. For one thing, if he *is* able to show that the two are congruent to a marked degree, he opens the artist to a charge of slavish imitation, or at least a decline in creative energy. More importantly, he is aware that the inventive imagination does not work with that kind of strict, logical inevitability. Milton himself said as much: "Who would claim that things which are analogous must correspond to each other in every respect?"[20]

Earlier in these pages it was proposed that there are certain degrees of congruence between experience and the work that reflects it, and that there are some genres—satire, or occasional poems, for example—in which the parallels between historical events and creative expression are consciously, deliberately intended. But when a poet draws on the broad experiences of his life, in the present instance a four-year-long war, to add substance and vitality to his lines, one should not demand of the experiential correspondence a degree of congruence that one would never require between a poetic image and a source in art or history. Indeed, insisting on such a strict one-to-one correspondence between life and art was what put nineteenth-century biographical critics in a bad light in the first place.

In brief, it is a premise of experiential criticism that when a poet draws upon life to enrich his art, the resultant image does not necessarily carry with it all the ideological and philosophical baggage that may have burdened the experience itself. Hence, Milton perceived of the struggle between good and evil in terms of armed conflict and sought to warn man of the crucial consequences of that struggle for the seed of Adam. In that endeavor, he drew on all the biblical, literary, historical, and iconographical resources of his vast learning to make that warning a compelling one. He further enriched this image of warfare with the language of real life, drawing on his time in public service, when England was party to a war broadly comparable to many of which he had read, a war, moreover, in which there were events whose inclusion would add to the vitality of his imaginative account. He had observed that

20. *YP*, 6:547.

political and military leaders who were planning to expand their domain or secure their borders expressed themselves in terms of occupying bridgeheads, establishing footholds, or upsetting what has come to be called the balance of power. In his use of this experience for artistic purposes, he is not necessarily reflecting his allegiance to one or the other of the belligerents; nor is he passing judgment on war itself. He simply recalls the shape of such conflicts: two great powers contending for a small corner of Europe, one a fading giant, the other a swelling youth, proud in its vigor and ambition. Within the outline of that conflict he traces a vision of how it goes with fragile man at such a time: great nations clash; some wax; some wane. In the end, "what I will is Fate," and so we take our solitary way, "hand in hand with wandring steps and slow."

The practice of pursuing all the implications of an experiential analogy in order to extrapolate elements of the artist's life or thought has produced so much confusion and contradiction that careful scholars have for years been reluctant to mine the rich lode of insight that the life can provide. Perhaps the best illustration of the inadequacies of this practice is the unsatisfactory conclusions about Milton's political allegiances that have been derived from the evidence of the poetry. Let us consider the political structures of Heaven and Hell. Heaven, of course, is an absolute monarchy; and we know what Milton thought of absolute monarchies. But to pursue the analogy to its ultimate conclusion is to arrive at William Empson's judgment that Milton thought God wicked.[21] On the other hand, Hell has many of the earmarks of a representative assembly, and more than one scholar has remarked on the parallels between the "great consult" in Pandemonium and a meeting of the English Republic's Council of State or the Long Parliament.[22] Thus it can be argued that since Milton was associated with these two bodies, the fact that he modeled his satanic state on them demonstrates that he thought both evil.[23] Of course,

21. *Milton's God*, especially p. 3.

22. F. R. Leavis, "Mr. Eliot and Milton," p. 19; J. Max Patrick, "Significant Aspects of the Milton State Papers," p. 324; David M. Miller, *John Milton: Poetry*, p. 23; Hunter, "Milton and Richard Cromwell," p. 259.

23. Harold E. Toliver, "The Splinter Coalition." Toliver does not mention this analogy specifically, but in his view Milton thinks "of all politics and temporal power as satanic substitutes for divine communion" and assigns "most of the achievements of statesmanship to Satan" (pp. 34–35). The "splinter coalition" in Hell represents all "the evils of the public state" (p. 48).

neither of these conclusions can be substantiated by what we know of Milton's political and theological thought. The fact that Professor Empson thought God wicked cannot persuade us that Milton did; and though Cromwell's secretary shared his frustration with the Rump, both recognized the importance of some kind of representative assembly to the governing of England. Faced with such contradictions, the literary scholar would seem justified in his conviction that art is one thing and biography quite another.

There is no need to go to these lengths, however. *Paradise Lost* is not a political testament; nor is it Milton's purpose to pass judgment on Charles I and the Protectorate, nor to encode a commentary on Restoration politics, as Christopher Hill implies.[24] Milton is warning his readers of the perilous condition of man in a universe where contending forces struggle for possession of his soul, and is using all the materials at his disposal, gleaned from learning and life, to make that message vivid and compelling.

One need not construe the poetry to discover Milton's political philosophy; he gave in his prose works a reasonably full account of his attitude toward governments as it had evolved to the time he began the composition of *Paradise Lost*. At the risk of oversimplification, it will be of value to summarize that attitude so as to compare it with what is to be found in the epics. Briefly, for him political institutions were a legacy of the Fall. There was no need for such cumbersome machinery to direct the affairs of man in the Garden, where he acted according to the natural law, hence was "naturally disposed to do right."[25] The Fall shattered that divine order, and man, having lost the gift of perfect obedience, became subject to passions controllable only by the imposition of codes. The clear white light of divine law was refracted into the spectrum of an oppressive Mosaic code, and man was forced to design his own imperfect laws to order his existence. The Incarnation altered man's status somewhat, releasing him from the Mosaic law and all that flowed from it, but not from the substance of that law, which is the "love of God and of our neighbour."[26] Until men subscribe to that substance, however, human law is required in a fallen society, as are institutions to administer it; and the burden of governments on a people is inversely proportional to their ability to govern themselves. The further they fall away from the love of

24. *English Revolution*, passim.
25. In *De Doctrina Christiana*, *YP*, 6:352.
26. *YP*, 6:532.

God and of neighbor, from virtue and inward liberty, the more they will be deprived of outward liberty. For the virtuous the yoke is a mild one, for the weak and corrupt it is heavy. In a free society of prudent, God-fearing people few laws are needed; but if a slothful and dissolute nation submits itself to a tyrant, its laws will multiply. In brief, men get the governments they deserve.

For a decade Milton served a government maintained in power by an instrument of force, the New Model Army. He supported the Republic not because he thought it an ideal arrangement, but because it was preferable to the only apparent alternative, a tyrannical monarchy. The Republican regimes gave promise, at least, of beginning the work of separating church and state and guaranteeing religious freedom for the English people. In *The Readie and Easie Way* he sketched out his own preference for a governing body, "a general council of ablest men" with life tenure who would resist tyranny and promote liberty of conscience so that the individual could seek perfection in the eyes of God and thus reduce his need for any government at all. The establishment of this perpetual senate, this "spiritual aristocracy" to use Don M. Wolfe's phrase, was to be accompanied by a sweeping decentralization of political power.[27] The chief business of the Grand Council would be foreign affairs, while the judicial, administrative, and some of the taxing functions of the central government were to be assumed by freely elected bodies in the counties. None of these civil institutions, of course, would interfere with the conduct of religion. When the English people rejected this design and called their "captain back for *Egypt*," it was a sign of their fall from virtue, their unworthiness and inability to govern themselves.[28] They surrendered their political freedom to a tyrant, who would govern their lives for them, and their religious freedom to priests and bishops, who would preside over the needs of their souls. They got the government they deserved.

It is immediately apparent, even from this cursory glance at Milton's political views, that none of the political structures of the epic poems much resemble his vision of the ideal government for fallen man. Only four are described in any detail, those in Heaven, Hell, Chaos, and Eden; oddly, the government closest to Milton's ideal is the one in Hell—but more on that later. If, in an examina-

27. *Puritan Revolution*, p. 63.
28. *YP*, 7:463, where the English are "perverse inhabitants" of the earth.

tion of these several structures, the critical imagination is disburdened of the necessity to reconcile them with the utopian vision of his prose, then the parallels between Milton's experience and the imagery may be fully explored. Relieved of the obligation to square life ideologically with art, one can search out those experiential influences which logic dictates are operative in the lines and arrive at some judgment about the function of these political structures in his art. Once again, it can be seen that this imagery serves to characterize evil, to dramatize its consequences, and to contrast obedience and disobedience to the word of God.

Heaven, it has been noted, is an absolute monarchy; but if the Almighty is to speak and act in the poems, it is difficult to conceive of him as anything other than absolute. Though almighty, God is not above artifice; he maneuvers things a bit in setting the stage for the Son to offer himself for man, and he clearly orchestrates the war. But he does not consult—and for good reason: Milton could not have him do so and still maintain his credibility as the Christian Deity. It is virtually impossible for the human imagination to visualize an "Omnipotent, / Immutable, Immortal, Infinite, / Eternal King" exchanging views or attending debate over his divine decrees.

Though to modern tastes the attendant angels may seem unnecessarily subservient, any more independent posture on their part would weaken the quality of absolute obedience the poet strives to portray. The court of God resembles that of any reigning monarch of Milton's time, where all the customary ceremonies are observed, to include the requisite bowing and scraping. When the disguised Satan takes his leave of Uriel, for example, he bows low, "As to superior Spirits is wont in Heaven / Where honour due and reverence none neglects" (3.737–38). This is not to suggest that Milton considered the rule of Heaven a model for human government. On the contrary, though in Christian liturgy and tradition God is quite properly a king, it is in imitating his absoluteness that earthly monarchs sin.[29] In *Pro Populo Anglicano*, for example, he argues that it is "a form of idolatry" for a people "to ask for a king who demands that he be worshipped and granted honors like those of a god." Again, for Milton, "the attribution of infallibility and omnipotence to a human being is the root of all evils."[30] To

29. I am indebted to Roland M. Frye for this insight.
30. *YP*, 4:369, 398.

demonstrate absolute obedience to the Almighty is something else entirely; God commands and his angels not only obey but exult in the act, singing hymns to praise the decrees of the Deity, "Whom to obey is happiness entire" (*PL* 6.741). Submission to a temporal king can diminish or demean a subject; obedience to the divine will can only enlarge and fulfill the faithful servant.

Chaos presides in similarly regal state, though Milton with a touch of levity calls him the "Anarch" of his kingdom. In a parody of Heaven he rules his noisy realm with Night as "Consort of his Reign" (2.963) and "next him high Arbiter / *Chance* governs all" (2.909–10), making up yet another unholy trinity. The source of Chaos's power is the ironic inverse of God's, however. The Almighty achieves divine order through perfect obedience, while Chaos perpetuates his rule by fomenting discord; he "Umpire sits, / And by decision more imbroiles the fray / By which he Reigns" (2.907–9).

Eden is an incipient patriarchy where Adam worships God and Eve worships God in him; when she upsets that mild hierarchy and he abrogates his civic responsibilities, all the trouble begins. Had they not sinned, "Orders and Degrees" would probably have evolved, jarring not with liberty and shadowing Heaven's hierarchies.[31] Some sort of political structure would have been needed after the children started arriving; but we catch only a glimpse of that lost opportunity when Michael tells Adam that Eden would have become

> Perhaps thy Capital Seate, from whence had spred
> All generations, and had hither come
> From all the ends of th' Earth, to celebrate
> And reverence thee thir great Progenitor. (11.343–46)

The most exhaustive treatment of the political process in Milton's epics is the description of the various convocations of the fallen angels, and it is in his portrayal of these bodies that he is most indebted to his own experience with warfare and politics. The devious debate in Hell has been much discussed, with emphasis on the lies, hollow rhetoric, false promises, masks, and manipulations of those in attendance.[32] Since this is, after all, a gath-

31. C. S. Lewis briefly imagines a prelapsarian future in *Preface*, p. 118.

32. John T. Shawcross, "The Hero of *Paradise Lost* One More Time," pp. 138, 142. Shawcross vividly describes Satan as one who "lies, deceives himself and oth-

ering of devils, it has been suggested that Milton uses that debate to condemn the governing bodies of his own time or even to demonstrate his disgust for all political process.[33] It is perhaps more appropriate, however, to consider the infernal council as the solution to an artistic problem than as a political statement. In a work that embraces all of human history the poet would not neglect a factor as important as the governments of men, but the time frame of *Paradise Lost* does not permit a thorough treatment of such matters. The poem ends as Adam and Eve depart the Garden with no need for a political institution more sophisticated than a patriarchal "Father knows best"; and Michael's swift documentary account of four thousand years of history simply does not allow for pause. Thus, though Hell is often interpreted as a parody of Heaven, the image of infernal rule may be looking in another direction entirely; it is perhaps more significant as a mirror of human government.[34] In describing the governing body of Hell, Milton takes pains that it appear as neither the best nor the worst of such institutions. As governments go, it must be said that the "Stygian Council" is not a particularly onerous one; its membership is fairly representative, selected "From every Band and squared Regiment / By place or choice the worthiest" (1.758–59), much as were the "Agitators" of the New Model who met in the spring of 1647 to politicize the army.[35] Satan presides as one "by merit rais'd / To that bad eminence" (2.5–6) and in Hell, at least, there is consultation. Devils debate, it would appear, and all sides are heard before issues are put to "popular vote" (2.313). The lords must be persuaded before any action can be taken, and no one is called upon to submit to coercion or act against his will. All of this seems in marked contrast to the ex cathedra decrees of Almighty God; but the concert of Heaven, Milton makes clear, is born of love while the unanimity of Hell arises from fear, pain,

---

ers, boasts without foundation, aggrandizes himself, sets up situations to promote himself like any con man in the daily tabloids." All of this is undeniable; but I write these words on the eve of a national election, acutely aware that these are the qualities not only of a "con man," but of any accomplished politician.

33. Some modern scholars have sensed in Milton the sort of disillusionment with the political process that may characterize our own age more than his. Joan M. Webber, in *Milton and His Epic Tradition*, suggests that Milton believed "one cannot put one's faith in any political system" (p. 121), and that he devalued "not only the Royalist cause but the Puritan as well" (p. 127).

34. Michael Wilding, *Milton's "Paradise Lost,"* p. 31.

35. Gardiner, *Civil War*, 3:477–95.

despair, and greed. In this regard, once more, the infernal council more faithfully mirrors its human counterparts.

The "great consult" is at once a representative assembly and a council of war. Satan strikes the keynote, "I give not Heav'n for lost" (2.14), and poses the question, "by what best way, / Whether of open Warr or covert guile, / We now debate" (2.40–42). Moloch, the old soldier, speaks for open war, saying, "what can be worse / Then to dwell here" (2.85–86);[36] but after his speech the debate takes an unexpected turn. Belial opposes any resistance at all, "open or conceal'd" (2.187), and Mammon seconds him, arguing that they should dismiss "All thoughts of warr" (2.283) and try to make the best of things. The assembly is divided—Moloch for war, Belial for submission, and Mammon for autonomy—but none of these positions is compatible with the intentions of Satan, and it is left for Beëlzebub to move the debate back on track. He argues that there can be no question of peace with God since they are already engaged in hostilities; "Warr hath determin'd us" (2.330), he says, and the only issue under consideration is how to pursue it. His final proposal is a nice compromise of the three positions: they will act, which placates Moloch, but not so as to invite destruction, calming the fearful Belial; and they will indeed build a new kingdom, which satisfies Mammon, in a place, however, "Neerer our ancient Seat . . . in some milde Zone" where they can "Purge off this gloom [and] heal the scarr of these corrosive Fires" (2.394–401). The plan appeals and all approve.

The debate in Pandemonium echoes many that were heard in London and Westminster during Milton's mature years, when England was almost continually in arms and questions of peace and war were discussed at length in both private conversation and public forum. The divisions within the "Synod of Gods" most closely resemble those that split the Parliamentary cause early in the civil wars. It will be recalled that though Parliament was committed to the war against the King, an important peace party prevailed in both Commons and the army, those who wished to debate not how to conduct or to win the war but how to bring it to an end. To be more specific, the opposing views expressed by Moloch and Belial are very close to those represented, respectively,

36. Hanford suggests that Moloch resembles Cromwell, with the "characteristic impetuosity and bluntness of a mere soldier" (*Handbook*, p. 198).

by Oliver Cromwell and the Earl of Manchester in the fall of 1644. Cromwell and his faction were pressing for a vigorous pursuit of the war while Manchester, like many Presbyterians, apprehensively sought accommodation with the King, for as the Earl is reported to have said, "If we beat the King ninety times, yet he is king still, and so will his posterity be after him; but if the King beat us once we shall all be hanged, and our posterity made slaves."[37] Belial's argument, and to a degree Mammon's, is in essence the same as Manchester's: we can't win, to oppose further will only do more harm, let's make the best of things.

Milton, of course, was not privy to the inner circles of government during the civil wars, but the issue of peace and war was never far from the minds of those committed to Parliament, and the confrontation between Cromwell and Manchester in the House of Commons was a cause célèbre. In later years, Milton was to sit in the councils of the Commonwealth where that same issue was discussed continually. There was little difference of agreement about the Irish and Scottish campaigns, it would appear, but the Council of State and the Rump were seriously divided over the wisdom of the Dutch War of 1652–1654. After the first surge of indignation at Van Tromp's surprise attack on the English fleet in May 1652, cooler heads began to prevail, questioning in particular why two great Protestant powers, who should more properly be in league against the anti-Christ of Rome, were fighting each other. Both Milton and Cromwell had strong reservations about the war, the latter reportedly responding to a Dutch petition in July 1652 with a promise that he would do everything in his power to bring about peace.[38] Thus, Milton approved of some wars, disapproved of others, and during these decades of conflict he would have heard all of the arguments on either side of the issue that had ever been devised by man.

Any effort to identify Milton's own views on peace and war with one or the other of the positions taken in the infernal debate would be fruitless. The longest and most eloquent argument against war is presented by Belial, and the narrative voice has nothing but scorn for his "words cloath'd in reasons garb" and his counsel of

37. See pp. 79–81 above.

38. Fraser, *Cromwell*, p. 408. Milton said of himself in *Pro Se Defensio* that no one in England "would less desire a war with [the Dutch], would wage one which had begun more pacifically, or rejoice more seriously when it was concluded" (*YP*, 4:742).

"ignoble ease, and peaceful sloath, / Not peace" (2.226–28). Mammon's advice to dismiss "All thoughts of War" (2.283) is greeted with applause, but no stretch of the imagination could associate his views with those of the poet. Milton, once more, is using this parliament of devils to mirror deliberations in the council chambers of fallen man. In both can be heard a great deal of impressive rhetoric. One cannot read Moloch's speech without some touch of admiration for his resolute spirit; he seems to reflect that quality Milton most admired in the Samnites, for whom "peace with slavery was worse than war with freedom."[39] Even Mammon seems to echo the pages of *Eikonoklastes* when he opts for "Hard liberty before the easie yoke / Of servile Pomp" (2.256–57). Belial's smooth speech, in which he pleads concern for the common welfare, is a model of reason, though compared to the others he sounds like a milksop.

It is all hollow, of course. Moloch is so blinded by rage that he doesn't care how many are destroyed in his attack on Heaven; he is quite content to lead the whole society to oblivion in his passion for revenge. Belial is interested only in his own skin, and Mammon is too obsessed with materialism to be much concerned with "Hard liberty." Satan has his own purpose, of course, a quest for personal glory; and to that end he has a plan prepared with a front man to propose it. He orchestrates affairs so that he can remain aloof from controversy and step forward dramatically after all the talk to offer himself as liberator. The assembly is swayed, first this way, then that. Their response to Moloch and Belial is not recorded, but they applaud Mammon for "Advising peace." They want release from suffering but are deterred from direct action by the memory of Michael's sword. Thus, Beëlzebub's proposal pleases them, and they welcome Satan's offer.

It is, in brief, not a very inspiring scene; but it is one that resembles any of the parliaments that come together from time to time to direct the affairs of a race that has lost the gift of perfect obedience to the word of God. Indeed, these "doubtful consultations dark" (2.486) are in some ways even superior to the deliberations of men, for as Milton says, "neither do the Spirits damn'd / Loose all thir virtue"; they know a statesmanlike gesture when they see one, however ambiguous the motive. Thus they praise Satan "That for the general safety he despis'd / His own" (2.481–83).

39. *YP*, 4:390.

Their final unanimity is a "shame to men," the poet chides; for "Devil with Devil damn'd / Firm concord holds, men onely disagree / Of Creatures rational" (2.496–98). This is but the way things are with men, for whom "true Libertie / Is lost" (12.83–84) since that first lapse; and Milton uses his experience in the higher councils of his government to give the account a richness and authenticity it might not otherwise have. Those bodies that ruled the English Republic were, again, not the best; they surely fell short of his visionary "spiritual aristocracy." Nor were they the worst, however; they were certainly an advance over the tyranny of Charles I. Milton, in an image that mirrors the human condition, simply draws on his experience of the representative, or consultative, assembly with which he was most familiar.

The governments of Milton's epics reflect yet another characteristic of the political institutions of men: they are in a constant state of change. Eve challenges the patriarchy of Eden when she insists upon acting independently of Adam, and after eating the fruit, she contemplates keeping her discovery a secret so that she may be "more equal, and perhaps, / A thing not undesireable, somtime / Superior" (9.823–25). Chaos complains that his borders are being encroached upon, first by the creation of Hell and then of the world. The rule of Heaven itself is mutable. When God announces, "This day I have begot whom I declare / My onely Son" (5.603–4), he initiates a new order in the celestial government, one obviously distasteful to Satan and his followers. And there is promise of more change to come. As Michael Lieb has ably demonstrated, the monarchy of Heaven is to undergo a gradual metamorphosis until the time when, as God tells the Son, "thou thy regal Scepter shalt lay by, / For regal Scepter then no more shall need, / God shall be All in All" (3.339–41).[40]

The change in the rule of Satan excites particular interest, however, since it somewhat resembles the experiences of the English Republic. It will be recalled that from 1649 to 1653 the Council of State acted as the executive body of the revolutionary government. Its members were elected annually by Parliament and, under the law at least, sat as equals in the conduct of public business. In fact, however, once he had returned from his campaigns in the fall of 1651, Oliver Cromwell was clearly the most powerful figure in

40. *The Dialectics of Creation: Patterns of Birth and Regeneration in "Paradise Lost,"* pp. 8–9, 85.

council, since he enjoyed towering prestige among the English people as a result of his victories and commanded the almost unqualified support of the English army. Under the constitutional system, however, it was still necessary for him to debate issues, marshal majorities, and strike compromises in order to pass legislation. In April 1653 he dissolved the Rump, and at the end of the year he was installed as Lord Protector under a constitution that reduced the Council of State to a largely consultative or advisory body, often referred to thereafter with the old monarchal designation of "His Highness' Privy Council." Cromwell acted more and more independently of the council, especially in foreign affairs, seeking their pro forma approval only on major issues.[41]

There are marked parallels between Cromwell's career and Satan's rise to infernal rule. At the first meeting of the "Stygian Council," Satan sits "by merit rais'd" on the "Throne of Royal State," but his position is not entirely secure. Most of his first speech to the "great Seraphic Lords" is devoted to justifying his position, to which he has been appointed, he reminds them, by their "free choice, / With what besides, in Counsel or in Fight, / Hath bin achievd of merit"; it is a "safe unenvied Throne / Yielded with full consent" (2.19–24). Decisions of state are arrived at, however, only by popular vote; and Satan must sit through debate in which all sides are aired and then maneuver, through Beëlzebub, to carry his position. It is apparent in *Paradise Regained* that as a result of his conquest of the world his status is much enhanced. He no longer maneuvers or persuades; he merely directs. When he "in mid air / To Councel summons all his mighty Peers" (1.39–40), it is only to inform them of his plans, for as he says, the danger "admits no long debate" (1.95); and the "gloomy Consistory" without more ado unanimously approves the designs of the leader who has now become "their great Dictator" (1.113). When they meet a second time, Belial intrudes with a brief speech but is insulted peremptorily into silence by Satan, who has little patience now with such talk. He has come only to keep them abreast of his progress and to select a band of assistant spirits "To be at hand, and at his beck appear" (2.238).

Certainly the most dramatic demonstration of the mutability of governments is the startling metamorphosis of Hell upon Satan's return from conquest of the world. The infernal rule disintegrates,

41. See pp. 102–4 above.

its council of "great consulting Peers" reduced to anarchy, their eloquence dissolved into "A dismal universal hiss" (10.508) in a mockery of their former unanimity. Meanwhile, outside Pandemonium the legions of Hell keep "thir Watch," standing "in station . . . or just array, / Sublime with expectation" (10.427, 535–36), the very image of discipline and obedience. Nothing could surpass the drama of that sudden degeneration from the order, precision, and pride of the parade to the venomous chaos of the snakepit, where the helpless forces of evil writhe in their sinuous curves and folds on the same fields where they had but lately marched "In perfect *Phalanx* . . . Breathing united force with fixed thought" (1.550–60). It is tempting to interpret this scene as Milton's judgment on the political and military institutions of his age, as a final, disappointed plague on both their houses after two decades of public service.[42] Such a reading is disturbing, however, for it demeans the poet, reducing him to the level of a misanthropic dropout who dismisses the value of those years of struggle and of his own sacrifices in the cause of religious freedom. That final dissolution of the order of Hell may be interpreted more broadly as an apocalyptic prophecy of the ultimate fate and futility of all the institutions of fallen man, not just a judgment on the seventeenth century. It may also serve as an infernal parody of the ultimate design of Heaven, when Christ's scepter will be laid by, all orders and degrees erased, and God himself "shall be All in All."

The political structure of Heaven, then, figures an order prevailing in a state whose citizens are capable of perfect obedience to the will of God. It is an order, sadly, to which man can only aspire; for having lost inner freedom through his lapse in the garden, he must forever submit to temporal rule. Man *can* aspire, however. In the utopian design of his *Readie and Easie Way* Milton envisioned a time when the authority of a strong national government could be decentralized for a people who had learned to govern themselves; but the English were unworthy of that vision and called their "captain back for *Egypt*." The rule of Hell is an image of how things are with man as a consequence of his disobedience, and Satan's rise from the status of the first among equals, one who shares power with his Stygian Council, to that of a "great dictator"

42. Wilding, "The Last of the Epics," pp. 113–14: "Milton's disillusionment with his countrymen in the Interregnum and with the Restoration" caused him to "withdraw from the present into history." See also Louis L. Martz, *Poet of Exile: A Study of Milton's Poetry*, p. 164.

who wields it unrestrained, foreshadows the fate of a people who continue deaf to the word of God.

* * *

It may be felt by some readers that this manner of interpreting military and political imagery in Milton's poetry does not provide for the degree of complexity and sophistication customary to most modern critical systems. It does not appear to allow for the subtleties and delights of a search for linguistic intricacies, a mining of the rich vein of myth, or a discovery of literary analogies; nor does it allow for the inductive leaps enjoyed by those pursuing the open-ended possibilities of psychoanalytic criticism. And it must be admitted that there is a kind of rigor imposed upon those who choose to examine the relationship between life and art; they labor under annoying restraints in analyzing a work of the imagination in the light of the facts of history. The imagination does not always rest easy in the company of fact, and the critical imagination in particular must insist on wide latitude in dealing with such insubstantial ingredients as tone, music, and the vagaries of the muse. Again, experiential criticism is not offered as an alternative to other critical approaches, but only as yet another to take its place at their side. Once released from the rigid and uncompromising insistence upon the one-to-one analogy between event and image, it may be found to allow sufficient complexity to satisfy the most sophisticated mind. Indeed, if anything proposed in these pages might be classified as a restraint on the critical imagination, it is simply the caution that when the art is explored for keys to the artist's thought, the conclusions somewhat resemble those arrived at in the examination of the chronicle of his days. Life is the raw material of art, the marble of Carrara from which Michelangelo shaped his splendid *David*; it is the element upon which the artist imposes his vision with skill of eye or pen. As such, art can never entirely free itself from life, even as those struggling *Captives* in the Accademia can never fully emerge from their essential stone.

When all is said, however, it must be admitted that the experiential critic will not fully share the pleasures enjoyed by those who devote themselves to the fascinating interplay of mind with mind or word with word. The value of the experiential perspective lies in its capacity to discern the rough outline, the scheme, or the frame of the artist's vision, the broad design within which he traces the delicate filigree of his expression, as in the present instance of the function of images of warfare and government in Milton's definition of evil. The feature that distinguishes experience from all but a few of the resources that an artist calls upon in the creative act is its entire dependence upon the faculty of memory (iconography comes to mind as another, particularly in the case of a blind poet). *Paradise Lost* owes much of its shape and power to what Milton could recall of women and rebellion, travel and teachers, gardens, ambassadors, courts, and parents (though, curiously, not of children)—and above all, his memory of evil. In its concern with this faculty, experiential criticism will find its chief value as a key to understanding art. As sources for poetic expression, experience and literature differ in that the latter is so often close at hand and hence remains unspoiled by the passage of time; one need only pull a book from the shelf or recall the words, and a work, no matter how ancient, may be said to live and participate in the moment. Should Milton have wished to make use of the wrath of Achilles in his lines, Homer's hexameters were but an arm's reach away, to read or have read, if they were not already etched in his mind. But how could he consult the experience of a London of 1643, Essex's army in decay, Rupert's cavalry cutting ever closer to the city, the parliamentary forces everywhere in retreat? And what of 1660? If he wished to convey some of the true shape of his own experience of fear or despair, he had no sources upon which to call save the dying coal of his own days. No experience can be retrieved with the same precision as a literary source—the memory fades, the mind plays tricks, lingering over some favored detail, leaving another in shadows. The particulars grow dim and over the years one recalls not so much "what it was" that happened as, more generally, "how things were" at the time.

In a way, this quality of the memory makes experience something of a touchstone for the artist, for that question is just the one we ask him: "How were things?" or better, "How are things?" We most admire the generic perceptions of the creative mind, for in them the artist touches the truth of our nature. We expect him to see in the particular acts of men a pattern common to the race and to define it in his art, stripped of parochial or transitory trappings, in such a way that we may recognize it as universally true. We expect him, in brief, to transcend the particular and show us the shape of things. He will, of course, define that vision in terms of particulars, and the aptness and decorum of his detail is a mark of his artistic achievement. But it is that generic shape for which the reader searches; while the particular may catch the attention and delight the eye, it is the vision that enlarges the spirit. Further, it is the vision that directs the choice of detail, either consciously or unconsciously, not the other way around. It is commonplace that time glosses over the experience of the past. If it was a happy time, one forgets the sadness; if a period crowned with triumph, the doubts and uncertainties of the trial will fade with the years, and the moment of victory will remain bright in the mind. If called upon to give an account of an event long past, one will recall those particulars that convey the quality and tone of the time as one remembers it. The creative vision will pierce to the meaning of that event, and the artist will select the detail which best expresses that meaning.

Thus Milton called upon his memory of king and counselor, senator and swordsman, Cavalier and Roundhead, to enrich his vision of the struggle between good and evil for the soul of man and to mirror the governments of a fallen world. But for a fuller appreciation of the complex interplay between experience and art, we must turn to the two great military and political images of his epics—the figure of Satan and the war in Heaven.

VI

Satan

O for that warning voice . . . (*PL* 4.1)

Marlowe's Mephistopheles first appears to Faustus as a dragon, which the learned doctor promptly dismisses as "too ugly to attend" on him. Milton also dismisses the dragon, except of course in book 10, where Satan exiting the poem resembles Mephistopheles entering the play. Milton further rejects the grotesque, cloven-foot satyr of medieval iconography and the pratfalling figure of ridicule who delighted the audiences of the mystery plays.[1] The poet surpasses these stereotypes of church and stage in creating a Satan of such complexity that readers centuries distant in outlook, differing widely in belief and sensibility, have recognized in the figure their own special perception of evil. Each age, of course, must reinterpret Milton's poetry according to its own lights. The experiential critic would caution only that, whatever echo of his own convictions the individual reader may find in such a figure, he be circumspect in attributing that same vision to the poet himself. The Devil *existed* for the seventeenth century, a metaphysical being palpably present in the affairs of men. For Milton the source of evil was ever that predatory enemy of man, not a socioeconomic condition or a psyche twisted by childhood trauma.

Whatever their cultural environment, scholars of even the most diverse views can probably agree on at least three characteristics of Milton's Satan: (1) He is a powerful, and for the most part successful, leader. After his defeat in Heaven, he achieves pretty much everything he sets out to do. (2) His efforts are, however, self-defeating, his successes serving only to intensify his own punishment. (3) He is a consummate liar and deceiver, seldom what he seems. These apparently straightforward lessons on the nature of evil, which might be heard from any pulpit in any age, are complicated immensely by the fact that each is conveyed by Satan in a different guise. First, he is the supernatural antagonist of God in

1. Frye, *Visual Arts*, pp. 71–72. Frye is unequivocal: "The devils of *Paradise Lost* could not be visualized in such a way as to appear simply repulsive. Nor could they be so presented as to appear ridiculous."

a cosmic war between good and evil. Second, he is an image of fallen man, in whom one may read the fate of those who lose themselves utterly to the power of evil. Third, in his deviousness he is the mirror image of good, illustrating the dilemma of Christians who love God and would shun the Devil but are plagued with the difficulty of distinguishing between the two.[2]

In these various roles Milton's Satan has aroused a broad spectrum of responses from generations of readers. As a demigod, the fearless and resolute adversary of an omnipotent foe, he excites either admiration or, given the futility of his cause, contempt. To Hazlitt he was "the clouded ruins of a god," the great rebel, a figure of awe to be admired for his courage and perseverance in the face of overwhelming odds.[3] On the other hand, Charles Williams found Hell "always inaccurate" and Satan ludicrous, worthy only of divine and human laughter for his foolish presumption.[4] For C. S. Lewis he was a "mere peeping tom."[5] As an image of suffering man, one for whom all good is irrecoverably lost, Satan engages pity. A. J. A. Waldock saw him as an actor in a human drama, one moreover with whom Milton sympathized as a being condemned to eternal suffering.[6] As the mirror image of good, he strikes fear into the hearts of God-fearing Christians who dread being tricked by the arch-deceiver into an eternity of hellfire and damnation. Any response to the character, whether it be awe, laughter, pity, or fear, is of course entirely appropriate, but only insofar as it reflects a single dimension of a protean figure. To appreciate fully Milton's vision of evil, they must all be considered.

This study will give little room to the ridiculous, or the comic, Satan, at whose antics we can smile with righteous satisfaction, chiefly because of serious reservations as to whether the historical Milton would have welcomed such a response from his readers. In attributing to the poet a more serious intent, particularly in the interpretation of the parallels between Satan and God, these pages will seem to slight the widely acknowledged reading of Hell as a

2. Frank S. Kastor, *Milton and the Literary Satan*. Kastor also finds Satan "trimorphic," but as Archangel, Prince of Hell, and Tempter.

3. William Hazlitt, "On Shakespeare and Milton," reprinted in *Milton Criticism: Selections from Four Centuries*, ed. James Thorpe, p. 108.

4. *The English Poems of John Milton*, ed. H. C. Beeching, intro. Charles Williams, p. xiii. Williams's essay first appeared in the 1940 edition.

5. *Preface*, p. 99.

6. *"Paradise Lost" and Its Critics*, p. 75.

parody of Heaven.[7] Milton is often said to be heavily ironic when he writes of the Devil, his purpose being to satirize evil. As Jacques Barzun has observed, "Like the cry of Fire, the cry of Irony is always believed, in the interests of one's safety: one does not want to get caught";[8] and any study that omits the satirical Satan certainly runs the risk of getting caught, that is, of being judged deaf to irony and dismissed as simplistic, or at best unsophisticated.

To avoid that oblivion, let me hastily acknowledge the wit and humor of John Milton.[9] His attacks on Salmasius and More are devastating in their ridicule of the personal life and intellectual pretensions of his opponents. *Paradise Lost* itself has many passages enlivened by a charming, dry humor; we have, of course, "No fear lest Dinner cool" (5.396) and the Son's playful "A nice and suttle happiness I see / Thou to thy self proposest, in the choice / Of thy Associates, *Adam*" (8.399–401), as well as the darker irony of Satan's "Awake, arise, or be for ever fall'n" (1.330). Satan does have some absurd moments, as when he squats "like a Toad" (4.800) at Eve's ear; and he puns outrageously at the success of his cannon in the war. The Paradise of Fools passage is consummate parody; Michael Lieb, with no little wit himself, has described the scatalogical effects of that "backside of the World" (3.494).[10] The target of all that anality is of course the monks, not the Devil, but Satan does not escape unsoiled. God himself has a laugh or two at the antics of men and angels, and presumably the reader is invited to join in. But once the parody starts, where does it end? A recent study, for example, carries that reading to the extreme of finding in *Paradise Lost* an "exposé of evil" in which the poet's "burlesque humor" unmasks "the grotesque incongruities of existence and the tragic absurdity of the universe," certainly a curious reading of a poem that proposes to "assert Eternal Providence / And justifie the wayes of God to men."[11]

7. This reading is so widely accepted as to hardly need documentation; but see especially Stein, *Answerable Style: Essays on "Paradise Lost,"* p. 19; Jackson I. Cope, *The Metaphorical Structure of "Paradise Lost,"* pp. 92–104; and T. J. B. Spencer, "*Paradise Lost*: The Anti-Epic," pp. 93–98. Others are cited below. Specific references to the war in Heaven as parody will appear in Chapter VII.

8. "Biography and Criticism," p. 487.

9. See also E. M. W. Tillyard, "A Note on Milton's Humour," in his *Studies in Milton*, pp. 71–81.

10. "Further Thoughts on Satan's Journey Through Chaos," p. 126.

11. John Wooten, "The Metaphysics of Milton's Epic Burlesque Humor," p. 259. See also Spencer, "*Paradise Lost*: The Anti-Epic," p. 93, for whom "in

Walter Raleigh remarked of Satan, "His very situation as the fearless antagonist of Omnipotence marks him either hero or fool"; and although Raleigh went on to conclude, "Milton is far indeed from permitting us to think him a fool,"[12] many have thought otherwise, finding in the futility of his resistance to God reason to see him as ridiculous. Charles Williams observes that "Love laughs at anti-love,"[13] C. S. Lewis finds Satan's pretensions everywhere "nonsensical,"[14] and many an able mind has pursued the thought, defending Milton from the heresy of declaring the Devil a hero. To say that Milton is laughing at evil is, to be sure, an effective strategy in defending him against the charge of admiring it; but laughter is so diverting, as well as infectious, that it can lead the unwary reader to unanticipated, and often troublesome, conclusions. Milton's satire can be read in two ways: first, when the figure of Satan resembles a god, he is said to look absurd by comparison; second, when the fallen angels sit in council or go to war, they are seen as a parody of human agents. In brief, when Satan looks like God, he ridicules himself; when he looks like man, he ridicules us. This Janus-like quality of the figure makes one wonder, to cite just one example, which way the unholy trinity is facing. Satan, Sin, and Death are widely interpreted as a parody of the Holy Trinity, their purpose a satiric demeaning of the rule of Hell; but since the Holy Trinity is nowhere mentioned in *Paradise Lost* and there is some doubt that the Third Person appears at all, there is nothing, in the poem at least, for the infernal trio to parody.[15] Since the only trinity to be found in the epic is in Hell (and perhaps in Chaos), then the figure can be read with equal reason as a parody of man, that is, as a travesty of his superstitious worship of that doctrinal inference—in brief, of his idolatry. The double-edged blade of parody thus allows for two contradictory conclusions about Milton's Arianism. Since the satire can cut either way, the reader cannot tell from the lines alone what Milton actually believed; he must look outside the poem to satisfy himself on that score.

Lastly, this pervasive reading of parody focuses so intently on tone rather than meaning that it can easily obscure the poet's pur-

---

some respects *Paradise Lost*, like *The Rape of the Lock*, is a kind of joke against the epic."

12. *Milton*, p. 133.
13. *English Poems*, p. xiii.
14. *Preface*, pp. 97–98.
15. Maurice Kelley, *This Great Argument*, pp. 106–22.

pose. Of course, there is no arguing tone—one hears what one hears. There is, however, a consensus on the effect of parody: it ridicules, prompting contemptuous laughter and an agreeable feeling of superiority. God, therefore, may be allowed an occasional chuckle, but man laughs to his peril. To scorn an enemy is to lower one's guard, to rest easy, ever a prelude to defeat; and it is difficult to imagine Milton wishing such a response from his readers. It was Charles Williams, again, who first brought to our attention that "irrepressible laughter in heaven" whenever fallen men or angels engage in one of their ill-conceived ventures.[16] C. S. Lewis would not go so far as to say that *Paradise Lost* is a comic poem, but he manages to have his cake and eat it too with the rather cryptic observation that "only those will fully understand it who see that it might have been" one.[17] God is certainly amused at times; Milton specifically mentions three occasions—when the rebels plot to try his omnipotence (5.237), when men attempt to chart the heavens (8.78), and when they raise the Tower of Babel (12.59). But to hear laughter everywhere in the lines and to propose parody as the prevailing tone of *Paradise Lost* is to misread the mind of a seventeenth-century Puritan poet, as well as the concerns of his God-fearing audience. Such interpretations assume that Milton has positioned his reader at the left hand of God and endowed him with such omniscience that he may look upon all the acts of men and angels as somewhat antic—the war in Heaven, the perilous voyage of Satan, the frantic scurrying of the sentinels outside Eden, and that silly domestic squabble between our first parents. But Milton's readers did not view events from the comfort and security of that airy perch; they were frail and flawed men who believed that as a consequence of these acts they were fated to live a brief and tragic existence in which they daily risked the fires of eternal damnation.[18] Milton did not perceive of man's struggles as absurd, nor did he wish to disarm his readers by mocking evil. He sought rather to warn them of its terrible powers.

In the final analysis, a reading of parody is unsatisfactory because it is too simple. While it pretends to a sophisticated com-

16. *English Poems*, p. xiii. 17. *Preface*, p. 95.

18. Joseph H. Summers, *The Muse's Method: An Introduction to "Paradise Lost,"* p. 41. Summers accepts the comic, but only as one of a number of possible perspectives internal to the poem: "From the point of view of Hell, Satan, Sin, and Death are heroic; from that of Heaven they are comic; from that of earth they may be terrifying agents of tragedy."

plexity, it is in fact reductive, both for the poet and the poem. That ringing laughter in Heaven drowns out all else, allowing for only one meaning, and that not a particularly enlightening one. To laugh along with God leaves the reader with little in the way of enrichment, and not much more understanding of evil than those who fear the Devil with naked superstition. Besides, satire makes for some strange bedfellows. A recent essay, for example, finds the war in Heaven "comic, absurd" and proposes therefore that Butler's *Hudibras* may be favorably compared with *Paradise Lost*, since they are satires both, and both parody warfare.[19] To deliver Milton from this choice of his associates, the present study will stress his words as warning, rather than as edifying entertainment. To neglect the parody and read Satan as a serious rather than comic figure admittedly takes some of the fun out of *Paradise Lost*; one does so only because to picture him as a buffoon is to slight the weight of that warning.

Satan, then, is powerful, self-defeating, and devious; he appears in the poems as demigod, man, and the mirror of good; and Milton uses political and military imagery to illuminate all these facets of the figure. Some of this imagery is obviously influenced by his public life, and perhaps a comment on the nature of experiential analogy as it applies to this specific figure will be useful at the outset. Perplexed Miltonists since the days of Addison have attempted to come to terms with Satan by suggesting that he is drawn from life. To cite but one such correspondence, there are times in *Paradise Lost* when he does indeed seem to resemble Cromwell:

> his face
> Deep scars of Thunder had intrencht, and care
> Sat on his faded cheek, but under Browes
> Of dauntless courage, and considerate Pride. (1.600–603)[20]

The pursuit of all the political and ideological implications of this comparison has inspired two different schools of thought. If, as one group has argued, Satan is analogous to Cromwell, then it can be safely said that Milton disapproved of Cromwell and all he

19. Wilding, "The Last of the Epics," passim.

20. In *John Milton, "Paradise Lost," Books I–II*, ed. John Broadbent, p. 39, Broadbent notes that "Milton admired leadership, like Satan's, in Cromwell." William Empson, in *Milton's God*, p. 74, is uncertain whether Satan is a satire on Charles II or on Cromwell. See also Hanford, *Handbook*, pp. 191, 238.

stood for, a view sympathetic with that comfortable figure, Milton the pacifist. On the other hand, it can be argued that since there is so much evidence that he admired Cromwell, we are free to conclude that he approved of Satan, a view the Romantics found attractive. Our knowledge of Milton, of course, persuades us that both of these conclusions are questionable. In the face of these frustrating contradictions between poetry and life, one might be tempted to simply dismiss Cromwell as an analogue, neglecting what may be a valuable key to the complex figure of Satan.[21]

Further confusion has arisen from the assumption that since Satan is the archetype of evil and morally corrupt, he must therefore be a bungling general, an inept leader, and an intellectual lightweight, deficient in all dimensions.[22] But life does not work thus and neither should we expect it of art. History will demonstrate that all successful leaders, however questionable their cause or moral persuasion, be they Ghengis Khan, Bonaparte, John Kennedy, Mao Tse-tung, or Martin Luther King, Jr., have certain qualities in common which equip them to sway large bodies of men and achieve positions of power. Milton watched the leaders of his own day at close hand and was able to note some of these common qualities: a tendency toward extravagant gesture, a mastery of rhetoric, a predilection toward action, an instinctive appreciation for the decisive moment, unswerving dedication to a cause, and physical courage, among others. Not infrequently, he may have observed, the burdens of office weighed so heavily that "care / Sat on" their faded cheeks. Satan, these pages will argue, was neither inept nor stupid, but a competent leader in much the same way that Cromwell was a competent leader; this need not imply, though, that Milton either admired Satan or disparaged Cromwell. The correspondence between the two means simply that he was artist enough to create such a commanding figure

21. *John Milton: "Paradise Lost" V–VI*, ed. Robert Hodge and Isabel MacCaffrey, pp. 45–49. Hodge struggles with the apparent contradiction, in which, as he puts it, "Milton seems to have taken exactly opposite sides in the divine and human spheres, or in poetry and life" (p. 45). His resolution seems at best strained: "A story that seems to discredit rebellion is really contrasting two forms of revolution" in which Abdiel is the real revolutionary, like Cromwell, and Satan represents the early generation of "ideologists," like Hampton and Pym. Milton "sides with the loyal angel against the rebel because the loyal angel is loyal to the revolutionary cause" (p. 48). If this sounds confusing, Hodge continues, it is because "Milton had some deep need to be confused." The confusion, I am arguing, arises only if one insists on the one-to-one congruence between poetry and life.

22. Lewis, *Preface*, p. 99.

from the materials of his experience, and an understanding of that creative process can only be obscured by reading all the weight of ideological inference into the analogy.

The most vivid portrayal of the power of evil is, of course, the great war in which "all Heav'n / Had gon to wrack, with ruin overspred" (6.669–70) had not the Almighty stopped it. The discussion of that image must await a later chapter, but there is a passage of equal force in book 1 where Satan restores his wasted army to order and hope after their shattering rout in Heaven. This passage demonstrates unusual insight on the part of Milton into the state of mind of defeated soldiers and the actions required to revive them, knowledge born perhaps of those early years of the civil wars when the despondent ranks of Parliamentary armies straggled back to London from their lost battles. In the summer of 1643, for example, Waller, shaken by his defeat at Roundway Down, returned to the city to inspire new hope in the citizens, who promptly proposed him as the commander of an independent force to be composed exclusively of London residents. That same summer, Essex, whose demoralized army, reduced to an ineffectual remnant by desertion and disease, had sat outside London scorned and ignored for so many months, revitalized the cause by marching a force of fifteen thousand men to the relief of Gloucester. Again, despite Essex's surrender of his entire army at Lostwithel in September 1644, the Parliamentary forces joined to attack Charles at Newark the following month.[23] All of London sank to despair at these defeats, only to surface time and again to new hope and effort in their wake.

Satan surveys a totally shattered force as he stands on that fiery shore in book 1. His is the supreme test of generalship, to restore an army sunk in the desolation and paralysis that follow defeat; and Satan's great accomplishment in the first two books, the source of the nobility that characterizes him in these early pages, is his success in overcoming his own despair and arousing his troops from their state of abject submission to a spirit of revived hope and defiance.

It is an imposing task. In brief, the problems that confront Satan are those that challenge the leader of any routed army:

1. Fear. The concern for personal safety, the strong instinct for

23. See pp. 49–53 above.

self-preservation, overshadows all other considerations in the minds of the soldiers. Each man thinks only of himself.

2. Loss of confidence in comrades and leaders. The essential cohesive force of any military unit, personal pride and fear of censure from fellow soldiers and immediate commanders, loses all influence with the individual.

3. Breakup of military organization. Paradoxically, fear prevents the soldiers from reforming the ranks of the army into the united force upon which ultimately their safety depends. Each seeks salvation in anonymity.

4. Loss of faith in the cause.

Satan addresses his problem in just this order. Recovering his own resolution, no mean feat in itself, he rouses Beëlzebub from a state of despair and immediately attacks the most formidable obstacle to his hopes—fear. To counter the great dread in his soldiers' hearts, he stings them with derision:

> have ye chos'n this place
> After the toyl of Battel to repose
> Your wearied vertue, for the ease you find
> To slumber here, as in the Vales of Heav'n?
> Or in this abject posture have ye sworn
> To adore the Conquerour? (1.318–23)

He also instills in them an even greater fear of their victorious enemy,

> who now beholds
> Cherube and Seraph rowling in the Flood
> With scatter'd Arms and Ensigns, till anon
> His swift pursuers from Heav'n Gates discern
> Th' advantage, and descending tread us down
> Thus drooping, or with linked Thunderbolts
> Transfix us to the bottom of this Gulfe. (1.323–29)

Satan's troops, stirred by his words, rise like "a pitchy cloud / Of Locusts" (1.340–41) and join him on the shore, "but with looks / Down cast and damp" (1.522–23). He must now restore their confidence in themselves and their leaders. Satan's appearance impresses many immediately; they are reassured

> to have found thir chief
> Not in despair, to have found themselves not lost
> In loss it self. (1.524–26)

But there is more to be done. As the rebel leaders gather about him on the shore, he passes among them, and

> with high words, that bore
> Semblance of worth, not substance, gently rais'd
> Thir fanting courage, and dispel'd thir fears. (1.528–30)

Here the general moves from man to man, with special words of encouragement for each. This is the crucial moment, for military discipline has not as yet been reestablished and the leader has only the force of his own personality to counteract the fears of his men; he must present an illusion of confidence he may not feel. The fact that Satan's words here have only the "semblance of worth" is of little import. It has been suggested that on occasion Milton seems to feel the necessity to undercut his own invention. According to A. J. A. Waldock, "Each great speech lifts Satan a little beyond what Milton really intended, so he suppresses him again (or tries to) in a comment."[24] But Satan is not being two-faced with his followers, nor is Milton letting his material get out of hand. Unless Satan wants to remain submissively in that fiery lake, he must rouse his troops; and this is the way it is done. The fact, therefore, that his words have not the "substance" of worth is not the point; their purpose is to spread throughout the command the warm glow of the commander's confidence, and in this they certainly succeed.

The next step is to reorganize the revived army, to reestablish discipline. Satan commands that

> at the warlike sound
> Of Trumpets loud and Clarions be upreard
> His mighty Standard. (1.531–33)

In response,

> All in a moment through the gloom were seen
> Ten thousand Banners rise into the Air
> With Orient Colours waving. (1.544–46)

There is a period of confusion as the units reform, but soon "they move / In perfect *Phalanx* to the *Dorian* mood / Of Flutes and soft Recorders" (1.549–51). Finally, "Breathing united force," they march in review and form a line, where

24. *Critics*, p. 79. The "comment" does not actually follow a "great speech," but unspecified words of encouragement in what Milton knew, as any Christian knows, was a lost cause.

> they stand, a horrid Front
> Of dreadful length and dazling Arms, in guise
> Of Warriers old with order'd Spear and Shield,
> Awaiting what command thir mighty Chief
> Had to impose. (1.560, 563–67)

Satan surveys his rejuvenated army, and "his heart / Distends with pride" (1.571–72), as well it might, for this is all his doing; he alone has restored his troops from their state of prostrate submission, where they had lain, inert and disordered "as Autumnal Leaves" (1.302), to this magnificent array of strength he sees before him. He is very much affected by the sight. When he observes their courage and loyalty to him and contemplates their fallen state, he cannot speak: "thrice in spight of scorn, / Tears such as Angels weep, burst forth" (1.619–20). These tears are not ignoble; they are a touch of compassion that adds dignity to his figure.[25] They reflect the emotions of a Lee after Gettysburg or a Rommel after El Alamein and may therefore be regarded as dramatically appropriate.

Satan must now instill in his men a renewed faith in the cause. His great speech to his troops is a masterpiece of martial rhetoric. Opening on a realistic note—for who, looking about, could deny his unhappy situation—he soon builds to a song of hope:

> For who can yet beleeve, though after loss,
> That all these puissant Legions, whose exile
> Hath emptied Heav'n, shall fail to re-ascend
> Self-rais'd, and repossess thir native seat? (1.631–34)

After a further appeal to their pride, he reveals a new strategy in the war, a counterattack against God through His new creature, man, concerning whom he will seek needed intelligence: "Thither, if but to pry, shall be perhaps / Our first eruption, thither or elsewhere" (1.655–56). Whatever happens, he tells his men, there will be action. They need not sit and rot; something can be done, and even now a plan of campaign is being developed. He concludes in a crescendo of pride, indignation, and defiance:

> For this Infernal Pit shall never hold
> Celestial Spirits in Bondage, nor th' Abyss
> Long under darkness cover. But these thoughts
> Full Counsel must mature: Peace is despaird,

25. Marjorie Hope Nicolson, *Milton: Poems and Selected Prose*, p. 16.

> For who can think Submission? Warr then, Warr
> Open or understood must be resolv'd. (1.657–62)

His words have all the effect he could have desired:

> out-flew
> Millions of flaming swords, drawn from the thighs
> Of mighty Cherubim; the sudden blaze
> Far round illumin'd hell: highly they rag'd
> Against the Highest, and fierce with grasped Arms
> Clash'd on thir sounding Shields the din of war,
> Hurling defiance toward the Vault of Heav'n. (1.663–69)

This is Satan's supreme moment in *Paradise Lost*, one in which he appears in his most elevated and noble guise as a warrior-prince.

Having raised his followers to this spirited pitch, Satan must devise means to keep them there, means, in the time-honored military tradition, "to keep the troops busy." Realizing that the best way to take his soldiers' minds off their troubles and to sustain their high morale is to give them something to do, he sets them to work building Pandemonium. Later, after the decisions of the "great consult" are announced, the army disperses temporarily; but this is not a demobilization such as that which takes place in peaceful and secure Heaven, where loyal angels are told to "inhabit lax" (7.162) the newly unpopulated regions of the kingdom. Satan instructs his troops to "intermit no watch / Against a wakeful Foe" (2.462–63) during his absence. This is no idle threat, the tyrant conjuring up foreign enemies to enhance his authority at home. Belial, warning of the power of Heaven, describes how the forces of God

> oft on the bordering Deep
> Encamp thir Legions, or with obscure wing
> Scout farr and wide into the Realm of night,
> Scorning surprize. (2.131–34)

Also, Raphael, perhaps even as they speak, is "on excursion toward the Gates of Hell" (8.231). As Satan departs, then, some of his legions march off to practice their battle formations and weaponry, others fall to marksmanship training with hilltops until "Hell scarce holds the wilde uproar" (2.541). The poets retire to compose epics celebrating the exploits of their military heroes while the more adventurous move off "in Squadrons and gross Bands" on "flying March" (2.570–74) to explore the kingdom.

Hell is alive with energy and activity in a militant display of the power of evil.

As any Christian knows, that power will ultimately be destroyed when Christ comes on the final day "to dissolve / *Satan* with his perverted World" (12.546–47). While the reader may take hope from the promise, that distant event offers little in the way of comfort in a world where the power of evil is all too painfully manifest. In this life, it would appear, the wicked flourish and a good man stands in need of solace as he struggles through his days. To encourage his embattled Christian reader, Milton presents yet another dimension of the nature of evil: the wicked are in pain, he says, and every ill act of theirs serves only to shape the design of their own defeat.

But Milton must demonstrate this dimension, not just say it, and therein lies the artistic problem. It was observed in an earlier chapter that the time frame of *Paradise Lost* provided little scope to elaborate on temporal governments, and the same limitation complicates a demonstration of the effect of evil on man. Brutish passions swarm momentarily upon Adam and Eve as an immediate consequence of their Fall, but they repent their sin, accept the punishment, and, though saddened and diminished, go forth into the world with hope and love renewed. In a sweeping spectacle Michael displays the wages of sin for the entire race—death, sickness, age, and war; but there are no humans in the narrative to demonstrate the horror and futility of those drawn on from evil to evil, no Macbeth gradually brutalized by the weight of his crimes. Michael gives only brief glimpses of the tyrants, dissemblers, and murderers of the world, little of the anguish of those lost to all good, living a Hell on earth, wracked by the pain and despair of their guilt.

It is, of course, in Satan that Milton presents such a figure, one in which the reader can contemplate his own fallen nature. Satan, as an image of man, embodies the message that evil defeats itself even as, to all outward appearances, it seems to be most triumphant. The poet traces this theme in two ways—by a dramatic representation of the psychological deterioration of Satan and by a poetic depiction of his decline in stature—and each is developed in military terms.

The psychological deterioration of Satan begins at that first convocation in Pandemonium. One aspect of the infernal debate sets it aside from any of the deliberations of men—the subject under discussion. The fallen angels are arguing the best means of continuing their opposition to a force newly manifested in the cosmos, the omnipotence of God. They had all sung about it during happier days in Heaven, but none knew what it meant until that cataclysmic appearance of the Son in the "Chariot of Paternal Deity." On the surface, any opposition to omnipotence would seem presumptuous in the extreme, and the apparent absurdity of the demonic pretensions has persuaded some that the whole scene is rather comic in effect.

A debate over how to make war on omnipotence does have its ironies, but they are not comic. They are instead tragic, the ironies of Sophocles, not Voltaire.[26] A grim fact of cosmic history stands as backdrop to the proceedings: the fallen angels must indeed oppose God's omnipotence in order to fulfill his divine plan. They have no idea of their fate, but the reader is forewarned at the moment Satan first raises his head above the burning lake. He could not perform even so much as that simple act, we are told, without "the will / And high permission of all-ruling Heaven"; further, he is permitted to act so as to provide occasion for the exercise of divine mercy and to perpetuate the punishment of the fallen angels, for God has

> Left him at large to his own dark designs,
> That with reiterated crimes he might
> Heap on himself damnation, while he sought
> Evil to others, and enrag'd might see
> How all his malice serv'd but to bring forth
> Infinite goodness, grace and mercy shewn
> On Man by him seduc't, but on himself
> Treble confusion, wrath and vengeance pour'd. (1.211–20)

Thus, in seeking to oppose the will of God, the fallen angels serve only, Oedipus-like, to fulfill it. Curiously enough, the despised Belial offers the most realistic appraisal of the situation. Of all the speakers he seems to appreciate best the lesson of their experience with omnipotence:

> Warr therefore, open or conceal'd, alike
> My voice disswades; for what can force or guile
> With him, or who deceive his mind, whose eye
> Views all things at one view? he from heav'ns hight

26. Tillyard, *Studies in Milton*, p. 55: "The irony promotes feelings more akin to the tragic than to the absurd and in no way diminishes the stature of the victim."

> All these our motions vain, sees and derides;
> Not more Almighty to resist our might
> Then wise to frustrate all our plots and wiles. (2.187–93)

They have been subdued, he continues, by "Omnipotent Decree, / The Victors will"; and the best course of action is to submit, for further opposition can only make things worse. It's all true! And the truth of it makes doubly curious the scornful characterization by the narrative voice. Is it really "peaceful sloath" to caution that a war against omnipotence would be fruitless? Is it "ignoble ease" to advise submission to an omniscient power who even at that moment "sees and derides" their deliberations? When arguing against a hopeless war, is one not counseling "peace"? I earlier expressed reservations about Waldock's suggestion that Milton occasionally was carried away by the speeches of Satan and felt obliged to warn his readers that he only "sounds splendid"; but something of that order may well be going on here, though in the inverse, of course, for Belial's speech doesn't even "sound splendid," however accurate his observations. Perhaps the whole thrust of his argument, which counsels abject submission to a tyrannical power, was so distasteful to the author of *Pro Populo Anglicano Defensio* and *Eikonoklastes* that he could hardly stomach his own words. In another sense, the whole action of the poem, as well as the substance of Christian doctrine, demands that the fallen angels reject the advice as contrary to the divine plan; hence who better to propose it than the dissolute god.

It is, then, the cosmic irony of their condition that in opposing God the fallen angels will only advance his purpose and increase their pain. The irony, moreover, is generically dramatic, for as "they sit contriving" they have no knowledge of their destiny; they desire only release from Hell and revenge for their defeat. Not until Satan lands on earth does he begin to understand the full meaning of their fallen state, that they can never leave Hell and that their pursuit of revenge will only plunge deeper the barb of that defeat. As Satan touches down atop Nephates, the narrative voice pauses to remind us of God's words, and Milton once more uses a military image to define the nature of evil. Satan's rage "boiles in his tumultuous brest, / And like a devillish Engine back recoiles / Upon himself." He can never escape his place of punishment,

> for within him Hell
> He brings, and round about him, nor from Hell

> One step no more then from himself can fly
> By change of place. (4.16–23)

Satan learns the second lesson quickly, recognizing almost at once the dimensions of his cosmic prison: "Me miserable! which way shall I flie / Infinite wrauth, and infinite despaire? / Which way I flie is Hell; my self am Hell" (4.73–75). But he does not yet realize the subtle trick that is being played on him, for he believes still that conquest will somehow ease his pain: "Evil be thou my Good; by thee at least / Divided Empire with Heav'ns King I hold / By thee, and more then half perhaps will reigne" (4.110–12). The reader can follow the slow dawning of awareness as Satan moves toward the dramatic recognition of the full horror of his fallen state. He first senses that something is wrong when he looks at the sun, only to find that he hates its beams. Next he sees Adam and Eve, an experience that fills him first with grief, and then, when they embrace, with pain: "Sight hateful, sight tormenting! thus these two / Imparadis't in one anothers arms" (4.505–6). He is not yet fully aware of what we already know, that the vision of light, or beauty, or happiness is misery for those lost to good.

Not until he is about to enter the serpent does he fully realize the extent of his punishment: "the more I see / Pleasures about me, so much more I feel / Torment within me, as from the hateful siege / Of contraries" (9.119–22). Only then does he abandon all hope of release from pain, realizing that his thirst for vengeance has only made him more miserable. He is in the divine trap; only in destroying can he find release from his "relentless thoughts," but in destroying he intensifies his anguish. He echoes the artillery image of the narrative voice, "Revenge, at first though sweet, / Bitter ere long back on it self recoiles," but that harsh knowledge does not deter him; he concludes with the fiercely defiant "Let it; I reck not, so it light well aim'd" (9.171–73). Given these lines, it is difficult to understand C. S. Lewis's characterization of Satan as "the horrible co-existence of a subtle and incessant intellectual activity with an incapacity to understand anything."[27] By the time he tempts Eve he thoroughly understands the penalties for opposing omnipotence. The ensuing indignity in Hell will only confirm for him the self-imposed fate of those who pursue evil. But for Milton's readers, the hopeless, almost heroic, rage of that final,

27. *Preface*, p. 99.

undaunted "Let it" is grim warning of the frightening power and resolve of the forces ranged against them.

Satan's psychological deterioration is complemented by an artistic decline in his stature from an "Arch Angel ruind" (1.593) to "A monstrous Serpent on his Belly prone" (10.514). Scholars agree in general that Milton, in a dazzling succession of poetic images, chiefly light-darkness and animal, deliberately degrades the figure;[28] but there is some dispute as to the regularity of the decline. John Peter, for example, finds it "a bumpy and uncertain curve," while Balachandra Rajan sees it exercised "evenly from the first books to the last."[29] Satan's decline as a military figure would seem to support Rajan's view that the process "is meant to be read poetically" from book 1 to book 10 and has little to do with the narrative sequence of advances and retreats of the adversaries, who are alternately generating evil from good and good from evil. At the lowest point of Satan's fortunes, for example, he appears in his most elevated martial guise, while at the moment of his greatest victory he is horribly degraded. As the reader makes his way through the lines, he watches the degenerative effect of evil upon the evildoer, a phenomenon that occurs not because of the success or failure of his efforts but simply as a consequence of his unrelenting opposition to the will of God.

A warrior's stature is determined ultimately on the basis of his performance in battle, most definitively by an individual encounter with an armed opponent. In book 1 Satan is a towering figure, the defeated general resolutely reviving his shattered armies and the imposing statesman restoring hope and purpose to his nation. He meets in every way the highest standards of courage, discipline, and determination that one can expect of a military leader. But we do not see him in battle. It is not until he approaches the gates of Hell that he is challenged to individual combat. Death confronts him, brandishing his "dreadful Dart" (2.672), and a battle impends: "Each at the Head / Level'd his deadly aime" (2.711–12). Sin intervenes before they can clash, and the outcome of the encounter is left in question; for though Satan is indeed powerful, Sin warns him to shun Death's "deadly arrow; neither vainly hope / To be invulnerable in those bright Arms" (2.811–12).

28. Nicolson, *A Reader's Guide*, pp. 186–89.

29. Peter, *A Critique of "Paradise Lost,"* p. 52; Rajan, *"Paradise Lost" and the Seventeenth Century Reader*, p. 105.

Combat threatens next in his encounter with Gabriel and the sentinels of Eden: "th' Angelic Squadron bright / Turnd fierie red, sharpning in mooned hornes / Thir Phalanx" (4.977–79), and Satan stands "Like *Teneriff* or *Atlas* unremov'd" with "in his graspe / What seemd both Spear and Shield" (4.987–90). The golden scales foretell the outcome, however, and he is forced to flee the field "Murmuring." The difference between these two challenges is subtle but important. In the first Satan is reconciled with his prospective opponent, and we are left in doubt as to who would have emerged victor; in the second, doubt is erased as he avoids battle, defeated without striking a blow, a much diminished warrior.

In book 6 Satan accepts the challenge and indeed a fight ensues, but on the two occasions when he engages in personal combat, he is soundly defeated, in a further decline of his martial stature (this aside from the fact that he loses the war, to be discussed in the following chapter). Abdiel strikes a blow from which Satan "back recoild," ending up "on bended knee" (6.194); but he recovers quickly to enter the fray. In his encounter with Michael, however, he is seriously wounded and "all his Armour staind ere while so bright" (6.334). Thus he appears as a warrior in one-on-one encounters with four separate opponents, emerging from each successively diminished: he is first reconciled with his adversary and then retires from the field with his strength still untested; and when he is finally committed to an exchange of blows, he is first knocked to his knees and then carried from the field in pain, "Gnashing for anguish and despite and shame / To find himself not matchless" (6.340–41). He is reduced from a warrior whose martial powers are only cast in doubt to a helpless casualty concerning whose vulnerability there can be no question. The next step in this "poetic" decline comes in book 9, where as a slinking coward he refuses even to face his adversaries, disguising himself to avoid altogether the "flaming Ministers" guarding Eden, those whose "vigilance" he dreads (9.156–57); and he is further degraded when after the Fall he flees the field at the sight of the Son of God, not "murmuring" this time, but "terrifi'd" (10.338), the ultimate disgrace for a warrior.

Satan's final appearance as soldier and statesman is in book 10, where he undergoes a series of startling transformations. He returns victor from Eden, having just conquered a new kingdom, but he enters the hall "In show Plebeian Angel militant / Of lowest order" (10.442–43). It is but a brief flash, inserted perhaps in a moment of levity; but it gives at least a hint that this whole process of degradation is consciously intended, for what a fall is here, from commanding general to lowly private. He reappears splendidly in "shape Starr bright" (10.450), reminding us briefly of his former grandeur, and then is suddenly humiliated, "A Dragon grown" (10.529), the very antithesis of the resolute, disciplined warrior-prince who stood with ponderous shield and massive spear on the edge of that flaming lake.

Satan is, then, in a sense digging his own grave by perpetuating his opposition to God; but when at the Last Judgment "Hell, her numbers full, / Thenceforth shall be for ever shut" (3.332–33), a host of human souls will be among those numbers. Milton's reader, while rejoicing in the promise of that final day, must contend with a more immediate problem, however: the terrifying possibility that his sins will condemn him to be one of those who "glut the Grave" (3.259). Of course, no man in his right mind would live his life so as to deserve such punishment, but to avoid that fate is terribly difficult, for man is weak and evil is deceptive. Even unfallen Adam was plagued with a flawed gift, his poor reason, which could be "by some faire appeering good surpris'd" and "dictate false" (9.354–55). Given the consequences of sin, few will deliberately choose evil; the problem is distinguishing it from good. The two came into the world like "twins cleaving together";[30] and if even Uriel, "The Sharpest sighted Spirit of all in Heav'n" (3.691), can be deceived, how is poor man to tell them apart?

Milton defines this third dimension of evil, its deceptive twinship with good, in the figure of Satan, the arch-deceiver; and the most effective expression of that quality is in the passages where he assumes the role of politician and diplomat. He shades the truth to gain advantage over those he seeks to corrupt, he assumes disguises and strikes poses to persuade them that he is not what he is, and he flatters to conceal his true purposes. Once again, it is going too far to conclude that since the Devil is a politician, Milton must have considered all public figures liars and dissemblers. As with soldiers and governments, there were some politicians he approved of and some he did not; but he doubtless observed that at one time or another they all will cloak designs, shift alliances, and conceal motives beneath a surface of easy words. Satan, as an im-

30. *Areopagitica*, *YP*, 1:514.

age of fallen man in an imperfect society, uses all these devices, and, save for his brief adventure as a toad in *Paradise Lost* and "an aged man in Rural weeds" (1.314) in *Paradise Regained*, he enjoys considerable success. As will be seen, even in his temptation of Christ he achieves what he sets out to do.

Satan's successes in court and council have been discussed in some detail and need not be reviewed further. In his most triumphant performance, that with Eve, though he speaks with all the flourish of a sophisticated courtier, the offer of fame and political power is not particularly effective. His overtures sadly miss the mark; for when he praises her as one "who shouldst be seen / A Goddess among Gods, ador'd and serv'd / By Angels numberless, thy daily Train" and as an "Empress" (9.546–48, 568), she is flattered but not overly impressed—indeed, she may well not know what he is talking about. The flattery perhaps softens her for his final pitch, but in the end he must turn to personal, rather than to public, enticements to persuade her that she needs "this fair Fruit."

Satan's most consummate performance as a deceiver is with Christ in the desert. Barbara Lewalski has written such a thorough and scholarly study of the Christ of *Paradise Regained* that I feel fortunate in being able to focus on Satan. She has left at least a few things to say from the Devil's point of view.[31] Actually, the temptations of Christ offer little in the way of dramatic tension, since he is never really tempted; nor does any Christian expect him to be. In an effort to animate the encounter, Milton takes pains to attribute human qualities to Jesus, afflicting him with some of the frailties of the race, among them a vulnerability to cold, hunger, ugly dreams, and moments of uncertainty. Of himself, Jesus knows only what his thirty years and the reading of Scripture have taught him, for the only divine revelation in his life thus far has been that approving voice at his baptism. He does not know why he is in the desert or why he must submit to the annoying attentions of Satan; he knows only that he must obey and endure and that somehow he will prevail in the end. He never doubts, but he does wonder; and Milton, perhaps feeling the need to insert some element of suspense into the narrative, shifts the scene to the anxious Mary at the opening of book 2, where we can catch a glimpse of a truly human response to Christ's predica-

31. *Milton's Brief Epic: The Genre, Meaning, and Art of "Paradise Regained."*

ment. His eye, sharper than Uriel's, sees through Satan's disguise from the start, however; and thereafter he is completely unaffected by the wiles of the Devil, affirming perhaps more than anything else the ancient wisdom that the value of a gift must be judged by the motive of the giver. Indeed, none of Satan's offers—wealth, fame, power, learning—are intrinsically evil; they all appear in Heaven and would surely have been features of an unfallen world. There is certainly nothing demonic about dinner; thus Satan, when he asks Jesus whether he would eat if food were set before him, receives the arch reply, "Thereafter as I like / The giver" (2.321–22). Christ rejects the things of this world not because they are evil in themselves but because they have been perverted by the Devil and turned from their proper purpose.

From Satan's point of view, however, these offers are temptations in every sense of the word. The question is, what is he tempting Christ to do? His purpose and his dilemma are defined in the first "gloomy Consistory" that he calls in midair. The fallen angels all know of the prophecy that the seed of Eve shall wound Satan's head, and he describes that prospect in terms of another war for control of earth. He reminds "his mighty Peers" of

> How many Ages, as the years of men,
> This Universe we have possest, and rul'd
> In manner at our will th' affairs of Earth. (1.48–50)

He then warns them that the appearance of the promised Messiah will threaten their freedom and power over "this fair Empire won of Earth and Air" (1.63). The question before them is the same as that shortly to confront the Jews, who for centuries had awaited their Deliverer: Is this the one? Satan remembers all too well God's "first-begot" whose "fierce thunder drove us to the deep"; but what of this new "Son belov'd":

> Who this is we must learn, for man he seems
> In all his lineaments, though in his face
> The glimpses of his Fathers glory shine. (1.89–93)

Something must be done quickly, he urges, "E're in the head of Nations he appear / Their King, their Leader, and Supream on Earth" (1.98–99) to end the fallen angels' "Raign on Earth so long enjoy'd" (1.125). Satan, of course, misreads the Messiah's "Kingdom" as temporal throughout, but readers can have little cause for smugness at this ignorance, for so did all but a few during his ministry, and many an archbishop since.

Satan's mission is to discover whether Jesus is God or man, and the chief purpose of the temptations is to prompt Jesus to reveal his identity by performing some act clearly characteristic of one or the other. The temptations of Christ have been classified and numbered in a variety of ways, but to my knowledge not from the perspective of Satan's mission to find out "Who this is."[32] When seen in the light of his effort to induce Jesus to act as either God or man, it can be said that there are but two temptations. The first, a request that he turn the stones into bread, in brief to perform a miracle, is a ruse to make him reveal himself as God. Failing that, Satan offers an elaborate series of gifts, "Rocks whereon greatest men have oftest wreck'd" (2.228), the acceptance of any one of which will identify Jesus as man. When all else fails, the resourceful Satan places him in a position where he has no choice in the matter: he must stand like God, or fall like man. Seen as Satanic strategies to make Christ act, the temptations assume a certain logical structure. The first and last are efforts to make him reveal himself as God, the first by appealing to him to perform a miracle and the last by forcing him to do so. Those between tempt him to act as a man. The initial two temptations ask him to respond to hunger, first as God and then as man; the final two attempt to force a response to fear, first as man and then as God. All between, those to wealth, fame, power, and learning, are efforts to prompt him to respond to worldly ambition.[33] Further, throughout the encounter the arch-deceiver assumes a variety of roles, each appropriate to the offer made. In the appeal to hunger, he poses as harmless "aged man" and prospective friend; in the appeal to ambition, as benefactor, counselor, and ally; in the appeal to fear, as bully and oppressor.

A Christian reader can be edified by Satan's discomfort and still delight in his performance, for Milton has endowed the figure with all the accomplished attributes of a consummate politician, diplomat, and courtier. Satan's purpose throughout is to entice Jesus to *do* something, but to the Devil's dismay all he does is argue, for the Messiah is an able debater himself. Satan is forced to

32. The perspective itself is not new, of course. See, e.g., *Paradise Regained*, ed. E. H. Blakeney, p. 96.

33. The structure of the temptations is, of course, variously interpreted. See Lewalski, *Brief Epic*, pp. 329–32; Burton Jasper Weber, *Wedges and Wings: The Patterning of "Paradise Regained,"* pp. 1–14; and Edward W. Tayler, *Milton's Poetry: Its Development in Time*, p. 256, n. 6.

shift ground constantly, posing alternately as a munificent benefactor or a mafioso enforcer; he must bargain like a bazaar tradesman and negotiate with the smoothness of a seasoned envoy; he is one moment an intimate confidant and the next an ominous bully; he coddles, fumes, threatens, confides, sulks, cajoles, fawns, and promises; and notwithstanding the obduracy of his adversary and the hopelessness of his mission, it is a fascinating performance.

In these various Satanic poses the dramatic interest of *Paradise Regained* is to be found, for certainly little tension is developed in the immovable Son of God. In a long speech just before he sweeps Jesus aloft, Satan seeks to justify the many disguises he has assumed to discover just what sort of "Son of God" this is; he argues that he had every right to approach his adversary and "By parl, or composition, truce, or league / To win him, or win from him what I can" (4.529–30). To that purpose he all but exhausts the possibilities of diplomatic activity, and one wonders how much the rich variety of the figure owes to Milton's own experience in foreign affairs. While few earthly emissaries have had to undertake a mission quite so challenging as that of persuading a god to do something he doesn't want to do, Milton during his time as secretary for foreign languages was associated with a number of diplomatic efforts, "By parl, or composition, truce, or league," in which the English encountered negotiators of comparable intransigence; and the experiences may have suggested to him some of the language and methods employed by Satan. In February 1651, for example, he was directed to assist in negotiations with the Portuguese ambassador to settle an undeclared naval war with that nation. The meetings dragged on until May when, with the differences still unresolved, Milton arranged for the ambassador's return to his homeland.[34]

Probably the most protracted diplomatic effort during Milton's active period of public service was that between the English and Dutch from 1651 to 1654. Intriguing parallels exist between England's role in this affair and Satan's temptations of Jesus. Both England and Satan employ similar strategies, beginning with an offer of friendship and union on the basis of a common cause, and following with a proposal of a political and then a military alliance. Both are rebuffed and resort to a threat, and finally a demonstration, of force, which fail to achieve the desired results.

34. *CSPD*, 3:203. See Fallon, "Filling the Gaps," p. 170.

There are, of course, important differences between the two initiatives, but they are sufficiently analogous to suggest that Milton may have had the historical experience in mind while shaping the strategies of his demonic negotiator.

The United Netherlands was an important commercial power in the seventeenth century, enjoying a prominence that outweighed its relatively small land area. According to the great French finance minister, Colbert, by 1665 Dutch vessels were carrying three-fourths of the trade of Europe; and this imbalance kept the country almost constantly at odds with its neighbors, including three wars with England during Milton's lifetime alone.[35] English temporal ambitions, however, often conflicted with her religious allegiances. Many Puritans, Milton included, entertained a strong respect and affection for the Dutch, who had so frequently offered haven for their persecuted brethren. Indeed, it was a Puritan dream, dating from the time of Elizabeth, that the two nations should be one; and it was in pursuit of this dream that in February 1651 the young Revolutionary government, in an excess of misguided zeal, sent a diplomatic mission to the Netherlands. That embassy, headed by Oliver St. John and William Strickland, placed before the Dutch a plan of political union, citing their long friendship and common struggle against Catholic powers. The offer was haughtily refused and the English were forced to withdraw rather hastily after suffering humiliating indignities, including a shower of mud and rocks from an outraged mob. Parliament retaliated with the Navigation Act, which was a serious blow to Dutch commercial interests; and in January 1652 the Netherlands dispatched ambassadors to negotiate the differences. There was a voluminous exchange of documents, all to no avail, and when the war started that summer the envoys returned home.

The United Netherlands, though wealthy and resolute, was small, with but a fraction of England's manpower and physical resources. The Commonwealth soon built a fleet that rivaled the Dutch, militarily if not commercially, and the war did not go well for the Netherlands. In May 1653 the Dutch dispatched another embassy under the able Hieronymus van Beverning to initiate peace talks; but unfortunately for them the English scored a signal naval victory at Garrard Sands the very next month, and another

35. Charles Wesley Cole, *Colbert and a Century of French Mercantilism*, p. 343.

at Scheveningen in August, effectively undercutting Beverning's bargaining position.

Oliver Cromwell, chief of state in all but name since the dissolution of the Rump in April, took an intense personal interest in the talks. As a result of the English successes, he clearly thought himself negotiating from a position of strength. Cromwell, though ambitious for commercial expansion, shared the feeling of many Englishmen in regretting a war between two Protestant powers who, it was thought, should more properly be united against the Catholic nations of Europe. Thus, in the negotiations he spoke as much of an alliance between the two states as he did of the differences that precipitated the war. The Dutch seemed agreeable enough to some kind of arrangement so long as certain commercial matters could be worked out, but they were completely unprepared for what was in store for them, for the English still cherished their old dream, and the secret deliberations of the Council of State went well beyond the question of a simple alliance. Finally, in a formal conference on 21 July, Cromwell presented the stunned Dutch envoys with the fruit of that debate—a sweeping proposal for a complete political and economic union of the two nations.

The proposal was animated by Cromwell's visionary scheme of a great league of Protestant nations to be built upon the foundation of an English-Dutch union. He had stretched out the negotiations with customary exchanges about grievances, indemnities, and alliances until he felt England strong enough to force that union. In arguing for the plan, he pressed repeatedly the obligation imposed upon the two nations by their common faith, insisting that they had a divinely ordained mission to unite against the anti-Christ in Rome. Though nothing was said of it publicly, Cromwell surely knew that the union would be dominated by England; but in his enthusiasm for the plan he confidently assumed that in the wake of English victories the United Netherlands was in no position to refuse. The Dutch were not fooled. In dispatches to his superiors Beverning appraised the plan realistically: "The Council did in express terms propose not the establishment of a league or union between two sovereign states and neighbors, but the making of two sovereign states one."[36] A fellow envoy ob-

36. Samuel Rawson Gardiner, *History of the Commonwealth and Protectorate*, 3:44. Gardiner is quoting from Beverning's diary.

served shrewdly that the council was probably using as a basis for its design the articles of union England had only recently imposed upon the Scots; and he concluded that the result would be virtually the same—the absorption of the United Netherlands into the Commonwealth of England.[37] Faced with such a prospect, the Dutch resisted, but they did not break off negotiations. Cromwell was eventually forced to abandon his position; and, fueled by English commercial interests, the war dragged on until May 1654, when it was finally settled on different terms altogether.

Milton was active on the periphery of these negotiations, certainly close enough to follow the talk of "parl, or composition, truce, or league" between the two nations. He was ordered to translate a document for the St. John–Strickland mission in 1651[38] and worked on another dealing with Cromwell's proposals of 1653.[39] He was responsible for the preparation of several documents during the prolonged exchange of early 1652 prior to the war;[40] and at about this same time he is reported to have asked Roger Williams to teach him Dutch, motivated perhaps by his involvement in the exchange of papers.[41] His personal reaction to the 1652 negotiations may be seen in his sonnet to Sir Henry Vane, whom he praises for his ability both to "settle peace" and "advise" on war, and specifically for the skill with which he unfolds "The drift of hollow states hard to be spell'd." The pun on Holland reflects his distrust of the motives of the envoys, whose duplicity the Dutch attack on the English fleet in May seemed to confirm. Though in the end the visionary scheme of union was discarded, it was a bold and exciting idea at the time, one which if realized would have had a profound effect upon the poet's faith and nation.

In one sense, the Satan of *Paradise Regained* approaches Jesus as an agent provocateur attempting to induce the Son of God to act so as to compromise himself. In another, he is an emissary to a

37. Abbott, *The Writings and Speeches of Oliver Cromwell*, 3:79.

38. *CSPD*, 3:116; not recovered. See Masson, *Milton*, 4:314.

39. *YP*, 5:665; State Paper 63.

40. *YP*, 5:560–621; State Papers 31, 32, 38. Milton was directed to translate two others which have not been recovered, SP 30 and 44. The *YP* editor rejects as Miltonic two accepted by *CW*; no. 43a, vol. 13, 131–37 (his SP 34); and no. 167F, vol. 18, 125–27 (see note for SP 44). John T. Shawcross in "A Survey of Milton's Prose Works" proposes that the Dutch Manifesto of August is arguably Miltonic (p. 353). *YP*, 5:620–21, rejects it (State Paper 47) on the basis that "objective evidence is slight."

41. French, *Life Records*, 3:127–28.

potentially hostile power, sent to uncover designs and propose alliances that would serve to neutralize the threat; and all his skills as politician, diplomat, and courtier are brought into play in the encounter. The parallels between England's initiative with the Dutch and Satan's mission with Jesus are best illustrated by considering the arch-deceiver in this latter role. He first appears to Jesus as an "aged man in Rural weeds" (1.314) but is quickly discovered. The "Arch Fiend now undisguis'd" immediately lays the groundwork for his mission. Concealing his purpose, he urges friendship, citing all that he has in common with Jesus, be he God *or* man—Satan is unsure as yet which but is covering all the options. He too has visited Heaven and, like the Son, has performed various duties for the Father, "For what he bids I do" (1.377). He protests that the enmity between himself and mankind has been greatly exaggerated; he is not their foe but in truth their benefactor. Nor does he rule them; rather he dwells as "Copartner in these Regions of the World" (1.392) in a "fellowship in pain" (1.401), a partnership which by implication Jesus, as man, is free to join. Surely, he seems to say, we can work together here as equals. Rebuked in his pretensions, he abruptly changes his posture and, abandoning all pretext of equality, becomes the fawning courtier, cloaking his intent in flattery: "thou art plac't above me, thou art Lord" (1.475). He pleads like an anxious petitioner that he not be denied further access to his Lord, "to talk at least" (1.485).

Having taken the measure of his opponent, Satan returns to his council to report in alarming terms that "an Enemy / Is ris'n to invade us, who no less / Threat'ns than our expulsion down to Hell" (2.126–28). He selects "a chosen band / of Spirits" (2.236–37) to assist him and reappears in the guise of genial host and aspiring friend, this time a courtly gentleman, to offer the now-hungry Jesus something to eat. Rejected yet again, he abandons the proposal of fellowship with long-suffering mock dismay at being misunderstood, "I see / What I can do or offer is suspect" (2.398–99).

Satan then takes a different tack. Though they can't be friends, he says, as practical men of affairs they can at least be associates. Christ is, after all, "unknown, unfriended, low of birth" (2.413), while Satan has powerful friends in important positions; and he is perfectly willing to act as counselor and benefactor to assist Jesus in fulfilling the prophecy that he will sit on David's throne. Christ will obviously need help, so Satan grandly offers him first wealth and then fame as necessary prerequisites to achieving his goal. It is essentially military fame that he proposes, citing as precedent the youthful exploits of Alexander, Scipio, and Pompey to prod the seemingly dilatory Messiah to be about his task. Jesus scorns their achievements, "what do these Worthies, / But rob and spoil, burn, slaughter, and enslave / Peaceable Nations" (3.74–76); and he derides the "herd confus'd, / A miscellaneous rabble" (3.49–50) who praise such deeds.

Rebuffed in his offer of the means of gaining David's throne, Satan switches tactics, tendering Jesus the throne itself, and the pattern of the temptations begins to emerge. Satan in the role of artful bargainer and negotiator is dangling before Christ all the things that men strive for—wealth, fame, power, and finally wisdom—in effect bidding on his allegiance, raising the offer step by step. Experience has persuaded him that every man has his price; and if one is patient, it is only a matter of time until it will be named. So he probes and postures, acting alternately put upon and grandly generous, keeping the pressure on with constant reminders of Christ's duty to *do* something, always withholding his best offer until last.

Power is offered in terms of kingdoms; and Satan shifts his pose here rather subtly from that of generous benefactor to worldly diplomat, an envoy from a larger power proposing alliance and bargaining for agreeable terms. The crown of Judea having been refused, he sweeps Jesus to the mountaintop and places before his eyes a dazzling panorama of the empires of the world, concluding with the longest military passage of the poem, the spectacle of the Parthian armies marching out of Ctesiphon to turn back the incursions of the Scythians.

It is a striking figure; one would have to turn back to books 1 or 6 of *Paradise Lost* for a comparable display of military glory. Christ's rejection of a Parthian kingdom and all "that cumbersome / Luggage of war there shewn me, argument / Of human weakness rather then of strength" (3.400–402) is often cited as evidence of Milton's antimilitary sentiments.[42] This reading, however, isolates the passage from the careful sequence that Milton has designed and disregards its function in the poem. Christ suc-

42. Tillyard, *Milton*, p. 306. Barbara Lewalski thinks otherwise: "There is no reason to suppose that Milton ever saw the Civil War as anything other than a patriotic defensive war" (*Brief Epic*, p. 271).

cessively repudiates *everything* offered him; he does not single out military glory for his scorn, but finds the splendor of Rome and the wisdom of Greece equally demonstrative of "human weakness rather then of strength." Scholars troubled by Christ's castigation of ancient learning, anxious that it may reflect a Milton turning his back on a lifetime of humanistic studies, err also in citing those lines out of dramatic context. Nothing that we know of him can support such a turnabout in his attitude toward the military, or toward learning, in his later life. This is the Christ of the New Testament speaking, the Son of God whose kingdom is not of this world; and his words are entirely appropriate to such a figure. Milton himself has cautioned us, "We should consider not so much what the poet says, as who in the poem says it. Various figures appear, some good, some bad, some wise, some foolish, each speaking not the poet's opinion but what is appropriate for each person."[43] If Christ has no need for arms, governments, or learning in his ministry, we are not free to conclude that Milton believed fallen man, whose kingdoms are very much of this world, could fulfill his destiny comparably unencumbered; nor, as Arnold Stein puts it, is Milton "trying to declare the business of the world bankrupt."[44] It is man's sad lot that he must struggle for salvation, and in that struggle he needs all the strength of voice and sword and pen he can muster. Those who find evidence in Christ's *contemptus mundi* of the poet entering a disillusioned and misanthropic old age, denying the value of a lifetime of service and study, have not consulted the chronicle with sufficient care. He was disappointed, certainly, with the course of events in Restoration England; but he apparently remained cheerful, worked hard, and published extensively, even returning to the arena of pamphlet warfare in the final year of life with *Of True Religion*.[45]

43. *YP*, 4:439; paraphrasing Aristotle, *Poetics*, 25.

44. *Heroic Knowledge*, p. 131.

45. Merritt Y. Hughes, in "The Christ of *Paradise Regained* and the Renaissance Heroic Tradition," takes to task critics who find in Christ's *contemptus mundi* "the self-portrait of a defeated old man." He further chides them (Raleigh, Grierson, and Tillyard) for suggesting that Christ's inaction is "a bitter confession from Milton that at last he has understood the futility of his own share in the defence of the Parliamentary cause" (pp. 254–55). Hughes argues on different grounds than those proposed here, of course, but he emphatically rejects the image of a Milton in despair after the Restoration. Despite Hughes's efforts, that view has prevailed. Hugh H. Richmond, for example, in *The Christian Revolutionary: John Milton*, finds *Paradise Lost* "the first and greatest epic of the pessimistic modern

The offer of Parthia is easily the most involved ruse of the cunning negotiator. He accurately identifies Parthia as the only rival to Rome for control of the Western world; but if it was the second most powerful empire of the time, it was a poor second at best; and Satan is at his most deceptive in exaggerating its importance. Milton may have presumed his readers' familiarity with Tacitus, from whom they would know that during Christ's adult life the Parthians were in constant trouble with Rome and that their forces were in fact rather rudely handled by Vitellius in the encounters.[46] Satan, of course, shows Christ nothing of this, instead stage-managing the spectacle of an apparently invincible army marching out of Ctesiphon to subdue the semibarbaric Scythians. And he artfully toys with time. Walter MacKellar notes that though Satan characterizes the Parthian invasion of Syria as having occurred "of late" (3.364), he is actually relating events of 40 B.C.[47] The same may be said of the spectacle spread before Christ, for the Parthians had had little trouble with the Scythians since the second century B.C., and any army moving out of Ctesiphon in Christ's time would have been moving west to confront the Roman Empire rather than east to subdue nomadic tribesmen.[48] Satan orchestrates and argues so as to mask the disturbances between the two empires, and in a final sleight of hand he justifies the choice of Parthia by grandly disregarding the fact that the Jews

---

European consciousness" (p. 128) and "the most comprehensive, vivid, and memorable discussion of the causes, conditions, and consequences of failure that has ever been written" (p. 140).

46. *Annals*, 6:31–37.

47. *A Variorum Commentary on the Poems of John Milton*, ed. Merritt Y. Hughes et al., 4:172.

48. All of the sources available to Milton—Josephus, *Antiquities*, 18 (4, 4), 96–105; Dio Cassius, *Roman History*, 58:26 and 59:27; Tacitus, *Annals*, 6:31–37—emphasize the troubles between Rome and Parthia in 32–37 A.D.; none of them breathe a word of a Scythian campaign. Indeed, Dio has the Parthian Antabanus allied with the Scythians (58:26). Milton could have assumed a fit audience familiar with these and earlier conflicts between the two empires, as well as the general inadequacies of the Parthian military (Dio, 60:15–30). Satan is not gifted with foresight, of course, but the knowledgeable reader, familiar with Trajan's conquest of Parthia in 115 A.D. (Dio, 68:26–30) and the empire's demise in the third century, would have appreciated the significance of Satan's offer of tainted merchandise. If one assumes Christ's birth in 4 A.D., by an intriguing coincidence even as Satan shows the Parthian armies marching out to subdue the Scythians, they were actively engaged with the Romans in Armenia and Syria (34–35 A.D.); but it is perhaps too much to attribute such nice historical ironies to the poet.

are in bondage to Rome and urging Christ to rush off on a wild goose chase to liberate the legendary ten tribes of Israel.

It is a stunning performance, the more so since Satan continues to manage affairs so as to keep his options open. When Christ rejects the "ostentation vain of fleshly arm, / And fragile arms" (3.387–88), Satan can raise the bid yet again. Rome is offered in a spectacle of political power rather than military pomp, but Satan is beginning to show the strain of his constant rebuffs. He is down to his last cards now and he is pressing. The power of Parthia was offered in a parade, a pageant in which the glories of the kingdom spoke largely for themselves. This time, however, Satan wants to leave nothing to chance; he accompanies the display of Rome with a running commentary, describing in glowing detail the beauties of the great city and listing the nations of the world, the "*Parthian* among" them (4.73), who appear to pay homage to the empire. He silkily congratulates Christ for his good judgment in preferring Rome "Before the *Parthian*" (4.85) and broadly hints that this is his final offer: "These having shewn thee, I have shewn thee all / The Kingdoms of the world, and all thir glory" (4.88–89).

Satan's tone changes markedly as Christ once more refuses the offer. Frustrated and angry, having failed in all his various roles as friend, benefactor, counselor, and envoy, he loses control completely and issues an outright bribe. "The Kingdoms of the world to thee I give," he rages, and in his fury blurts out the terms of agreement: "if thou wilt fall down, / And worship me as thy superior Lord, / Easily done, and hold them all of me" (4.163, 166–68). A skilled negotiator will withhold his terms until he has received some indication of interest; but Satan has quite come apart—he is like an obsessed poker player who, with all his cards showing, blindly raises the bid against a winning hand, refusing to believe that he has lost. Completely frustrated in his effort to trick Christ into performing some act that would reveal him as man, Satan irrationally demands it of him, letting slip what had obviously been his intention all along and, incidentally, exposing the lie that he ruled only as "Copartner" with man. Barbara Lewalski feels that this "price tag of idolatry" applies to the offer of kingdoms alone;[49] but I think she would agree that something would have been demanded at any stage of the negotiations, even for din-

49. *Brief Epic*, p. 280.

ner. Satan's language throughout implies that he is offering free gifts, but acceptance would never have been without cost, and the price would always have been the same, acknowledging him as "superior Lord." As Christ seems to know well, a deal with the Devil is no deal at all.

Satan, undaunted by yet another humiliating repulse, regains his composure long enough to tender Christ the gift of the wisdom of the ancients; but his anger bursts out again when, his final offer refused and "all his darts . . . spent," he demands in bewilderment and indignation, "What dost thou in this World?" (4.372). The tempest that follows is an act of frustrated and vindictive rage, but it is also one more effort to force Jesus to reveal himself as man, this time through a show of fear.[50] Failing that, the ever-resourceful Satan places Christ in a position where he will be compelled to act either as man or as God. At the pinnacle of the temple, where Satan observes ironically, "to stand upright / Will ask thee skill" (4.551–52), Christ must either respond with fear and fall from the height, thus revealing himself subject to the laws of gravity like any human, or perform a miracle and stand. Satan finally has his answer; but at the moment of the success of his mission, it is he who falls, as evil once more "recoils" on the evildoer; and Christ is borne up triumphantly to Heaven, where the angelic choirs sing of his victory, which has "frustrated the conquest fraudulent" (4.609).

At the risk of belaboring the obvious, let us review briefly the parallels between the real and imagined negotiations. Satan's oblique offer to rule "Copartner" with Jesus and his subsequent effort to establish himself as a helpful friend resemble the design of the Strickland–St. John mission to the Netherlands in 1651. In one of his state letters concerning that embassy, Milton protests, like Satan, that the English intentions had been misunderstood. The English ambassadors, the letter claims, arrived with "the offer of friendship and a very binding alliance" with the Dutch, but their friendly overtures of "brotherly amity and a very binding league" were rebuffed. When all the talk proves futile, Satan resorts to force, first indirectly with the tempest and then overtly with the physical removal of Jesus to the temple; similarly, the English first imposed the Navigation Act and then declared war. Both efforts achieve only part of the desired effect. Further, Satan's

50. Elizabeth Pope cites a number of references for this reading, but rejects it in *"Paradise Regained": The Tradition and the Poem*, pp. 87–89.

bargaining strategy in the offer of kingdoms bears the mark of Cromwell's devious deliberations with the Dutch ambassadors in 1653. Both assume they are negotiating from a position of strength, Satan who rules "th' affairs of Earth" with "all / The Kingdoms of the world" to offer Jesus, and Cromwell with English victories to press upon Beverning and his embassy. Both keep their true intentions cloaked, Satan with what appear to be gifts and Cromwell with vague discussions of alliances and indemnities. In the end each attempts to impose a settlement that will leave him in a position of dominance, Satan as "superior Lord" and Cromwell as head of a union that would leave the Netherlands little better off than Scotland. Throughout the negotiations each presses his prospective ally with the moral obligation to submit, Jesus to fulfill his divinely destined role "to sit / On *David*'s Throne" (4.146–47) and the Dutch to join in the sacred struggle against the anti-Christ in Rome. The English, Milton claims in that same letter, were ever conscious of the higher cause, "looking not so much to our own interests as to those of all Protestants."[51] In each case, the effort fails.

One may not wish to presume so far as to claim the Anglo-Dutch negotiations as a "source" for the encounter between Satan and Jesus, for the two are certainly dissimilar in many respects; but the provocative parallels must persuade us that the experience influenced in part the substance of Milton's art. He was at times closely associated with international diplomacy during his period of public service, and even in the semiretirement of his later years, when he was on the sideline of affairs, his ear remained attuned to the nuances of diplomatic exchange and the subtle play of power. He knew it all—the stilted facade of protocol, the give and take of guarded debate, the careful wording and artful veiling of purpose, the uncertain ceremony of treaty and alliance, and the sudden sword of war—and that experience served him well as he turned it to his purpose and shaped the figure of the powerful and deceptive enemy of man, rallying his troops, presiding at council, clashing in battle, or dissembling with Christ.

Satan deceives on yet another level, however, especially in *Paradise Lost*; for while outwitting the various figures he encounters, he can also disarm the unwary reader. It is difficult not to admire his resolution in Hell, his parliamentary skill in Pandemonium, or

51. *YP*, 5:665; State Paper 63.

his persuasiveness with Eve, and even to delight in the doublecross of Chaos and the little trick he plays on Uriel. He is fascinating as he manipulates others to advance his designs; and the reader may well find him a pleasure to observe, even as we are drawn to the theater time and again to watch Richard III work his wiles on the hapless House of York. It is perhaps too much to say, with Stanley Fish, that Milton deliberately traps the reader into admiring sin or, with A. J. A. Waldock, that the poet sometimes slips into that sin himself, but there can be no question that Satan often "looks good" to us.[52] Once one has discarded the notion that Milton made Satan an accomplished politician, warrior, and diplomat because he thought ill of all such people, it is possible to consider this phenomenon from another point of view. Milton rejected the grinning caricature of medieval art, the Devil of cloven foot and pointed tail, as well as the grotesque monster of Tasso's *Jerusalem Delivered*, whose "yawning mouth . . . foamed clotted blood" and scattered "kindled coals about / Hot sparks and smells that man and beast would choke."[53] He did so because an acquaintance with these highly imaginative shapes is of little value to a Christian trying to recognize evil in his daily life. The Devil incarnate is more likely to appear as one of the politicians, warriors, or diplomats who direct the affairs of men.

The great dilemma of mankind is how to distinguish between good and evil, not between angel and monster. How does one tell a good from an evil politician when they sound much alike, a good from an evil general when they both win battles, or a good from an evil diplomat when it's hard to believe what any of them say? Satan illustrates man's problem convincingly. He is an accomplished politician, adroit and persuasive in promising his followers independence from an oppressive regime, freedom to seek their own destiny, and equality of opportunity. Of course, this is not true independence, true freedom, or true equality; Milton need not belabor the fact that the Devil is a liar for his fit-but-few audience—his point is just how true the false can sound. Satan is presented in these admirable, even heroic, proportions to illustrate our dilemma and to underscore the message that Milton never tires of repeating: any moral judgment of a man's deeds must

52. Fish, *Surprised by Sin: The Reader in "Paradise Lost,"* passim; Waldock, *"Paradise Lost" and Its Critics*, pp. 78–79.

53. *Jerusalem Delivered*, trans. Edward Fairfax, 6:7–8.

be made, not on the basis of his words or appearances, but on whether he acts in obedience or disobedience to the will of God.

Thus, it is argued here that Milton, in order to give weight to his warning, depicted Satan as the powerful adversary of God, one who holds sway over this "perverted world." His efforts are self-defeating, to be sure, but man can draw small comfort from his sufferings, which are but a mirror in which man can see the fate of those sunk in evil. The Devil is deceptive and thus most dangerous, for in man's voyage on the bewildering road to salvation, he may lose the way at any turn where evil looks good to him.

VII

The War in Heaven

. . . Their respective forces were drawn up in battle array and separated after a fairly even fight.—*De Doctrina Christiana*

Was this your discipline and faith engag'd,
Your military obedience, to dissolve
Allegeance to th' acknowledg'd Power supream?—*PL* 4.954–56

Since the time of Samuel Johnson, critics have found book 6 of *Paradise Lost* something less than satisfactory. He put an incisive finger on the problem when he complained of the incongruities caused by the "confusion of spirit and matter" in the account; and readers since have chided the poet for weighing down the angels with cumbersome armor, intruding on Heaven with artillery, and filling the air with hills, all artistically indecorous, it is said, and evidence of a flagging imagination. Many scholars have detected serious prosodic flaws in the lines, including awkward syntax and meter, unnecessarily inflated language, and an uncertain command of the material.

Among those who rise to defend the poet, a number argue that once the reader knows what the poet is about, these faults will all seem virtues. They propose that book 6, like all the military imagery in *Paradise Lost*, is a parody of human warfare and that once this is understood, the awkwardness, inflated language, and apparent uncertainty will be correctly perceived as deliberate effects entirely appropriate to an essentially satirical passage, malaprops, if you will, on an epic scale.[1] Arnold Stein says of the war in Heaven, for example, that the "dominant mood . . . is like nothing so much as a scherzo, a kind of great scherzo, like some of Beethoven's—with more than human laughter, too elevated and comprehensive, and reverberating not to be terribly funny."[2] The angels on both sides are "absurdist comedy actors" according to another

1. Martz, *Poet of Exile: A Study of Milton's Poetry*, p. 210: "Is the writing simply awkward and inflated and unsure, or is it a deliberate creation of heroic parody?"

2. *Answerable Style*, p. 20. See also J. B. Broadbent, *Some Graver Subject: An Essay on "Paradise Lost,"* pp. 219–20.

study, and the exchange of hills is "a passage of grotesque comedy" in yet another.[3]

This reading of the war in Heaven is so widely accepted that one hesitates to admit not hearing the laughter. In assigning a very different and somewhat more serious role to Milton's military imagery, I may perhaps rest under some obligation to explain this curious deafness, if for no other reason than to forestall the observation that since I fail to see the humor, the joke is on me. As Joseph Summers observes, "Every reader has only his own reading of any poem—what the poem seems or has seemed to him—to go by," so one can certainly not deny that the laughter is there, since so many have heard it.[4] One can, however, question whether Milton meant it to be there—and about this some reservations may properly be expressed.

The intended effect of parody is to ridicule or demean; thus it was observed in the previous chapter that in those parodical readings where Satan is said to resemble Christ or God, he makes a fool of himself, and when he mirrors human action he makes fools of us. The second part of this effect concerns us here, the observation that Milton sprinkled so many uniforms about so as to ridicule human warfare. At the heart of this reading lies the premise that Milton detested war and warriors in all forms and so considered them fit subject for satire. Though many scholars regret that he should have undertaken this criticism at all,[5] it is certainly inconceivable to them that he would devote over twelve hundred lines, ten percent of the entire poem, to the causes and conduct of a war for any reason other than to ridicule or criticize it.[6] My reservations about this reading may be summed up under three heads: (1) It diminishes the artistic achievement. (2) The effect produced is peripheral to the poet's purpose. (3) It presumes an ideological orientation that is not otherwise demonstrable.

In comparing the war in Heaven with its literary predecessors,

3. Wooten, "The Metaphysics of Milton's Epic Burlesque Humor," p. 259; Wilding, *Milton's "Paradise Lost,"* p. 35.

4. *The Muse's Method*, p. 187.

5. Peter, *A Critique of "Paradise Lost,"* p. 79: "It leaves us wondering what all the fuss has been about, and why the battle should have been reported with such fidelity and at such length."

6. Revard, "Milton's Critique of Heroic Warfare," passim. While Revard and I agree that Milton had a more serious intent, we see that intent differently. Many of my reservations about a parodical reading may be applied with equal force to a critical one.

scholars propose that Milton deliberately parodies those who *write* about human warfare; and while the relationship between *Paradise Lost* and its ancient models is not our subject here, a word or two about the genre of the passage might not be out of place.[7] There can be, of course, no mistaking Milton's arch tone when he expresses his disregard for those who dissected "With long and tedious havoc fabl'd Knights / In Battle feign'd" (9.30–31). Since Aristotle, however, burlesque and parody have been considered a decidedly lesser form of literary art, and one wonders at readings that find so much ridicule in a work intended to take "no middle flight."[8] It is probable that Milton could write bad poetry if he chose, as could Shakespeare (Orlando's execrable verses in *As You Like It* spring to mind); but one must question whether he would place a book and a half of deliberately awkward, inflated, and unsure poetry at the very heart of his great work. The artist who openly invites comparison with Homer and Virgil and then does no more than satirize them may be suspected of doubting his own powers. Milton, we can be assured, entertained no such doubts, and hence had no need to diminish their achievements in order to enhance his own.

However one interprets the "purpose" of *Paradise Lost*, whether one accepts the poet's expressed intent to "assert Eternal Providence, / And justifie the wayes of God to men" or derives some comparable formula from its lines—these pages, for example, focus on the poem as warning—it is difficult to comprehend what a parody of human warfare adds to his "higher Argument." Wars, armies, and generals are marks of our fallen state, as are politics, governments, and senators. To parody them is to mock our fallen state and Milton surely had higher purposes in mind. It has been seen how pervasive military imagery is in *Paradise Lost*—Hell in arms, war in Heaven, sentinels at Eden, Raphael on reconnaissance, Michael in uniform, and so on—indeed there is so much that if its only purpose is to ridicule human warfare, one might suspect that the subject had become something of an obsession with the poet; for such mockery adds little to our understanding of God's ways to men. Warfare is not a cause but a consequence of sin, like governments and gout; and though foolish, it is but one,

7. Webber, in *Milton and His Epic Tradition*, p. 211, is only one of the most recent scholars to find Milton "burlesquing epic conventions."

8. *Poetics*, IV.

and perhaps not the worst, of our follies. If all that imagery is meant only to mock the military, then it must be considered an unfortunate digression from the poet's larger purpose.

These are, admittedly, somewhat subjective misgivings, but questions of more substance may be raised by examining the implied assumptions about Milton's attitude toward the military. Certain unstated premises are preconditions of any parodical intent: (1) The object of the parody must be considered worthy of satirical treatment. (2) The object must be associated with a device that will demean or ridicule it. (3) The writer must be convinced that his readers will be sufficiently familiar with both object and device to agree with him on these implicit characterizations. For example, the chivalric tradition is considered by many a subject worthy of satire. To parody the tradition, one depicts the knight-errant as a doddering antiquarian, his squire as a dimwitted laborer, his lady as a tavern wench, and his heroic adversaries as harmless shepherds or merchants, to say nothing of windmills. Finally the writer must be assured that his readers are as well versed as he in the difference between, let us say, a lady and a tavern wench. Thus, the proposal that Milton intended book 6 as a parody of warfare assumes that he considered Satan and his followers appropriate subjects for satire, that he thought presenting them as military figures would serve to demean them, and that he felt confident his fit-but-few readers would agree on both counts. Earlier chapters, it is hoped, have been persuasive in raising serious doubts whether John Milton of London or his seventeenth-century audience thought the Devil a figure of fun, and also whether men who had looked to the New Model Army as a spiritual model would think that handing a man a sword and shield would automatically make him look like a fool.

In brief, to assume that Milton is parodying warfare is to accept premises about his sentiments that are not otherwise demonstrable—indeed, the study of his prose and early poetry leaves one with the strong impression that he had nothing but respect for the figure of the soldier and that he thought warfare a perfectly legitimate and often laudable human activity, though he had very definite ideas about which were the righteous warriors and which the just wars. Thus, evidence that he disliked soldiers or that he hated war is to be found *only* in the lines of *Paradise Lost*, and perhaps only by those who themselves consider soldiers ludicrous and war sheer folly. Again, one cannot argue with those who hear laughter in Heaven. It may be regretted that the "scorn, scoffing, laughter, deriding, contempt, disdain, vanity, and folly" heard by Arnold Stein everywhere in the lines of book 6 may deafen the reader to other, more essential meanings to be found there; but if one hears laughter, then laughter there is.[9] Those who do not hear it need not be dismissed as lacking in appreciation of wit, however—it is entirely possible for them to get the joke and just not think it funny.

The charge of inflated language is somewhat more difficult to address than the logic of parody, for the issue is one of style. It is perhaps fair, however, to ask the terms of reference for this evaluation. War is a violent and terrifying experience, and all descriptions of battle tend to employ highly charged language. Few passages in literature or history can match the intensity of such a time—Harry of Monmouth before Harfleur, perhaps, "Stiffen the sinews, summon up the blood, / Disguise fair nature with hard-favor'd rage" (Henry V.3.1.7–8) and Tolstoy's account of Austerlitz—but no one who has been through that searing experience will be heard to complain that a verbal narrative of battle exaggerates its effects. There are, to be sure, many readers for whom an account of battle holds little appeal, for whom a narrative of the gory splendors of a Waterloo or a Gettysburg would be, if not distasteful, at least tedious. Book 6 may indeed sound inflated when compared to less spectacular passages in the poem, since descriptions of battlefields and gardens make different demands on the language; but when placed beside similar narratives from Homer or Tolstoy, it certainly holds its own. Indeed, to some ears it has the solid ring of authenticity. Marjorie Nicolson writes of the World War I veteran in her class who responded to one of her lectures in which she discussed the commentary on the deficiencies of the passage:

> My student said that he had read widely in the contemporary war-literature that was pouring from the press, trying to find some expression in prose or poetry for what he had felt, but found nothing until he came to book 6 of *Paradise Lost*. There he found scenes which recalled those he had experienced and others he had imagined at night in his dugout, warfare on a vast scale, with two great armies drawn up on opposing fields, each wondering but never sure what Satanic new engine of destruction might be used against them the next day.[10]

9. *Answerable Style*, p. 22.
10. *A Reader's Guide*, p. 260.

My own reading, as one who has also been under fire, seconds this appreciation; for there are in Milton's account passages that evoke powerfully the confusion, the deafening clamor, the pain, and the fearful grandeur of that experience. It is a remarkable performance for one who never saw battle.

Though one can praise Milton's account of battle, it is also fair to say that the war in Heaven does have certain deficiencies. Its defects, which are largely dramatic in nature, may be traced in part to Milton's limited experience of war. He had seen armies in retreat, on parade, and marching to battle; he had heard soldiers address Parliament, had watched them stand guard and sit in council, and had applauded their assumption of political power—but he had never seen a battle (we can say this, I think, with some assurance, on the basis that if he had, he would certainly have told us about it). Hence the war in Heaven is probably the most extended passage in *Paradise Lost* that owes nothing to his personal experience. He had felt pain, love, anger, defeat, the temptations of the flesh, and a sense of injured merit; he had heard debate, sat in gardens, contemplated the stars, sought fame, rebelled against authority, lost his sight, and languished in prison. Even his description of Hell may owe something to a visit to the Phlegraean Fields outside Naples, as Marjorie Nicolson suggests;[11] and Heaven holds many of the delights of the English countryside, where "with fresh Flourets Hill and Valley" smile (6.784); for, as Raphael says, "Earth hath this variety from Heav'n / Of pleasure situate in Hill and Dale" (6.640–41). But for the experience of battle Milton was entirely dependent upon the accounts of friends or descriptions in history or literature. Thus book 6 probably owes more to the poet's classical models than any other extended passage in the poem, and as a derivative of Homer and Virgil, it may lack that intimate pulse of life to be felt in the thunder of Satan's defiance, "Better to reign in Hell," the sweetness of Eve's love, "With thee conversing I forget all time," or the depths of Adam's despair, "O Conscience, into what Abyss of fears / And horrors hast thou driv'n me."

The dramatic deficiencies of the account arise chiefly from the intractable nature of the myth—a war between two forces, one of which is omnipotent. Creating a measure of suspense with such

11. "Milton's Hell and the Phlegraean Fields," pp. 500–513. See also *A Reader's Guide*, pp. 194–95.

material is difficult enough, but Milton's laying on the Almighty with such a heavy hand certainly doesn't help matters. First, the "Eternal Eye" sees all and God smiles at the thought of defending himself against the rebels, then Abdiel scoffs self-righteously at Satan, "fool, not to think how vain / Against th' Omnipotent to rise in Arms" (6.135–36). God limits the might of the angels, puts an edge on Michael's sword, and allows the exchange of hills to go just so far:

> and now all Heav'n
> Had gon to wrack, with ruin overspred,
> Had not th' Almightie Father where he sits
> Shrin'd in his Sanctuarie of Heav'n secure,
> Consulting on the sum of things, foreseen
> This tumult, and permitted all. (6.669–74)

He finally sends his "Second Omnipotence" (6.684) into the war. The Son tidies up the battlefield and then with only "half his strength" (6.853) expels the rebels. Milton's message that man, acting of his own free will, brings woe upon himself is all but lost in a war where God is so much the puppetmaster manipulating all to his purpose. How much less powerful the first two books would be if the reader were so continually reminded that all is going according to plan. We are told at the outset that Satan acts through the "high permission of all-ruling Heaven" (1.213) and reminded briefly once again (1.366), but God keeps his distance and events can take a recognizable course. When Sin opens the gates of Hell, it seems an act of defiance against a God who had expressly forbidden it (2.776). We are reminded of God's hand only obliquely when we learn that "She op'nd, but to shut / Excel'd her power" (2.883–84). At least there is no parenthetical "permission granted" as when the loyal angels begin heaving hills: "(behold the excellence, the power / Which God hath in his mighty Angels plac'd)" (6.637–39). How much more satisfactory book 6 would have been, for example, if Milton had followed the structure of *Paradise Regained*, where God appears only briefly in book 1 and then is heard no more, leaving the struggle entirely to Christ as a model for human action. And it is not too much to say that the message of book 9 would have been seriously compromised had God been so much in evidence, peering with his "Eternal Eye" and permitting all.

At times Milton's ambition to soar "above the Olympian Hill" seems at cross purposes with his intention to account for "Mans First Disobedience." Perhaps his own lack of experience in battle led him to lean too heavily on his classical models and in creating the battlefield of Heaven he was too conscious of the one at Troy, where the gods were constantly meddling in the action of the combatants. In his desire to surpass Homer he may have fallen into the artistic trap of following him too closely.[12]

Admittedly then, the Almighty meddles more than we could wish; but to complain that the war lacks interest because the outcome is predetermined is to complain too much. The *Iliad* is not less compelling because we know that Achilleus will finally subdue Hektor or that Zeus, brooding over the battlefield, will manipulate things to that end; indeed the ironies of the account draw substance from that foreknowledge. Even C. S. Lewis, who finds the ironies of book 6 comic, denies that the humor arises from the reader's knowledge of the outcome. As he says, "The criticism that the war in Heaven is uninteresting because we know beforehand how it will end, seems to miss the point."[13] One does not read battle accounts, be they in *Revelation* or Herodotus, to learn who wins. On the other hand, any tale of combat, if it is to maintain interest, must create a certain degree of tension or suspense. It can operate at any of three diminishing levels of uncertainty and still be satisfactory to its readers: First, ideally, it is most interesting if the reader has no idea of the outcome. Second, since this is rarely the case, the combatants must at least be free agents and have a chance to influence the outcome, even though the reader knows they will fail. Third, if the combatants have no power to affect the outcome and the reader knows of their fate, they must at least remain unaware of their helplessness—they must *think* they have a chance. For example, a reader engrossed in an account of the battle of Gettysburg is certainly aware that Lee lost this critical engagement but also that the Confederate army came perilously close to victory. He is reading on our second level of uncertainty, and the account is entirely satisfactory. If, however, the narrative is written on the third level and the reader knows that no matter what the soldiers do, no matter how clever or courageous they are, no matter how skillful their commanders, some deus ex

12. David Daiches, *Milton*, p. 198: "The nearer Milton approaches the defiances and conflicts of the classic epic the less convincing *Paradise Lost* is."

13. *Preface*, p. 127.

machina is going to appear finally out of the clouds to decide the battle, his interest may indeed lag. Any step below this level, to the point where the soldiers themselves realize that it is all hopeless, will certainly lose the reader. If one of Pickett's men is observed searching the sky for some sign of golden scales, the book will find itself back on the shelf.[14]

Milton's problem was that the very nature of Heaven makes it difficult to maintain the action at even this third level of uncertainty. For one thing, the angels are all but omnipotent. They cannot die, and it is difficult to imagine them as wounded. Further, from the very beginning the cards are stacked against the rebels. Homer was able to maintain tension in the *Iliad* because, even though there are supernatural powers influencing the outcome of battle, the gods themselves are rather evenly divided and somewhat unpredictable. In Heaven only one side has the services of this super-supernatural agent, and the only suspense arises from uncertainty as to *when* he is going to act. These and other characteristics of the heavenly host make them thin material for a convincing war.

Milton's unfortunate emphasis on omnipotence has persuaded many that the power of the Almighty is the essential meaning of book 6 and that the poet sought only to assure his readers that the forces of good are indeed more powerful than the forces of evil. Assuming such a purpose, one may well find the pretensions of the rebels absurd, their hopeless rebellion somewhat comic, and the accounts of their debates and conspiracies as amusing as a tale of the congress of mice that resolves to bell the cat. The victory of the Messiah is surely a comforting demonstration of the superior power of the forces of good and a confirmation that evil will be overcome in the end. But this seems a pale purpose; these are matters concerning which Milton and his seventeenth-century readers could be expected to agree, and he can have felt little need to press such articles of faith. He surely had a deeper design than simply to remind his readers that all will be well in the final day. Omnipotence, in brief, is not the point of the war in Heaven.

Two of Milton's purposes, of course, were to embellish his biblical sources and to compose an epic poem in the classic tradition;

14. Stephen Vincent Benét, *John Brown's Body*, p. 300. On the second day at Gettysburg, "Greek-mouthed Warren," watching the action at Little Round Top, sees "a dip in the scales"; but it is purely a rhetorical figure. Benét eschews the supernatural.

these he fulfilled with an account of the war in *Revelation*, which he adorned with scenes of general and individual combat in the manner of Homer and Virgil. The account met his readers' expectations for passages of martial narrative; but the details of the war have raised questions about just how well he did it. Why was Heaven made to endure a three-day battle?[15] Why were Michael and the Son limited to half-strength, a device which in Michael's case almost assured that he would be powerless to accomplish the task God had put to him? Why did Milton encumber his angels with armor and introduce a cosmic anachronism in the cannon? Centuries of scholars have posed such questions in finding the account cumbersome, unrealistic, and inartistic.

Milton's purposes were more than literary, of course; he not only imitates, but also transforms his sources to his own ends, and any judgment on the success or failure of his images should be based on an understanding of those ends. To consider first the question of Michael's strength: on the surface the limitations placed upon him seem acts of an arbitrary, overly manipulative Deity; but those restraints must be examined as part of a larger design by which the poet develops the true meaning of that "First Disobedience." The war in Heaven is a vivid lesson in the causes and effects of disobedience; it is as well a forceful illustration of its opposite, perfect obedience to the will of God. The account of the war is precipitated by a rather offhand remark by Raphael. He is discussing in general terms the happy future of the race—part of his mission is to "advise [Adam] of his happie state" (5.234)—and he comments, somewhat casually, that all these rich rewards will be man's, "If ye be found obedient" (5.501). Puzzled, Adam asks innocently,

> But say,
> What meant that caution joind, *if ye be found*
> *Obedient*? can we want obedience then
> To him . . . ? (5.512–15)

Raphael replies with a discussion of free will and ends his remarks, "And som are fall'n, to disobedience fall'n, / And so from Heav'n to deepest Hell" (5.541–42). How does one describe disobedience to a creature who doesn't even know the meaning of the

15. The scholarly discussion of the three days offered by William B. Hunter, Jr., would seem to obviate the need for further consideration here. See his "The War in Heaven: The Exaltation of the Son," in *Bright Essence*, pp. 123–30.

word? One must describe the law that is disobeyed, the presence of free will that makes disobedience possible, the motives and manner of disobedience, and, most important of all, the consequences. One must describe, in brief, sin. The war in Heaven is Adam's education in the nature of sin, concerning which he has only a vague understanding. Of course, the angel could have said simply, "Now this was our experience with evil up there. One day God decreed that we would all adore His Son, but Satan and about a third of the angels refused. For their disobedience God banished them all to Hell. You make sure the same sort of thing won't happen down here." Such an explanation, however, would not have satisfied the needs of the inquisitive Adam, who is trying to understand the nature of this danger. Raphael, in order to make the idea of evil at all comprehensible, puts it in terms of the narrative of a war. (This discussion must beg the question of Adam's ability to comprehend warfare in the first place. One is tempted, in a moment of whimsy, to imagine him scratching his head and murmuring, "What in the world is a gonfalon?").

The lesson is long, and it is dramatic; for the concept of disobedience to the will of God is not easy for unfallen, or for that matter fallen, man to grasp. Indeed, for all its impact Raphael's lesson fails, and as a consequence Adam's progeny have since been burdened with the laborious pursuit of learning in an effort "to repair the ruins of our first parents by regaining to know God aright." After the Fall, Adam begins the schooling of the race, not, however, under the tutelage of the genial "sociable Spirit" (5.221); this time he attends the stern Michael. After hearing the exhaustive account of man's sorry history and the shining promise of Christ's return, Adam remarks, rather pathetically, "Henceforth I learne, that to obey is best" (12.561), in tragic contrast to the innocent time when he could not even comprehend disobedience. He has, it seems, forgotten everything Raphael told him and must start all over again. It will be a slow, weary process, this "regaining to know God aright," and one will not always have an angel as tutor.

In Raphael's narrative, Adam also receives a lesson in obedience. God sends Michael into battle with stirring words, commanding him to assault the rebels "with Fire and hostile Arms,"

> and to the brow of Heav'n
> Pursuing drive them out from God and bliss,
> Into thir place of punishment. (6.50–53)

The archangel is denied sufficient power to achieve the victory, however. God both limits the might of the angels and restricts the size of his army to a force "Equal in number to that Godless crew" (6.49), effectively assuring that Michael will fail. God has reasons for this curious behavior, and they are soon made clear; he orchestrates the war so as to glorify the Son, and the stalemate on the second day sets the stage for that event. He does not explain all this to Michael, however, an omission which has led at least one critic to accuse him of "devious and dubious" conduct toward the commander of His armies.[16] Given God's larger purpose, however, the restraints make good sense indeed. In military terms Michael is put in charge of what can be seen as a "secondary attack," an essential element of any sound offensive plan. A commander in battle may assign a number of such missions to conceal the location and strength of his main effort, and each must be pushed energetically if that effort is to succeed. He does not, therefore, always inform his subordinates that they are engaged in a secondary attack, which may have little chance of success, lest they fail to conduct the operation with the necessary vigor. Such tactics were employed frequently enough in the Civil War to have come to Milton's attention, even if he were not familiar with the principle from his reading. In the Second Battle of Newbury, for example, Manchester's proposed frontal attack on the Royalist position was designed to fix the enemy so that Waller's more powerful main thrust from the rear could surprise and overwhelm him; and since it was precisely Manchester's tardiness and lack of energy in pursuing his secondary attack that doomed the plan, the tactics became the focus of Cromwell's complaint against his commander in the widely publicized debate that followed.

It is possible, therefore, to explain the Almighty's conduct toward Michael quite satisfactorily in terms of human warfare, and Milton may be seen as achieving a degree of verisimilitude in the account. The entire discussion of God's "deviousness," however, misses the point of the passage, which is the quality of Michael's response to his orders. It is, in fact, entirely immaterial whether he knows if he can succeed; his devotion to the Almighty is such that he would have acted with no less energy *even if he had known*. The archangel illustrates for Milton's readers what is meant by absolute obedience to the will of God. At the heart of this vast definition of the consequences of disobedience, the poet has placed a

16. Peter, *Critique*, p. 81.

vivid lesson in the nature of its opposite, which is no less complex and difficult to comprehend. There are examples enough of disobedience in the poem—Satan and his followers, Eve, Adam, the entire race in Michael's narrative—but the alternative must be defined as well. Milton clarifies its meaning through the words and actions of the loyal angels, not in the war alone, but throughout the poem, and he does so largely in martial terms. Gabriel gives the image explicit expression when, confronting Satan outside Eden, he chides the prince of Hell for his rebellion and demands of him, "Was this your discipline and faith ingag'd, / Your *military obedience* . . . ?" (4.954–55; italics mine).

As an analogy, "military obedience" is most apt, indeed may be the closest parallel in human terms to the paradoxical condition of those who, endowed with reason and will, surrender both in acts of absolute obedience to the word of God. In battle, success hinges on the ability of a commander to concentrate his forces swiftly to exploit an enemy's weakness or answer his attack; and that ability depends on the immediate and unquestioned obedience of his subordinates. In the heat of battle there is little time for explanations, none for debate. Soldiers are often called upon to obey when they have no concept of what is in the mind of the commander. To a subordinate, the assigned mission may appear foolhardy, unnecessary, frivolous, or doomed to failure; but victory may turn on its success, and he must carry it through without hesitation. Milton admired this quality in Cromwell's troopers, whom he praised as "an army obedient to his command in all things," and his imagination turned to them as a "corporal form" of spiritual obedience to the divine will.[17]

The analogy of "military obedience" is developed elsewhere in the poem. Raphael's much-maligned reconnaissance to the gates of Hell comes to mind as another example (8.229–46).[18] He leads the expedition simply because "such command we had," knowing full well that the devils dare not "without [God's] leave attempt" to erupt from Hell. The angel understands God's purposes only imperfectly but accepts the mission without question for, as he says, the Almighty often sends them "upon his high behests / For

17. *YP*, 4:668–69.

18. Waldock, *"Paradise Lost" and Its Critics*, pp. 105–6, finds the passage an example of "sheer clumsiness" on Milton's part; Wilding, *Milton's "Paradise Lost,"* p. 67, thinks it "makes God seem like some madman playing with toy soldiers."

state, as Sovran King, and to enure / Our prompt obedience." Gabriel's mission is yet another instance. He is ordered to establish a "strict watch that to this happie Place / No evil thing approach or enter in" (4.562–63), a charge which proves beyond his powers. He is certainly aware of the difficulties, for he observes to Uriel, "hard thou knowst it to exclude / Spiritual substance with corporeal barr" (4.584–85). This mild complaint is about as far as any of the loyal angels go in questioning the will of God. Indeed, it could be argued that Gabriel's devotion may be of a yet higher order, for it would appear that he performs his duties *knowing full well that he will fail.* While Satan is yet winging his way "Not farr off Heav'n" (3.87–88), God delivers his judgment on a yet unfallen Adam, "Dye hee or Justice must" (3.210); and though Gabriel is at his post outside Eden at the time, celestial communications being what they are, it may be presumed that he knows Satan would succeed. God implies as much later when he greets the "Powers return'd / From unsuccessful charge" and reminds them, "I told ye then he should prevail" (10.34–40). While Gabriel's state of knowledge may be open to question, there can be no doubting Raphael's. He was among the heavenly host that heard God's judgment on man and hence knows that his mission to warn Adam "to beware / He swerve not" (5.237–38) will be to no avail, that it is in fact but the Almighty's means to fulfill "All Justice" (5.247).

Thus, in their demonstration of military obedience, the loyal angels give meaning to the concept of absolute submission to the divine will. Michael enters battle under restraints that prevent victory; Raphael leads what seems a pointless expedition "toward the Gates of Hell"; Gabriel stands watch with a force he knows unequal to the task; and Raphael undertakes a mission he has been told will fail. Each enters on his duties without question or doubt and returns to sing God's praises regardless of success or failure. Milton tells his readers that those who obey God do not always triumph, that their missions will often seem frivolous, and that at times their cause will appear, indeed may be, hopeless; and Michael completes the lesson when he tells Adam of the consequences of perfect obedience for fallen man—frustration, isolation, persecution, and sacrifice in this life, but joy and union with the Father in the next.

Once persuaded that omnipotence is not the point of the war in Heaven, the reader may find it possible to overlook the annoying intrusions of the Almighty and examine the battle as one would any other. Raphael throughout is "lik'ning spiritual to corporal forms" (5.573), of course; but for the narrative to carry its intended weight those "corporal forms" must bear as close a resemblance to human actions as possible. If the sequence of events and the structure of Milton's war are considered in the light of those political and military forces that shape the conflicts of man, the battle emerges as very convincing. Human wars are analyzed in terms of causes, aims, strategy, tactics, armament, and relative combat power; and Milton's celestial battle bears up rather well when examined in such terms.

The causes of war are studied under two headings, immediate and long-term, the latter being the underlying conditions—economic, ideological, or political—which set two nations, groups of nations, or groups within a nation at odds to provide the potential for armed conflict. In early seventeenth-century England, for example, these conditions included the long struggle between king and Parliament for political power, the growing antagonism between religious groups, and, as Christopher Hill has demonstrated, the widening gap in the prosperity of economic and social classes.[19] The long-term cause of the war in Heaven is God's decision to grant his angels free will. If they have the right to decide, they have the potential to disobey. The fact that God created the conditions that make war possible does not make him culpable for the conflict, however, any more than responsibility for the English Civil War can be placed at the feet of Martin Luther. Milton is quite definite about this; with God's very first words in *Paradise Lost* he justifies that decision, "Not free, what proof could they have givn sincere / Of true allegiance, constant Faith or Love" (3.103–4), and denies responsibility for the consequences, "they themselves decreed / Thir own revolt, not I" (3.116–17).

An immediate cause of a war is an event that sparks that potential into flame, a Sarajevo or Pearl Harbor that suddenly incites opposing forces to line up in a posture of hostile confrontation. The spark that set off the English Civil War is variously identified, depending on the focus of the inquiry; but certainly the most provocative act was the King's armed intrusion into Commons in

19. A persistent theme of Hill's. See, e.g., *Change and Continuity in Seventeenth-Century England*, p. 281: "The Revolution was caused, ultimately, by economic developments which could not be absorbed within the old régime."

January 1642, after which Parliament insisted on assuming control of the militia. The two parties lined up in adamant opposition over this question. Charles had given in on almost every issue up to that point, but he accurately recognized that without his traditional authority over the military, he could no longer be king. The immediate cause of the war in Heaven is clearly God's announcement that "This day I have begot whom I declare / My onely Son" (5.603–4); and his tone on that occasion can only be described as provocative:

> him who disobeyes
> Mee disobeyes, breaks union, and that day
> Cast out from God and blessed vision, falls
> Into utter darkness, deep ingulft, his place
> Ordaind without redemption, without end. (5.611–15)

Free will implies the capacity to disobey, but it is only a latent potential until explicitly expressed as a feasible alternative. It is indeed curious that the first mention of disobedience in cosmic history, as defined by *Paradise Lost*, should be heard from the mouth of God himself. The war may not be God's fault, but certainly he creates the conditions that make it possible and provides the occasion that sparks it.

When one turns from the question of causes to a consideration of the "war aims" of the opposing sides, however, the picture grows murky. Prior to the battle, the moral and political positions of the two sides are spelled out in the verbal exchange between Abdiel and Satan, though the actual motives of the two principals are only vaguely alluded to, on Abdiel's part because he does not as yet know God's purpose, on Satan's because he is reluctant to reveal his full intent. The exchange, however, is of particular interest in its echos of the great debate of Milton's own time. Indeed, if the war in Heaven resembles anything in the poet's experience, it is the civil wars, not so much in the narrative of the fighting itself, which probably owes more to Homer than to history, but in the cross fire of debate over grievances, provocations, and political theory that precedes the action. Abdiel and Satan justify their positions in terms remarkably similar to those expressed by apologists for king and Parliament in the English Revolution; but, paradoxically, Abdiel's passionate expression of loyalty to God sounds like nothing so much as a *Defensio Regia*, and Satan's rebuttals like Milton's defense of the English Republic. For example, Abdiel challenges Satan:

> Canst thou with impious obloquie comdemne
> The just Decree of God, pronounc't and sworn,
> That to his only Son by right endu'd
> With Regal Scepter, every Soule in Heav'n
> Shall bend the knee, and in that honour due
> Confess him rightful King? (5.813–18)

Thus Salmasius: "This, moreover, is what makes good subjects: when they obey the will of God by showing due honour to the king whom God has set up."[20] Again, Abdiel:

> unjust thou saist
> Flatly unjust, to binde with Laws the free,
> And equal over equals to let Reigne,
> One over all with unsucceeded power.
> Shalt thou give Law to God, shalt thou dispute
> With him the points of libertie . . . ? (5.818–23)

And again, Salmasius: "After [the people] yielded all these privileges to the power of one, he judges and he proposes laws as he wishes for the assembly—that is the whole people—and they are binding upon all."[21] These arguments for absolute obedience and unquestioned loyalty to the Deity encompass all the elements of a defense of monarchy.

Satan's justifications for his rebellion, on the other hand, almost echo Milton's vindication of the English Republic. This is Satan, for example, addressing his followers from his throne in "The Quarters of the North": Can God "introduce / Law and Edict on us, who without law / Erre not?" (5.797–99); and Milton in *Pro Populo Anglicano*: "to give civil laws to men not subject to laws is foolish and laughable."[22] Satan argues that the angels are "Equally free" and "ordain'd to govern, not to serve" (5.792,802). Milton in *The Tenure of Kings and Magistrates* observes that no man "can be so stupid to deny that all men naturally were borne free," and further, "born to command and not to obey."[23] When Satan casts scorn on the loyal angels, who, he says, "through sloth had rather serve, / Ministring Spirits, traind up in Feast and Song" (6.166–67), he echoes Milton's frequent charge that England un-

20. *YP*, 4:1004. 21. *YP*, 4:1022. 22. *YP*, 4:365.
23. *YP*, 3:198–99.

der the kings was "Nearly ruined by luxury rather, to make it less conscious of its servitude."[24] Examples could be multiplied, but they would only further confirm the perplexing impression that the Devil in attacking the monarch of Heaven sounds like Milton lashing out at the King of England and that the loyal Abdiel expresses views with which Clarendon, Salmasius, and More would find themselves thoroughly comfortable.

One cannot conclude from these resemblances that Milton was a closet monarchist all this time and that his true sentiments surfaced only when he was possessed by the muse.[25] Milton is quite deliberate in these characterizations, for it is essential to his purpose that the forces of evil be seen as having a case. To present Satan's cause as anything other than reasonable—to caricature him, that is, as an adamant Leveller, an irresponsible anarchist, or a wild-eyed revolutionary zealot—would only undercut Milton's message that man's reason may be "by some faire appeering good surpris'd / . . . dictate false, and misinforme the Will" (9.354–55). It is the politician's art to explain alternatives in such a way that his own position appears in the best possible light. Thus, Satan presents himself as the champion of freedom as opposed to slavery, of equality as opposed to servitude; he is the foe of oppression who offers his followers the hope of victory, prosperity, and independence. Milton puts his most forceful arguments in defense of freedom into the mouth of the Devil to underline in the most dramatic way how difficult it is for man to distinguish the false from the true. These are, after all, the same arguments trumpeted by terrorists and tyrants, as well as sincere servants of the people; and Milton means us to know that those who make the best speeches do not always do so for the best motives. The debates must be compelling; they must make sense so as to illustrate how easily the words of men may lead us astray from the word of God.

Satan's expression of intent is intriguingly analogous to the position assumed by the Parliamentary leaders in the Civil War. Until the final months they were careful not to attack the King directly, expending their wrath rather on his counselors and ministers, those who, they complained bitterly, had misused the powers delegated to them and unjustly oppressed the people. Satan's first speech in "The Quarters of the North" is directed against the Son,

24. *YP*, 4:430.

25. The question is raised by Robert Hodge in *John Milton, "Paradise Lost," Books V–VI*, p. 45, but only rhetorically.

not the Father. Only after Abdiel's challenge does Satan, in ironically ambiguous terms, reveal his intention "to begirt th' Almighty Throne / Beseeching or besieging" (5.868–69). Indeed, we never hear from Satan an explicit challenge of God himself or, until after his defeat, any hint of ambition to overthrow him. He seeks only to limit the tyranny of Heaven, he claims, and restore the traditional prerogatives of its citizens. The rebel position is that they "can allow / Omnipotence to none" (6.158–59); and Satan affirms to Michael, again ambiguously, his determination "here however to dwell free, / If not to reign" (6.292–93).

So much for Satan's "Why We Fight," insofar, that is, as his private intents are translated into expressions of public policy. The actual war aims of the principals are revealed as the action unfolds. Satan's objectives are relatively straightforward—he "thought one step higher / Would set" him highest (4.50–51)—but to understand the mind of Milton's God will require some study. His war aims cannot be defined in familiar terms, for it is certainly inadequate to say that he is defending his throne, since it is never endangered. The Almighty's purposes must be considered on another level entirely: it is not a matter of why he goes to war but why he allows it to be fought in the first place. There is no question that he permits the battle or, in abstract terms at least, why he does so. God foresaw the conflict, as Raphael explains,

> and permitted all, advis'd:
> That his great purpose he might so fulfill,
> To honour his Anointed Son aveng'd
> Upon his enemies, and to declare
> All power to him transferr'd. (6.674–79)

Before sending Christ into battle, God tells him,

> Two dayes are therefore past, the third is thine;
> For thee I have ordain'd it, and thus farr
> Have sufferd, that the Glorie may be thine
> Of ending this great Warr.

He has, he says,

> this perverse Commotion governd thus,
> To manifest thee worthiest to be Heir
> Of all things, to be Heir and to be King
> By Sacred Unction, thy deserved right. (6.699–709)

The war, as Allan Gilbert observes, "has for its idea the place and function of the Divine Son."[26] Even before the battle, the Messiah foresees that the plottings of the rebel angels will be "Matter to mee of Glory" (5.783); and indeed, it may be said that any discussion of God's purpose in permitting the war can ultimately be condensed into that single word, *glory*. The concept of the glory of God pervades *Paradise Lost*, as it does Christian liturgy. Milton's God predicts the consequences of the fall of both Satan and Adam: "in Mercy and Justice both, / Through Heav'n and Earth, so shall my glorie excel" (3.132–33). The Son asks him about the fate of the fallen Adam: "wilt thou thy self / Abolish thy Creation, and unmake, / For him, what for thy glorie thou hast made?" (3.162–64). In the end Adam recognizes that his *felix culpa* will bring "To God more glory" (12.477). The war must be considered as only one of the events of the poem—the promotion of Christ, the creation, fall, and redemption of man, and the final destruction of the world—that are designed to add somehow to the glory and honor of God. Merritt Hughes comments on this doctrine:

> It is necessary to see the historical process from the world's creation to its end as begun for the glory of God and ending in the glory of both man and God, as the creeds of the Calvinist churches affirm. . . . The enhancement of God's glory by man's sin had been declared by several theologians and poets before Milton, and once Christ's atonement for that sin has been accepted, the enhancement of God's glory and the justification of his ways to man ineluctably follow.[27]

But what is this glory which seems to be God's war aim? Any attempt to rationalize the concept runs afoul of the logical contradiction at the heart of any doctrine proposing that the act of worship, or any act of man for that matter, can add a cubit to the already infinite stature of God. To say that we bring glory to God is an admission of our inability to comprehend the very thought the phrase hopes to define; it is the "O Altitudo" of man's desire to understand God's ways. Despite the difficulties, we persist. The universe is said to glorify God, and since it does we may conclude that he intends it to do so. Glory may be seen, then, as a synecdoche

26. "The Theological Basis of Satan's Rebellion and the Function of Abdiel in *Paradise Lost*," p. 42.
27. "Milton and the Sense of Glory," p. 119.

for God's plan; it is that part of his purpose which for the moment he has thought fit to reveal to us.[28] As a glimpse of the divine intent, the concept of glory is precious to men; but the human imagination, shackled to the concrete, translates the concept into terms of solemn procession, ceremony, celebration, and the bending of knees, of *Te Deums* and coronations, for though these may reflect God's meaning imperfectly, such trappings are the closest parallel in the human experience to the divine vision.

As Dr. Johnson noted, words describing a spiritual being, be it God, angel, or devil, carry the burden of their own contradiction. To describe the Infinite in finite terms, one must show the Source of Motion moved, the Omnipotent uneasy, the Omniscient in doubt, and the Most High reaching yet higher. But the only alternatives for a believing Christian are to stop talking about God at all, or to lose oneself, like St. Dionysius the Areopagite, in the mystical act of worship, making no effort to comprehend.[29] If Milton's poem is to be an argument to justify, not simply praise, God's ways, he must show those ways in terms of speech and action; and the actions of his Almighty cannot be entirely mysterious. As C. M. Bowra has observed, "God is an essential character in his story and must appear in his own person."[30] There must be some rational dramatic motivation for his doing the things he does—otherwise *nothing* is justified. In *De Doctrina Christiana* Milton describes the Creation as

> the act whereby GOD THE FATHER PRODUCED EVERYTHING THAT EXISTS BY HIS WORD AND SPIRIT, that is, BY HIS WILL, IN ORDER TO SHOW THE GLORY OF HIS POWER AND GOODNESS.[31]

In *Paradise Lost* all of God's actions are justified in similar terms. If *glory* is to be Milton's metaphor for God's purpose or plan, then

28. In *De Doctrina Christiana*, bk. I, chap. 2, Milton observes, "We ought to form just such a mental image of him as he, in bringing himself within the limits of our understanding, wishes us to form" (*YP*, 6:133). See Kelley, *This Great Argument*, pp. 72–74; and Roland Mushat Frye, *God, Man, and Satan*, pp. 7–13, 70–94. Frye's work remains the clearest discussion available of the theory of accommodation.

29. The most memorable study of these two approaches to an understanding of God is Charles Williams's *The Figure of Beatrice*. In this lovely book Williams refers to the two modes of worship as the Way of the Affirmation of Images and the Way of the Rejection of Images (pp. 8–9 and passim). Milton's, like Dante's, is clearly the former.

30. *From Virgil to Milton*, p. 212.

31. *YP*, 6:300.

the metaphor must be played to the hilt if it is to carry the weight intended. If it really is glory, and it is certainly something of that nature, then it must be as glorious as our limited knowledge of the word will permit. Milton offers earthbound images of glorification and depends on the music of his lines to convey the sense that they are really a great deal more. Some readers, of course, are troubled when God occasionally sounds like Louis XIV; for them, the music is not enough to dispel the distaste for a Deity revered with all the obsequious and ostentatious ceremony generally employed in the presence of an earthly monarch and endowed with some of the unpleasant characteristics of such a dignitary—anger, authority, inflexibility, and a demand for military pomp and majesty. Indeed, many of Milton's fellow Puritans themselves disapproved of any effort to present the mind and person of the Deity, whether it be with glass or stone or a performance of the Passion. For them the paradoxes and incongruities were an unsurmountable aesthetic obstacle.

Milton uses political and military imagery extensively, in the convention of Christian liturgy and doctrine, to describe the divine purposes. God is King, his Son the "Heir" to the throne. The angels are ranked in "Orders, and Degrees" (5.591) like any hierarchical nobility, and the lesser orders observe appropriate deference to the greater. They all acknowledge the Almighty's supremacy with due ceremony:

> lowly reverent
> Towards either Throne they bow, and to the ground
> With solemn adoration down they cast
> Thir Crowns. (3.349–52)

God holds court, issues decrees, commands armies, and punishes offenders like any earthly monarch, all to the accretion of his glory.[32] But Milton is not satisfied with this traditional picture of the rule of Heaven, nor is he willing to end all inquiry with a simple, reverential acknowledgment of the "O Altitudo" of man's desire to know God's ways. That tough and probing mind did not easily

32. Milton, as has been observed, fully accepts the traditional image of God as a king; indeed, in *Paradise Lost* he adorns the figure to emphasize his superiority to any earthly monarch. They sin who presume to imitate the Almighty, as do Satan and, more recently, Charles I. As Milton says in *Eikonoklastes*, "He who desires from men as much obedience and subjection, as we may all pay to God, desires not less than to be a God, a sacrilege" (*YP*, 3:532–33).

accept such limitations on human reason, and so in *Paradise Lost* he transcends the conventional glory to encompass a more complex vision of the divine purpose. Some consideration of that broader vision will help put the discussion of war aims into perspective.

Milton's God describes himself as filling "Infinitude" (7.169); though he may withdraw his "goodness" from space, by definition he cannot withdraw himself.[33] It is through creation that he defines himself; thus the warring atoms of Chaos, as well as men, angels, Hell, and the world, are all particularized and individuated manifestations of his nature, part of the "Infinitude" he fills. He is, at the same time, a distinct being, "substantially express'd" to his creation through the Son.

Milton's God creates out of himself, so anything that is made of him cannot cease to be him. Raphael says as much when, in describing to Adam the future of the human race, he explains that everything he sees about and above him is made from "one first matter all, / Indu'd with various forms, various degrees / Of substance" (5.472–74). Raphael defines the act of creation both as an event in cosmic history and as a continuing phenomenon. God is the "Author and end of all things" (7.591), the conventional alpha and omega of existence, from whom "all things proceed, and up to him return" (5.470). God's purpose is achieved, it would appear, by a differentiation of the divine substance, as he creates *ex Deo*, and a reintegration of the "various forms, various degrees" back into himself. The process is carried out both consecutively and simultaneously, for God is everywhere present in time and space; but man, himself locked in time, sees the Deity as one engaged in a dynamic *egressus-regressus* of his being, or what J. H. Adamson has called a "cosmic systole and diastole."[34] Milton gives the process a political dimension when Raphael defines for Adam his prelapsarian destiny. Men are to be the subjects of an immortal monarch, whose bodies, if they remain dutifully obedient, "may at last turn all to Spirit" (5.497); but for a time they must dwell on earth "till by degrees of merit rais'd / They open to themselves at length the way / Up hither" (7.157–59). The Fall does not alter the final end of man, but his body now seems fixed in nature; it will enjoy no slow metamorphosis to spirit, "Im-

33. Kelley, *This Great Argument*, pp. 122–30.
34. "The Creation," pp. 92–97.

prov'd by tract of time" (5.498). In his corrupt state, man can only "Up to him return" through death, which God provides as "His final remedie" (11.61–62).

The angels are also undergoing a metamorphosis, though of a somewhat different kind. They do not change in substance, but rather in their relationship with the Son; and Milton leans heavily on political imagery to define what appears to be a merging of the two natures into one. The exaltation of the Son before the war, as has been noted, occasions a change in the governance of Heaven, one which Satan sees as a usurpation of power, a "Yoke" newly imposed upon them. Abdiel defends the act not as an elevation of one above the others, but as a leveling of power: "he the Head / One of our number thus reduc't becomes" (5.843–44). It is difficult, though, to dismiss the impression that God's announcement sounds very like a monarch anointing a royal heir, one moreover who must somehow prove himself. His victory over the rebels more than achieves that end, of course; he returns "Victorious King, / Son, Heir, and Lord, to him Dominion giv'n, / Worthiest to Reign" (6.886–91).

The apparent contradiction of the Son being raised and lowered at once may be better understood if one considers his ambiguous relationship with the Father. On the surface at least, the heir of an immortal monarch could not be said to anticipate a very promising political future. Thus he is "to be Heir and to be King" at once. As such an heir, of course, he cannot accede to the throne, but as king he already sits upon it; he thus partakes of the nature of both. The complex question of Milton's Arianism need not concern us here; though all the votes are not in, a strong case has been presented that from the evidence of *De Doctrina Christiana*, at least, he subscribed to a fairly orthodox subordinationist doctrine.[35] In *Paradise Lost*, however, the ambiguity of the political imagery implies a somewhat different status. As "Heir" and "Son" he is subordinate to the Father; but he is also "King," and despite the troublesome double throne (3.350), it is difficult to imagine there being *two* Kings of Heaven. The political imagery would seem to add weight to the intriguing suggestion made by C. A. Patrides that *in the poem* God and Son are, in fact, one.[36] Patrides

35. See, for example, W. B. Hunter, "Milton's Arianism Reconsidered," pp. 50–51.

36. See his "The Godhead in *Paradise Lost*: Dogma or Drama?"

cites Milton's practice of referring to the Son as "God" whenever he is not in the company of the Father, to which may be added the obvious ambivalence of the angels even on those occasions when the two are together, as when they celebrate the creation of the world:

> Great are thy works, *Jehovah*, infinite
> Thy power; what thought can measure thee or tongue
> Relate thee; greater now in thy return
> Then from the Giant Angels. (7.602–5)

Throughout *Paradise Lost* the Son is described as the Father manifest. God declares him "Son in whose face invisible is beheld / Visibly, what by Deitie I am" (6.681–82). He *is* the Father, appearing in such form as the Deity, otherwise too dazzling for the "brightest Seraphim" to look upon, chooses to reveal himself to his creation.

In this sense Abdiel's claim that the begetting of the Son represented a leveling of the Deity can be better understood. In arguing with Satan about the genesis of the angels, Abdiel asserts that "by his Word the mighty Father made / All things, ev'n thee" (5.836–37); but apparently this is an article of faith for him, not based on personal knowledge, for he raises no objection to Satan's reply that "We know no time when we were not as now" (5.859). There is no evidence that prior to the moment when the Father "begot" the Son any of the heavenly host had ever seen "the Word." He did not rise from the ranks; he emanated from the Godhead; hence his appearance in a shape like their own is interpreted as the Deity's desire to be "one of [their] number." The Son first expressed the Father "substantially" *in angelic form*, foreshadowing the Incarnation, when he would appear in yet more humble shape as one of the numbers of men.[37]

But the status of the Son as "King" is itself subject to change. As he enters battle, he proclaims, "Scepter and Power, thy giving, I assume, / And gladlier shall resign, when in the end / Thou shalt be All in All" (6.730–32). The Father later confirms this vision of the future, predicting a time when "thou thy regal Scepter shalt lay by, / For regal Scepter then no more shall need, / God shall be

37. Albert C. Labriola, "'Thy Humiliation Shall Exalt': The Christology of *Paradise Lost*," pp. 31–36. Addressing the subject from a different point of view, Labriola comes to the same conclusion.

All in All" (3.339–41). His reign will end when there is no further need for distinction between master and servant, monarch and subject, at a time when all political divisions, ranks, and hierarchies will disappear. Christopher Hill likens this mysterious denouement to the Marxist doctrine of the final withering away of the state, which, though a bit mind-wrenching, is not altogether *outré*; for the political imagery employed strongly implies that the cosmos will undergo a great *regressus* to a condition in which God shall once again be the "All" he was before he set himself the task of creation.[38]

Thus, in *Paradise Lost* the Father is manifested in the Son, who by his acts reveals the nature and purpose of the Deity. In each of the four episodes of the poem where he appears prominently, he demonstrates a different trait of the Godhead: in the war he displays the power of the Almighty;[39] the "Six days' work" illustrates his creative energy; when he offers himself for man, he expresses God's love; and in judging the sinners of Eden, he exercises the Father's mercy and justice. This process of revelation is accompanied by *egressus* or differentiation of the divine substance. God creates out of his infinite self the warring atoms of Chaos, Heaven, the angels, Hell, the world, and finally man, all of which are destined in turn to undergo a *regressus* or reintegration back "up to him," as men's bodies turn all to spirit and angels join nature with the Son, who in the end will be revealed as the Deity himself. "The World shall burn" and all creation return to God, who will then be "All in All." Milton defines at once the history of the cosmos and the passion of any moment in that chronicle when the devout Christian prays to be truly one with God; and in a brief glimpse of that final order, the poet gives the purpose, end, and meaning of what is proclaimed in the tongues of men as "Glory."

The war in Heaven can be seen, then, not as an unfortunate digression on the evils of warfare, but as an integral part of Milton's poetic vision, one of a series of events that reveal the nature of God, and as a stage in the differentiation of his infinite substance—in brief, as a reflection of the divine purpose. The angels

38. *Milton*, pp. 304–5. Empson, in *Milton's God*, p. 144, suggests that God, like Cromwell, is planning his own abdication; but Hill's analogy is more apt. Milton clearly conceives of a situation in which all political distinctions will be erased as natures merge; he does not envision a simple transfer of power.

39. The identity of Father and Son is underlined by the apparent absurdity of a "Second Omnipotence." Could there possibly be two?

are divided into those who obey and those who do not, even as later the sons of men will be divided into the Cains and Abels of the race. God permits all, his "war aim" being to glorify the Son, that is, to reveal the power of the Almighty. Thus the fact that the rebel angels face an omnipotent enemy, which excites the laughter of those who find the war comic, is quite beside the point. If the Messiah is to be effectively elevated to the position of "Heir" and "King," he must confront a credible foe and demonstrate a power something short of absolute. An exercise in omnipotence would amount to overkill and be contrary to God's purpose; thus Milton has the Son exert but "half his strength" so that the defeat of the rebels can be appreciated in human terms.[40] The divine plan is advanced by the differentiation of the angels into warring factions; and in a revelation of the power of the Almighty, the Son is seen as sharing in the nature of the Father.

Quite aside from these abstract questions of causes and aims, however, the actual battle must be convincing, though again not to persuade us of the obvious, that omnipotence will triumph or that peace is preferable to war. Were that Milton's meaning, he might well have depicted the rebel angels as figures of ridicule—ragtag bunglers, mindless automatons, or the anguished monsters of medieval iconography cringing under the sword of Michael. But he did not. Rather, the rival armies are evenly matched, their soldiers equally valorous, their leaders comparably adept; and Satan seems godlike, an "Idol of Majestie Divine" (6.99–102). This even balance of forces in a vast military image at the heart of *Paradise Lost* illustrates, as do many of the martial figures of the epics, the complex nature of evil. It is powerful, a force so great that it can shatter the very order of Heaven. And it is again the deceptive mirror-image of good; the two are as twins "cleaving together." Abdiel is perplexed and indignant at the sight of the approaching rebel army:

> O Heav'n! that such resemblance of the Highest
> Should yet remain, where faith and realtie
> Remain not; wherfore should not strength and might
> There fail where Vertue fails, or weakest prove
> Where boldest; though to sight unconquerable? (6.114–18)

40. Milton is either unaware of, or in an exercise of poetic license winks at, an essential property of infinity: half of it is still infinity. Similarly, half of God's strength would still constitute omnipotence—but we nitpick.

Why don't the evil *look* evil, he complains, echoing man's dilemma; and if, as we are told, evil promotes weakness, why are they so strong? Satan seems a match for Michael; he "that day / Prodigious power had shewn, and met in Armes / No equal" (6.246–48); and when the two clash, no "odds appeerd / In might or swift prevention" (6.319–20)—no odds, that is, until he feels pain. And in that pain we see yet a third quality, evil again "recoiling" upon the evildoer.

An examination of the tactics and weapons employed will reveal how successful Milton is, despite the difficulties involved, in giving the account a degree of verisimilitude. It is in the description of the first day of battle that the poet displays his mastery of the art of martial narrative. The lines themselves thunder:

> now storming furie rose,
> And clamour such as heard in Heav'n till now
> Was never, Arms on Armour clashing bray'd
> Horrible discord, and the madding Wheeles
> Of brazen Chariots rag'd; dire was the noise
> Of conflict; over head the dismal hiss
> Of fiery Darts in flaming volies flew,
> And flying vaulted either Host with fire.
> So under fierie Cope together rush'd
> Both Battels maine, with ruinous assault
> And inextinguishable rage; all Heav'n
> Resounded, and had Earth bin then, all Earth
> Had to her Center shook. (6.207–19)

It is, moreover, an accurate description of the conduct of battle, though one of an earlier time than Milton's, before the musket had replaced the bow. When the two armies are still some distance apart, the archers unleash their arrows into the opposing ranks, after which the forces close to engage in hand-to-hand fighting. The outcome is in doubt, "long time in eeven scale / The Battel hung" (6.245–46), until Satan challenges Michael and their encounter reveals the fatal weakness of the rebel forces: "then *Satan* first knew pain" (6.327).[41] This mysterious vulnerability appar-

41. The fact that Satan brings forth Sin "in miserable pain" need not be attributed to Milton's uncertain control of his material. Sin is sufficiently vague about the timing of her nativity to allow for the event to have happened during the night of the first day, with plenty of time left over for their incestuous dalliance. "Mean while Warr arose" (2:767), she says rather vaguely, meaning "at about the same time." Satan must *act* in disobedience to God, not just contemplate it, before

ently afflicts all of his followers simultaneously, for with Satan's defeat the tide of battle suddenly turns as Milton follows quickly with accounts of the victories of loyal angels, Gabriel, Uriel, Raphael, and Abdiel, in personal combat.

Milton is careful to avoid any implication that the vulnerability of the rebel angels is God's doing; they are "to such evil brought / By sin of disobedience" (6.395–96). Pain afflicts them only after the battle has been joined; the rebels engage in an open act of defiance before they begin to suffer the consequences of their sin. Pain is a self-inflicted torment, the first in a long series of changes Milton describes as the effect of sin upon the sinner, that metamorphosis the rebel angels undergo as they gradually fall away from their original untainted brightness. In this sense book 6 complements the image of the fading glory of Satan and the slow coarsening of the fallen angels' spiritual substance; they experience the capacity of evil to inhibit good in angels and men simply because they sin, and not because God so directs.

Only the fall of night prevents the complete rout of the rebels in what has now become an uneven fight (night invariably put an end to major action on seventeenth-century battlefields). Satan, "undismay'd," calls a council of war to evaluate the situation, opening with a speech reaffirming their hope of victory. Those who read the war as comic are particularly amused by him here, where he questions the omnipotence, and by inference the omniscience, of God. But to hear divine laughter in counterpoint to his lines, or to dwell on the obvious and call him a liar, is to ignore the public demands of his position as a military leader with a battle on his hands, one in which his forces may have suffered a setback but which they have by no means lost. He praises his followers and holds out the hope of success on the next day—what else would we have him do?—and though we may know that his cause is doomed, it certainly doesn't seem so to him. As he says, they have survived a day of battle against a foe who had claimed to be all powerful, and much may be seen in that. This is not false hope; the chronicle of human wars records the defeat of many an army so described—such as the Persians at Marathon or the French at Agincourt. The problem, however, is pain; for if they are to pre-

Sin is born and pain appears. As Adam tells Eve, "Evil into the mind of God or Man / May come and go, so unapprov'd, and leave / No spot or blame behind" (5:117–19).

vail, some means must be devised to balance the tactical advantage enjoyed by the enemy. As Nisroch puts it, they must find a way to "offend / Our yet unwounded Enemies, or arme / Our selves with like defence" (6.465–67). Can tactics be developed that will enable them to surprise and overwhelm the enemy at a distance before he has a chance to close "the rough edge of battel" and bring to bear his superiority in hand-to-hand combat?

It is an artistic and dramatic problem for Milton; he must even the odds. At this point a complete rout of the rebels simply would not do, not for God's purposes, nor Raphael's, nor his own; things must be so ordered that Christ's intervention is the triumphant event it is meant to be. It would be stretching credulity to have God, who is too much in evidence as it is, step in and suddenly change the rules. Thus, Milton has Satan, as the resourceful leader, invent the cannon; and of those who have found the introduction of artillery into Heaven indecorous, none so far has offered a more artistic alternative.

The solution is ingenious. Satan shrewdly examines the relative combat strengths of the two forces and detects the only tactical weakness of the loyal angels: though "Invulnerable, impenitrably arm'd" and "unobnoxious to be pain'd / By wound," they can be "from thir place by violence mov'd" (6.400–405). He mines materials from their "dark Nativity" in the soil of Heaven, shapes his weapons, and employs them skillfully and effectively on the next day. Raphael, a veteran of the battle, heightens the dramatic intensity of the action with an eyewitness account: at first sight of the cannon, "we suspense, / Collected stood within our thoughts amus'd, / Not long" (6.580–82). The former "Victor Host" is "Level'd":

> none on thir feet might stand,
> Though standing else as Rocks, but down they fell
> By thousands, Angel on Arch-Angel rowl'd, (6.590–94)

where they languished, baffled by this new development. The result is a stand-off. The rebels cannot close with their enemy because the loyal angels have all the advantage in close combat; held off by the "devilish Enginrie," the loyal angels cannot attack to bring their advantage to bear. They are dismayed:

> What should they do? if on they rusht, repulse
> Repeated, and indecent overthrow

> Doubl'd, would render them yet more despis'd,
> And to thir foes a laughter. (6.600–603)

Satan is triumphant, as well he might be, but here he commits a tactical blunder. This is the critical juncture of any battle, one recognized by a seasoned commander as that moment when victory and defeat hang in delicate balance, when a temporary advantage gives him the opportunity to seize the initiative and press home the attack. Satan, however, lets the moment pass; instead of attacking, he puns. It is irrelevant to observe that there is little he *can* do; the same might have been said of him the night before, when all options seemed closed to him. Of course the Son will waste the rebels; but, once again, omnipotence is not the point. Satan contributes to his own defeat by failing, through pride, to press his advantage. In pausing to gloat over the discomfort of his enemies, he allows them time to recover from their surprise, regroup, and devise a means of response. Milton exposes the fatal flaw of those who march to war for personal fame rather than the glory of God. As he had expressed it earlier, "Glorious deeds don to ambitious ends, find reward answerable, not to thir outward seeming, but to thir inward ambition."[42] Pride makes vulnerable those who pursue "ambitious ends"; since their only cause is themselves, they are wont to lose sight of any larger goal and bask in the glow of a momentary success. It is not so much that Satan is "disgusting" here, as some would have it;[43] the point is that he is completely ineffectual as a commander in battle, so preoccupied with idle self-congratulation that he is blind to the opportunity to exploit the very advantage his resourcefulness has created. It is not an uncommon occurrence in combat and is often the prelude to a startling turn in the fortunes of opposing sides; but it is a remarkable psychological insight for one who, like Milton, was unused to battle.

The loyal angels must nullify the damaging effects of the cannon or fail their mission. They must somehow return missile with missile—and so they turn to the hills. That this mountain-tossing should receive so much unfavorable attention is a bit puzzling. John Peter, for example, refers to the "Disney-like panoramas" of the scene, and A. J. A. Waldock imagines that "even Milton

42. *YP*, 3:429–30.
43. Hughes, *Complete Poems*, p. 179.

giggled" when he described the exchange.[44] The moving of mountains is not an uncommon image in literature, and the scene is sufficiently foreshadowed in *Paradise Lost* so as not to come as a surprise. In book 1 "the force / Of subterranean wind transports a Hill / Torn from *Pelorus*" (230–32); and in book 2, when the fallen angels disperse each to his task, some of them "with vast *Typhoean* rage more fell / Rend up both Rocks and Hills" (539–40). The fact that heaving hills is one of their military exercises prepares us somewhat for the scene to come. Again, when Abdiel strikes Satan, it is as if he "had push't a Mountain from his seat" (6.197).

Whatever the decorum of the image, it is certainly sound tactics for the loyal angels. They wisely direct their first missiles at the troublesome cannon, effectively neutralizing "those cursed Engins triple-row" (6.650), and then take aim on the demoralized troops themselves. The rebels respond in kind, however, and the result is a chaotic brawl with overtones of a wild, barbaric age:

> Warr seem'd a civil Game
> To this uproar; horrid confusion heapt
> Upon confusion rose. (6.667–69)

All is to God's purpose, however; he instructs the Son:

> Ascend my Chariot, guide the rapid Wheeles
> That shake Heav'ns basis, bring forth all my Warr,
> My Bow and Thunder, my Almightie Arms
> Gird on, and Sword upon thy puissant Thigh. (6.711–14)

The Son appears on the battlefield in the Father's flashing chariot, resplendent in God's "Almightie Arms," "attended with ten thousand thousand Saints" (6.767), the reserves held back on the first day. He instructs the loyal forces to withdraw, leaving him to face the rebel hosts alone; for

> not you but mee they have despis'd,
> Yet envied; against mee is all thir rage,
> Because the Father, t'whom in Heav'n supream
> Kingdom and Power and Glorie appertains,
> Hath honoured me according to his will. (6.812–16)

44. Peter, *Critique*, p. 77; Waldock, *"Paradise Lost" and Its Critics*, p. 112; Stein, in *Answerable Style*, p. 24, visualizes it as an exchange of custard pies.

With a single, spectacular display of the power of the Almighty, he expels the rebels and returns "Sole Victor from th' expulsion of his Foes" (6.880) to his triumph in Heaven.

Thus the war ends, its goals fulfilled. Adam has learned what is meant by disobedience and by obedience; and he has received a vivid lesson in the nature of evil—in the fury of battle he can sense its power, in the speeches of Satan he can hear its deception, in the wounds of the rebels he can feel its self-defeating corruption, and in the victory of the Son he can rejoice in its ultimate destruction. God has glorified the Son, and through the Son, himself. Milton, handicapped by theological and dramatic limitations that did not trouble Homer or Virgil, has created a scene of epic battle that in many ways surpasses both. And if the reader may have found himself in sympathy with Satan's talk of freedom and equality, or had he admired the Devil's fortitude in the face of defeat and pain, he may well ponder how difficult indeed it is in our life to distinguish between truth and falsehood, between virtue and decadence; for nowhere in Milton's epics do the forces of good and evil resemble one another so closely as when they first clash along those "ridges of grim War."

VIII

Two Warriors

> I once again
> Defie thee to the trial of mortal fight,
> By combat to decide whose god is god,
> Thine or whom I with *Israel*'s Sons adore. (*SA* 1174–77)

If the account of the war in Heaven owes the least to Milton's experience of life, *Samson Agonistes* perhaps owes the most; for no other figure from his pen so powerfully evokes the image of the poet himself, one of the "Princes of Exile," in Louis Martz's excellent phrase, excluded "from the community of men by the loss of eyesight, and then by political isolation."[1] The parallels have been so widely rehearsed that brief mention of a few will suffice: Samson the blind champion of the Israelites bound in chains, Milton the blind champion of the English Republic cast into prison; Samson whom a timid nation would not follow to freedom, Milton to whom the "perverse inhabitants" of England were deaf; Samson who can no longer fight for the God of Israel, Milton whose voice is stilled by the Restoration; Samson who finally defends his God, Milton who justifies his. In each analogy, for Samson's strength we read Milton's words.[2]

One element of this identification gives pause, however: that which discovers in the play evidence of the poet's retreat to the inner life, his rejection of the active in favor of the contemplative sphere. A. S. P. Woodhouse, who dates the play from 1660–1661, detects in Samson's lines the voice of a Milton who had "retired to the citadel of his own inner life." Woodhouse describes those years as a time when the poet's world was "in ruins around him, and himself blind, in hiding from his enemies, disillusioned, embittered, and alone," and the play as perhaps "our fullest and most

1. *Poet of Exile: A Study of Milton's Poetry*, pp. 79–80; as he explains, it is a phrase he borrows from St.-John Perse.

2. Hanford, *Handbook*, pp. 290–92; Tillyard, *Milton*, pp. 346–54. The autobiographical analogy raises the question of the dating, of course, but the reader will recall my early resolve to stay clear of that controversy. For a bibliography of material on the issue, see William Riley Parker, "The Date of *Samson Agonistes* Again," p. 175. The latest, though we can be sure not the last, word is in Radzinowicz, *Milton's Mind*, pp. 387–407.

authentic record" of that experience. While Woodhouse acknowledges that this was "far from Milton's normal mood" in old age, others who date the play much later than he have heard that same voice.[3] Joan Webber is among the most recent of Milton scholars to find in his epics (though not in *SA*) signs of a descent into self. The words dot her pages as they do the literature of our age: self-consciousness, self-awareness, self-knowledge, self-integration, self-examination, self-regard. She concludes, as have many, that Milton found the inner life true, the outer false.[4] This picture of his mind draws substance from the words of his great sonnet, where he praises those "who only stand and waite," and from the invocation to book 9, where he scorns those epic poets who write of nothing but battle, leaving "the better fortitude / Of Patience and Heroic Martyrdom / Unsung" (31–33).[5]

But contemporary accounts clash with those who picture post-Restoration Milton as a sequestered recluse soured by disappointment, isolating himself from the world and penning ironic renunciations of the values that shaped his half-century of living. He was surely made of sterner stuff.[6] After the initial distress of deprivation and imprisonment, he recovered his resolve and resumed work. Though certainly disappointed by the return of the monarchy, he was by all accounts a cheerful man who received visitors graciously, enjoyed a song, entertained at table, and, until afflicted with gout, kept his health and figure with frequent walks. Blindness was a limitation, of course, and it compelled him to seek solace in the life of the mind, which one of his studious bent would have found not uncongenial anyway. But it was ever his conviction that men had a moral obligation to act in the world; thus in the final years he published widely and even returned to the pamphlet wars with *Of True Religion*. If his works reveal anything, it is a mind that has struck a careful balance between the active and con-

3. *The Heavenly Muse*, pp. 315–17.

4. *Milton and His Epic Tradition*, p. 49, e.g.: "The human search for self-realization and self-transcendence also makes use of the unconscious mind, not in an attempt to get back to the beginnings, but both to accept and to transcend the human self-consciousness that has been achieved." Milton's epics, she concludes, can aid our consciousness, so "desperate to pierce beyond itself into a more creative and spacious kind of awareness" (p. 216).

5. William O. Harris, "Despair and 'Patience as the Truest Fortitude' in *Samson Agonistes*."

6. Radzinowicz, in *Milton's Mind*, p. 116, cautions against finding in Samson evidence that "Milton's reaction to his party's collapse was a complete retreat from political thinking into pure other- or inner- worldliness."

templative life, a balance seen more clearly if one places beside the great sonnet on his blindness the lesser one to Cyriack Skinner, in which he speaks of his lost sight much as a veteran would of an honorable wound suffered in "Libertyes defence." The first a private, the second a public sentiment, they do not contradict, rather they complement, showing the inner and outer life in thoughtful equilibrium, both valued, both real.

Inasmuch as our first parents fail the test of patience and there is little occasion in *Paradise Lost* for martyrdom, heroic or otherwise, one must turn to *Paradise Regained* for a demonstration of "the better fortitude."[7] There the Messiah submits to the physical and psychological assaults of Satan and "stands" immovable against them, a model for the triumph of patience. Yet even here we are reminded that his spiritual trial and toughening are not ends in themselves but a preparation, an exercise in "the rudiments / Of his great warfare" (1.157–58) before he enters on his ministry. In Samson, Milton describes a fallen man, however, not the Son of God, a man, moreover, much like himself, one who has struggled through spiritual and physical affliction to achieve an inner resolve and then, like the Messiah, gone on to assume his destined role in the world.

If Milton's figures do descend into self, they do not stay there. To gain inner fortitude surely asks them patience, but once achieved it invariably leads to action, at times ending in heroic martyrdom, at times not. The works are woven with the recurrent pattern of defeated spirits that rise from despair to hope and action—Satan in Hell, Adam in his lost paradise, Samson in chains. Though not given to despair, even the loyal angels, discouraged by the fury of the cannonade, "stood / A while in trouble; *but they stood not long*" (6.633–34; italics mine). Each perseveres for different reasons, some less admirable than others—Satan because of his diabolical energy and hunger for revenge, Adam because he is buoyed by a vision of man's redemptive destiny, Samson because he rediscovers his strength and role in the battle between God and Dagon, and the loyal angels because the Almighty gives them the power—but they all act.

Among recent studies of Milton's drama is one by Jackie DiSalvo,

7. Fish, *Surprised by Sin*, p. 181, quotes H. R. Swardson, *Poetry and the Fountain of Light*, p. 143. Of *Paradise Lost*, Swardson asks, "Does Milton really think he is singing 'the better fortitude of Patience and Heroic Martyrdom'? Where? What space and prominence does he give to it?"

in which she cites Puritan sermon literature to illustrate one of the moral foundations of the English Revolution, "the repudiation of ease and the emphasis on disciplined activity," and to remind us that Puritans saw the heroes of the Old Testament as soldiers committed to engagement in "The Lord's Battells."[8] With some daring, she proposes Cromwell and the New Model soldier as patterns for Samson, using Milton's own words persuasively in support of the analogy; and her argument is so effective as to prompt the thought that in Samson, Milton finally realizes his perception of himself as a soldier in the wars of truth, defending with his words what the New Model trooper defended with his arms.[9]

Milton's Samson is a soldier of God, faithful to the biblical source.[10] The Nazarite of Judges is a warrior-prince, a man of violence who dies a heroic martyr in one final, catastrophically violent act. His weapons and tactics are somewhat unorthodox, to be sure, but appropriate to one of superhuman strength. He is destined from birth as one who will "begin to deliver Israel out of the hand of the Philistines,"[11] and he sets about his life's work with enthusiasm, slaughtering Philistines whenever the opportunity presents itself and provoking occasions when it doesn't. He is a military and political leader whom the timid Israelites cannot muster the courage to follow. Most of the martial detail of the biblical account appears in Milton's lines; the killing of the lion, the removal of the Gaza gates, and the slaughter of the thirty at Ashkelon and the thousand at Ramath-lechi are all mentioned, some more than once, in order to set before us the image of the fallen warrior-prince, "O change beyond report, thought, or belief!" (117). The only warlike incident not included is the burning of foxes' tails and the subsequent slaughter, omitted perhaps be-

8. "'The Lord's Battells': *Samson Agonistes* and the Puritan Revolution." See Radzinowicz, *Milton's Mind*, pp. 111–79, for an exhaustive treatment of political imagery. I find little to argue with in Radzinowicz's development, save for occasional moments when she seems to demean Samson's martial prowess, preferring to see him as an intellectual or spiritual force (pp. 155, 173n, 174). I think him a nice balance—but we quibble.

9. DiSalvo, "The Lord's Battells," pp. 57–58. Radzinowicz has reservations about the analogy (*Milton's Mind*, p. 173n) but characterizes Samson elsewhere as "a Commonwealth hero" (p. 113).

10. Judges 13–16.

11. Judges 13:5. In lines 38–39 Milton ignores the "begin to" of the original but he includes it in line 225. It is an irony of the play that Samson's sacrifice does not deliver the Israelites. See John Shawcross, "Irony as Tragic Effect: *Samson Agonistes* as the Tragedy of Hope," p. 296: "Samson is one of a long line of Judges, none of whom liberates Israel from bondage."

cause that adventure seemed almost too frivolous for the tragic figure the poet sought to create. The chorus expands on his prowess, how he "Ran on embattelld Armies clad in Iron, / And weaponless himself, / Made arms ridiculous" (129–31), an echo of the Christ of book 6, against whose power the weapons and shields of the rebel angels are useless. The message of both is clear: none can stand in battle against those whom God has armed. Samson's abject servitude, however, underlines the qualification imposed by divine justice: he will prevail only so long as he maintains that inner strength and virtue from which his power flows.

In the course of the play Samson is confronted by yet another warrior, one who serves a false god. The closest parallel in *Paradise Lost* to the encounter between Samson and Harapha is perhaps that between Gabriel and Satan in book 4, where the two square off for a battle that never takes place, as Satan flees "murmuring" upon the appearance of the golden scales, even as the giant withdraws sputtering ineffectual threats. Samson's triumph is of a different order, however, for he has no deus ex machina to dissuade the enemy; he must subdue Harapha through the sheer magnitude of his spirit. One of the most telling points in DiSalvo's essay is one made earlier in these pages: there were some warriors that Milton liked and some he didn't. She characterizes the encounter between Samson and Harapha as "a confrontation between two different kinds of soldiers." [12] And so it is, for in placing opposite Samson a warrior of a different mold, Milton finally juxtaposes two men, not angels or gods; and in the contrast he puts in sharp relief the qualities essential to a "true warfaring Christian."

Samson is anything but patient; and his inner life, like his outer, is a mess. The great, flawed "Nazarite of God" longs to act and is close to violence throughout the play. He is but a step away from tearing Dalila "joint by joint" (953); he challenges Harapha thrice to battle and threatens the officer darkly, "Perhaps thou shalt have cause to sorrow indeed" (1347). He speaks briefly of the "internal peace" (1334) he finally gains but promptly stalks off to the Temple of Dagon determined to *do* something, though, it would appear, he is not as yet sure what (1387–89, 1423–26); and it is an inspiring sight for the chorus, who in the first scene had found him enthralled by self-pity. As the play opens, he has lost all faith in his inner strength and, paralyzed by guilt, wishes only for "speedy

12. "'The Lord's Battells,'" p. 52.

death, / The close of all my miseries, and the balm" (650–51). This despair arises from two factors, the first a cause and the second a consequence of his condition of servitude. Agonizingly aware that his helplessness is his own doing, brought about by "impotence of mind" (52), he is immobilized by a sense of unworthiness and berates himself for "foul effeminacy" (410) and "Shameful garrulity" (491), accepting his slavery as just, a "servil mind / Rewarded well with servil punishment" (412–13). Again, he despairs because as a consequence of his moral and physical weakness, he is denied the destined role as defender of his Lord against false usurpers; he laments that "all the contest is now / 'Twixt God and *Dagon*," for he can no longer "enter lists" to champion the God of Israel (461–63). In his rejection of Dalila's "fair enchanted cup, and warbling charms" (934), he purges himself of guilt and emerges somewhat at peace; but he is still the thwarted champion, lacking confidence in his strength, now returned with the growth of his hair.

The encounter with Harapha dispels the second source of his despair and renews his faith that he may once more enter battle to determine "whether God be Lord, / Or *Dagon*" (477–78). The revival of his confidence is gradual, however, his first responses to the blustering giant being but ironic retorts. Harapha has come, as he announces condescendingly, out of curiosity, to see for himself if all those stories are really true. Samson responds with a curt taunt, a one-line aside, addressed to no one in particular, "The way to know were not to see but taste" (1091). Harapha's haughty reply receives a direct retort this time: "Boast not of what thou wouldst have done, but do / What then thou would'st" (1104–5). Finally, patience thrown to the winds, Samson rises angrily, spoiling for a fight, and issues three successive challenges to battle. He will put "*Dagon* to the test, / Offering to combat thee his Champion bold" to determine "whose God is strongest, thine or mine" (1151–55). Harapha's arrogant rebuff rouses him further and he defies the giant again "to the trial of mortal fight, / By combat to decide whose god is god" (1175–76). When Harapha refuses yet a third dare to "single fight," Samson is triumphant—he is Hercules:

> Go baffl'd coward, lest I run upon thee,
> Though in these chains, bulk without spirit vast,
> And with one buffet lay thy structure low,

> Or swing thee in the Air, then dash thee down
> To the hazard of thy brains and shatter'd sides. (1237–41)

This is God's soldier, then, the inner strength of his conscience restored, confidence in his physical prowess renewed—God's champion eager to translate his faith into action, to "enter lists" once more. He is again the warrior-prince who had been the scourge of the Philistines, and the chorus rejoices in the transformation: "Oh how comely it is and how reviving / To the Spirits of just men long opprest!" (1268–69). The Israelites are edified, but timidity limits their understanding of just what has happened to him. To their bound vision, a Samson restored to an "Heroic magnitude of mind" (1279) is still but a helpless, blind man "Whom Patience finally must crown" (1296). Patience, as it turns out, is far from his thoughts; he has not achieved this difficult victory over himself to no purpose. He rises, like so many of Milton's figures, indeed like Milton himself, from adversity to action and devotes his gift of physical power, now seconded by an inner strength of conscience, to the destruction of the enemies of his God.

Samson, then, is Milton's image of the soldier of God, one whom the poet invested with the same qualities he admired in Cromwell: "Commander first over himself, victor over himself, he had learned to achieve over himself the most effective triumph" before entering battle.[13] But if Samson is his ideal warrior, Harapha represents all that Milton found detestable in the soldier. There are hints in him of a Homeric hero, to be sure, in his pompous recital of lineage and mocking regret for the lost opportunity to achieve honor and glory; but the overwhelming impression is that of a chivalric knight.[14] Earlier in life Milton had demonstrated his disregard for the false values of the chivalric code, which to his mind was little more than a devious facade erected to mask corruption and brutality. He scorned a tradition that had shaped the tinsel grandeur of the royal court, concealing under the pretense of doing God's work an allegiance to anti-Christ and the depraved ambition of the medieval church to wield secular power. He discarded Arthur as unfit for epic song and attacked the king and his

13. *Defensio Secunda*, *YP*, 4:668. For a very different reading see F. Michael Krause, *Milton's Samson and the Christian Tradition*, pp. 128–29, where the author insists that Samson undergoes a temptation to violence and, saintlike, successfully resists it. For Krause on patience, see pp. 15–16, 98n.

14. Hughes, *Complete Poems*, pp. 535–36.

courtiers for disguising tyranny with fine words decked out in chivalric trappings. In *Eikonoklastes*, for example, one can delight in the obvious relish with which he pounces upon each of Charles's references to his "honour."[15]

The medieval chivalric code proposed a union of two natures that according to reason could never be joined in a single person. The knight was called upon to be courageous, physically powerful, and furious in battle, and at the same time demonstrate all the virtues of the Sermon on the Mount.[16] In the early Middle Ages the tradition probably appealed most strongly to the women, who, hoping perhaps to curb some of the unrestrained brutality of their lords, urged them to stay in court and talk of love rather than ravage the countryside. If these hopes were not fully realized, the tradition did impose a moderating influence on medieval warriors, who by any standards could only be described as barbarous thugs.[17] Those who insisted upon exercising their martial prowess were at least persuaded that they should do so in a cause that would advance the kingdom of God. Thus, a veneer of humility, piety, and mildness thinly covered the warlike spirit of men, who could ride forth righteously to slaughter Turks by the hundreds and return to court, there to blush, stammer, and grow faint at the sight of their lady—or so the story went.[18]

It is questionable just how well the literary tradition translated into real life;[19] but one of the knight's high missions was to protect the weak and helpless, those who could be expected to inspire sympathy in the breast of a warrior striving to emulate the Savior's meekness, and it was considered dishonorable for him to attack an unarmed man. Harapha represents the unregenerate barbarian who twists this ideal of concern for the weak to hide his fundamental cowardice.

15. *YP*, 3:456–57, 460, 466–67, 478, 497, etc. See, especially, p. 539, where the word "honour and civilitie" are defined as "complement, Ceremony, Court fauning, and dissembling" in "the language of the Courtier."

16. The most recent, and most readable, treatment of the influence of the chivalric tradition on medieval life is Barbara W. Tuchman, *A Distant Mirror: The Calamitous Fourteenth Century*. The code, she says, was "intended to fuse the religious and martial spirits and somehow bring the fighting man into accord with Christian theory" (p. 62).

17. Ibid., chaps. 2–5, gives an indelible account of the brutality of the age.

18. Maurice Valency, *In Praise of Love*, written with rare humor and insight, remains a classic. See also Tuchman, *Distant Mirror*, pp. 62–63.

19. Ibid., p. 62: "Chivalry was a moral system, governing the whole of noble life. That it was four parts in five illusion made it no less governing for all that."

The giant's responses to the various challenges of Samson chart a gradual decline in his stature as self-assurance slowly leaks from his arrogant frame.[20] To Samson's first oblique taunts he replies with the boisterous confidence of an overbearing bully. "Dost thou already single me" (1092), he protests in mock-disbelief, and then goes on to declaim haughtily that it would be dishonorable for him to fight with a blind man, particularly one, he jibes, who smells so bad (here the bully may be seen glancing about to ensure that all appreciate the joke). Samson then challenges Harapha openly, offering a duel in which, armed with only an "Oak'n staff," he will oppose the giant in all his "gorgeous arms" (1119–23). Harapha is somewhat taken aback and stands on his dignity, shocked that Samson would "thus disparage glorious arms / Which greatest Heroes have in battel worn" (1130–31). On the surface, this challenge does seem a bit foolhardy for a blind man. It gains credence, however, if one recalls Milton's often-repeated expression of confidence in the efficacy of the single blow from an arm guided by righteousness—the "two-handed engine" in "Lycidas," for example, which "Stands ready to smite once, and smite no more," or Abdiel's "noble stroke" (6.189) that felled Satan. Again, when Michael and Satan prepare to clash, "Uplifted imminent one stroke they aim'd / That might determine, and not need repeate" (6.317–18), and indeed "one stroke" of Michael's sword is all that is needed. Milton's God helps those who help themselves, of course; thus the conditions that Samson prescribes for the encounter are cleverly designed to give a single blow every chance of success:

> Therefore without feign'd shifts let be assign'd
> Some narrow place enclos'd, where sight may give thee,
> Or rather flight, no great advantage on me. (1116–18)

Samson, of course, does not disclose his tactics at the time; only when Harapha retreats do we discover what Samson had in mind, as he taunts the defeated giant with a threat to "with one buffet lay thy structure low" (1239).

20. Anthony Low, *The Blaze of Noon*, pp. 158–59. Low finds him in the tradition of the "Renaissance comic braggart." Nicolson, *A Reader's Guide*, p. 367, calls him "a taunting braggart prize-fighter, who has come to gloat over a fallen champion." On the other hand, Don Cameron Allen, *The Harmonious Vision*, pp. 91–92, finds Harapha's first speech "that of a genuinely valorous man" who speaks "honestly and generously."

In responding to Samson's first challenge, Harapha, suspecting that his opponent will have more than an "Oak'n staff" in his corner, accuses him of calling upon "some Magicians Art" (1133) to even the apparently unfair odds. Samson disclaims any such skills, and the giant, now somewhat uneasy, falls back on his reputation; a prisoner of war, he protests, is "no worthy match / For valour to assail, nor by the sword / Of noble Warriour, so to stain his honour" (1164–66). On being challenged a second time he becomes visibly agitated and lashes out at Samson as "A Murtherer, a Revolter, and a Robber" (1180). From his earlier, almost reasonable, condescension at the idea of fighting a blind man or a prisoner, he is now reduced to impugning the reputation of his challenger to hide what is evidently a growing fear. He would apparently prefer to exchange insults rather than blows. When "singled" once again, he responds weakly that it would be beneath his social standing; "no man of arms will deign," he says, to fight with "a Slave enrol'd" (1224–26). Harapha then withdraws, his cowardice revealed beneath all that talk of valor, honor, and glory. "His Giantship" stalks off to report these indignities to the Philistine lords, like some sulking schoolboy threatening to "tell on" his tormentor. His final remark amounts to a blustering "You'll regret this," unmasking all his feebleness of spirit and impotence of arm.

Critics have suggested that the encounter between Samson and Harapha has overtones of a confrontation between Puritan and Royalist soldiers.[21] Milton may well have called upon his memory of the God-fearing troopers of the Army of Saints as he fashioned his image of Samson, but he also had in mind those other soldiers of God, the loyal angels of *Paradise Lost*, and this most dramatically in the quality and consequences of Samson's obedience. Like Michael and Gabriel, Samson finds his strength insufficient to accomplish his divinely appointed task, that of delivering Israel from the "Philistine yoke" (39). Like Raphael, his efforts seem futile from the start—the Israelites do not have the courage to follow him to freedom, and even his final sacrifice fails to liberate them. Like the angels again, he finally obeys the word of God with no concern for life or honor and with no regard for prospects of defeat or victory. Unlike them, however, Samson must struggle with his flawed nature to achieve a spiritual state that makes obedience possible. Unlike them again, he despairs over his failures—he

21. DiSalvo, "'The Lord's Battells,'" p. 52.

doubts, regrets, and longs for death to end his suffering. Further, he hears no explicit command thundering from the mouth of God, only that inner voice he must accept on faith. He is a man, not a god, and so must overcome formidable obstacles to emulate the angels.

The angelic nature is to be "absolutely obedient to God in all things,"[22] so they obey without question. They are created with free will, of course, and hence have choice; but there is no evidence, save for Gabriel's mild complaint about the corporality of his sentinels, that they ever think twice about the commands of the Almighty. So in union are they with the Godhead that when they obey him, it is never *against* their will; there can be no qualifications or doubts for those so empty of self-concern that God's will indeed *is* their own and angelic thought but an instant echo of the Deity's. For them, the will is the deed. Should an angel disobey but once, he

> breaks union, and that day
> Cast out from God and blessed vision, falls
> Into utter darkness, deep ingulft, his place
> Ordaind without redemption, without end. (*PL* 5.612–15)

For an angel to so much as entertain doubt would cloud the perfection of that bond between his mind and the Almighty's. Thus, even in the face of apparent defeat, when the loyal angels fall before the fury of the cannonade, there is no wavering, no irresolution or perplexity about an omnipotent Lord who permits them to be so humiliated. They seek only to obey, and so quickly devise an alternate means to continue their mission. It must be admitted that the hurling of hills may not seem a tactic particularly well designed to drive the rebels "from God and bliss" (6.52), as they had been ordered, but it is at least a temporary expedient, illustrating their determination to persevere despite the setback.

For fallen man, obedience is a very different matter, perseverance more of a problem. His is a flawed nature and his bond with the Almighty imperfect to begin with; doubts and questions arise as a matter of course to a being whose understanding is discursive rather than intuitive. Hence God can be more merciful with human than he can with angelic disobedience, like a father who can forgive behavior in a toddling child that he would condemn in an

22. *De Doct-ina Christiana*, *YP*, 6:345.

older brother. Flawed man can only aspire to that complete surrender of will and reason attained by angels; he must struggle to achieve that emptying of self which makes them a perfect instrument of the divine will. This is no easy task, as Milton knew well. Obedience was a constant problem with the Parliamentary forces, and the New Model went through a long period of inner conflict and debate over its allegiance to King or Commons, Presbyterian or Independent. During the Anarchy, it took a serious examination of conscience to decide whether Parliament or the army was the godly party; and if conscience dictated the latter, then one had to choose between Fleetwood, Lambert, or Monk. The self intervenes, clouding the issue with thoughts of safety, family, or gain, and frail man falters. In *Samson Agonistes* Milton dramatizes the anguish, despair, and triumph of one who must struggle with his fallen nature to achieve a spiritual state even approaching that of a Michael, who stands to receive his hopeless charge to expel the rebels from the plains of Heaven.

The play opens with Samson, as we have seen, wrapped in self-pity and paralyzed by guilt, but by the time Harapha retires "somewhat crest-fall'n" (1244) the once-despondent slave is a different man. Composed, even humble, he is angry at no one. Of most importance, he is no longer angry at himself. Purged of despair over blindness and his servile state, relieved of anguish at his lost privilege as "a person separate to God" (21), he no longer prays for death but awaits it calmly, as he would a "friend" (1263). He stands ready, emptied of self, to receive the divine command, which comes as "rouzing motions" that dispose his thoughts "To something extraordinary" (1382–83).[23] In obeying that voice, he does indeed end his suffering and fulfill the destiny foretold him; but he first had to surrender his despair and accept his exile before he could realize that final triumph.

Samson's exchange with the Philistine officer defines his state of mind and demonstrates the victory over self. Blindness is no

23. In the play the phenomena is foreshadowed by Samson's explanation for his marriage to the woman of Timna: "what I motion'd was of God, I knew / From intimate impulse" (222–23). In contrast, the marriage to Dalila received no such divine sanction, for as he says, "I thought it lawful from my former act" (231). In consequence, he escapes the treachery of the first but is snared by the second. Don Cameron Allen, *The Harmonious Vision*, p. 94, compares Samson's obedience to that of Christ in *Paradise Regained*, whom "some strong motion" led into the wilderness (1 : 290–91) for reasons he could not fathom.

longer a problem for him, it is hardly mentioned; and his defiance shows him no more enthralled by despair. Once again conscious of his status as a Nazarite, he vows to do nothing that would sully that name. But there is no rancor in his responses—he no longer hates his captors. Roland Frye has observed that in Medieval and Renaissance iconography Michael always appears sweetly composed during his combat with Satan, exhibiting no anger or indignation at the iniquity of the Devil; he "seems serenely aloof and spiritually at peace" as he does God's bidding.[24] Samson cannot achieve that perfect composure—his replies to the officer are not without some heat—but he exhibits none of that fierce desire for revenge so prominent in the account of Judges; he complains only that the Philistine insistence robs him of his newfound "internal peace" (1334).

The exchange with the officer serves yet another purpose: it illustrates that Samson has a choice, "If I obey them, / I do it freely" (1372–73), and that if it were left to him, he would most emphatically choose *not to go*. Indeed, the prospect of performing for the worshippers of Dagon is grossly repugnant to him. An appearance at the temple, he tells the officer, would be for him "The worst of all indignities" (1341). When the fearful chorus tries to reason with him, he is even more adamant, declaring that a Nazarite would be "prostituting" his gifts by appearing "in place abominable." There is no mistaking his mind: "Besides, how vile, contemptible, ridiculous, / What act more execrably unclean, prophane?" (1354–62). To obey the officer would "displease / God for the fear of Man, and Man prefer, / Set God behind" (1373–75) and incur the anger of a jealous Deity. Milton makes it abundantly clear that Samson's sudden change of mind is in response to those "rouzing motions" and not to any importunities by the timid chorus or further threats from the officer, who returns only after the decision is made. It is also clear that when Samson rises to accompany the officer he does so in spite of his better judgment, he obeys though every fiber of his being cries out against it. He leaves assuring the Israelites that he will do nothing unworthy of "Our God, our Law, my Nation, or my self" (1425), though he had but moments before declared his conviction that to submit to the Philistines' commands would be a disgrace to all four.

24. *Milton's Imagery and the Visual Arts*, pp. 53–54.

No celestial being is called upon to struggle so with his conscience or to act against conviction. The angels' "military obedience" is an expression of the perfect bond that unites them with the Godhead, not a triumph over doubts about His judgment or uncertainty about their ability to fulfill His commands. When God decrees that all shall worship the Son, those who obey do so in happy accord, and those who refuse act with equal conviction. There are no doubts on either side, no wrestling with conflicting allegiances, no struggle with conscience or anguish over inadequacy. They either embrace God's will or pursue their own, and the battle lines are drawn by that issue alone. Samson, unlike the angels, must struggle with his frailties to do God's bidding; thus his triumph over self to become an instrument of divine intent is more heroic in human eyes, and the example of his obedience a surer guide for the race.

Samson Agonistes is Milton's final word on warriors. Over the years, from that first encounter with them, when the sheltered scholar had addressed the "Captain or Colonel" in the language of his learning, Pliny and Euripedes, the forge of experience had shaped his vision until he could finally offer his times a powerfully wrought image of the faithful soldier of God.

DiSalvo argues that in the confrontation between Samson and Harapha, Milton explores "the relationship between faith and action."[25] He does so, I would add, by presenting a dramatic contrast, not between those who act and those who "only stand and waite," but between the causes and consequences of two modes of action. Milton condemns a certain breed of warrior, again not because he is a warrior, but because he serves a false god, and is therefore himself false. Those who enter the struggle under such banners will be corrupted by the very cause they espouse; the meanness of their purpose will distort their values until they are unwilling to fight except for some shallow personal honor, and then only when it is convenient, picking and choosing opponents who will enhance their name. The forces of evil are formidable, like Harapha, but they carry within them the seed of their own defeat, an inability to dedicate their arms to any cause larger than themselves. In this regard, Harapha is a cousin of Satan, congratulating himself over the success of his cannon when he should be pursuing his tactical advantage. The true warfaring Christian an-

25. "'The Lord's Battells,'" p. 53.

swers to the word of God, whether it comes to him thundering from a cloud or in the mysterious form of "rouzing motions," and he obeys whether it directs him to some seemingly fruitless task or sends him to certain destruction. In the end, allegiance to a false god will only sap a warrior's courage, erode his will, and render his strength a feeble instrument, powerless in the face of a righteous Saint-in-Arms.

Afterword

. . . calm of mind, all passion spent.

A thousand volumes attest to the elusiveness of the poet of *Paradise Lost*. His voice is so varied that one can catch in the lines only quick glimpses of a protean figure surfacing in one form, only to be replaced in sudden succession by yet another. He is to be heard in Satan's defiance and God's commands, in Samson's lament and Eve's love song, in Adam's doubt and Abdiel's loyalty; he can be sensed in Christ's patience, in the awesome sweep of Michael's arm, and perhaps even in the sensuality of Belial. The artist, like God in his universe, is everywhere in his work—*and nowhere.*

The generations of scholars, sensing that the voice represents one human spirit reaching out to touch another, seek to know him better; but as they search out the man in his lines, what they so often see mirrored back is the image of their own best selves: Charles Williams finds a gentle Christian, moved by love and faith; William Empson, a troubled mind, grappling with the spectacle of an unjust God; William Riley Parker, a good, gray poet, dreaming of his first love; B. A. Wright, a man of peace, lashing out at the madness of war; Christopher Hill, an impassioned revolutionary, incensed by economic and social injustice; Arnold Stein, the conscious artist, rising to the challenge of the masters of his tale; Joan Webber, a searching spirit, seeking solace and truth in the warm cave of self. This rich response is the ultimate tribute to the poet, for each image is in fact a true one; his poetry embraces them all. Every reader, in seeking to know the poet better, has in the end come to know himself.

What, then, is to be said of the John Milton of history, Mary Powell's husband, Cromwell's secretary, Salmasius's adversary, the scourge of kings and sightless champion of the Army of Saints? Of what value is he to this endeavor? The artist silvers the mirror of his art with the metal of all his days, an amalgam of spirit, flesh, and mind distilled from the base matter of his life. He may reveal in his writing an inner life of which his neighbor had little knowledge, or he may choose to conceal much he would not have the world to know, and this with some success despite our second-guessing at his unpremeditated lines. But one of Milton's fearless mind would never lead a reader astray. What he is in his art, he was in his life, though transfigured; and while we have but a scattered chronicle of that life, those who search out the man in his lines can surely reconcile the poetry with that chronicle. The man we find may not always be to our liking—the granaries of a poet's art can store a strange and separate seed—but his history cannot be denied. One enters the realm of Clio here, a demanding mistress who asks accountability to her laws, particularly of those who stand in awe of the artist or who have fallen under the spell he weaves; for neither state of mind encourages that disinterested reflection she expects of her servants.

While Clio can be a killjoy at times, a probing of the chronicle, however fragmentary, will serve the scholar well, for the days of John Milton of London were a rich resource for the poet of *Paradise Lost*. This study can only begin to explore the mystery of how the one flows into the other, of how the life is transfigured into art. I write in the fond hope that younger and more agile minds may find in these pages some cause to search further for that elusive stream of creativity.

Works Cited

Primary Sources

Abbott, Wilbur Cortez, ed. *The Writings and Speeches of Oliver Cromwell.* 4 vols. Cambridge: Harvard University Press, 1937–1947.

Archer, Elias. *A True Relation of the Marchings of the Red Trained Bands of Westminster, the Green Auxiliaries of London, and the Yellow Auxiliaries of the Tower Hamlets, under the command of Sir William Waller, from Monday the 16. of Octob. to Wednesday the 20. of Decemb. 1643.* By Elias Archer Lieftenant to Captain William Archer. London, Printed for Edward Blackmore, dwelling at the Angel in Pauls-Churchyard, 1643. BM 101. b. 64.

Aristotle. *Poetics.* Translated by Gerald F. Else. Ann Arbor: University of Michigan Press, 1967.

Barriffe, William. *Militarie Discipline: or the yong artillery man. Wherein is discoursed and showne the Postures both of Musket and Pike: the exactest way, etc. Together with the Motions which are to be used, in the exercising of a Foot-company. With divers and severall formes and figures of Battlee; with their reducements; very necessary for all such as are studious in the Art Military.* London, 1635. Guildhall Library, London, Mss. A. 9. 1. no. 23.

B[arriffe], W[illiam]. "The Names, Dignities and Places of All the Collonells, Lieutenant-Collonels, Serjant Majors, Captaines, Quartermasters, Lieutenants, and Ensignes of the City of London . . . ." London, 1642. BM 669. f. 6. (10).

Benet, Stephen Vincent. *John Brown's Body.* Garden City, N.Y.: Doubleday, Doran, 1928.

Browne, Sir Thomas. *The Works of Sir Thomas Browne.* 2 vols. Edited by Geoffrey Keynes. London: Faber and Gwyer, 1928.

Burton, Robert. *The Anatomy of Melancholy.* 3 vols. Edited by A. R. Shilleto. London: G. Bell and Sons, 1926.

Calendar of State Papers, Domestic Series, Commonwealth. 13 vols. 1875. Reprint. Edited by Mary Ann Everett Green. Vaduz: Kraus Reprints, 1965.

Dale, T. C. *The Inhabitants of London in 1638. Edited from MS 272 in the Lambeth Palace Library.* London: Society of Genealogists, 1931.

Dante. *De Monarchia.* Translated by Herbert W. Schneider. New York: Liberal Arts Press, 1957.

Dio Cassius. *Dio's Roman History.* Translated by Earnest Cary. The Loeb Classical Library, vol. 7. London: William Heinemann, 1924.

"The Ensignes of the Regiments of the Rebellious Citty of London . . . taken as they marched into Finsbury Feilds, being their last General Muster, Tuesday, Sept 26th, 1643." London, 1643. Guildhall Library, London, A. 6. 5. no. 6 in 14.

French, J. Milton. *The Life Records of John Milton.* 5 vols. New Brunswick: Rutgers University Press, 1949–1958.

Gardiner, Samuel Rawson, ed. *The Constitutional Documents of the Puritan Revolution, 1625–1660.* 3d ed. Oxford: Clarendon Press, 1962.

Herbert, George. *The Works of George Herbert.* Edited by F. E. Hutchinson. Oxford: Oxford University Press, 1959.

Josephus, Flavius. *The Antiquities of the Jews.* Translated by William Whiston. London: George Routledge & Son, n.d.

Lithgow, William. *The Present Surveigh of London and England's State; containing a Typographical Description of all the Particular Forts, Brestworks and Trenches newly erected round the Citie, on both sides of the River, with the several Fortifications thereof.* London, 1643.

Machiavelli, Niccollo. *The Discourses of Niccollo Machiavelli.* 2 vols. Translated by Leslie J. Waller, S.J. London: Routledge and Kegan Paul, 1950.

"The Manner of the March and Embattelling of the Trayned Bands and Auxiliaries of the City of London . . . performed on Tuesday the 26. of September 1643." London, 1643. BM 102. a. 14.

May, Thomas. *The History of the Parliament of England, which began November 3, 1640, with a Short and Necessary View of Some Precedent Years.* London, 1647.

Milton, John. *Milton: Poems and Selected Prose.* Edited by Marjorie Hope Nicolson. New York: Bantam, 1962.

———. *Complete Prose Works of John Milton.* 8 vols. Edited by Don M. Wolfe et al. New Haven: Yale University Press, 1953–1983.

———. *John Milton, Complete Poems and Major Prose.* Edited by Merritt Y. Hughes. New York: Odyssey, 1957.

———. *John Milton: "Paradise Lost: Books I-II."* Edited by John Broadbent. Cambridge: Cambridge University Press, 1972.

———. *John Milton: "Paradise Lost: Books V-VI."* Edited by Robert Hodge and Isabel MacCaffrey. Cambridge: Cambridge University Press, 1975.

———. *Paradise Regained.* Edited by E. H. Blakeney. London: Scholartis Press, 1932.

———. *The English Poems of John Milton.* Edited by H. C. Beeching. Introduction by Charles Williams. The World's Classics, vol. 182. London: Oxford University Press, 1940.

———. *The Works of John Milton.* 18 vols. Edited by Frank A. Patterson et al. New York: Columbia University Press, 1931–1938.

More, Sir Thomas. *Utopia.* Translated by H. V. S. Ogden. Arlington Heights, Ill.: AHM, 1949.

Rabelais, Francois. *Gargantua and Pantagruel: Selections.* Arlington Heights, Ill.: AHM, 1966.

Raikes, G. A. *The Ancient Vellum Book of the Honourable Artillery Company.* London: Richard Bentley, 1890.

"September 29, 1642. The Persons to whom the Militia of the Citie of London is Committed, for saftie of the said Citie, have thought fit, and hereby Declare." London, 1642. BM 669. f. 6. (79).

Tacitus. *The Complete Works of Tacitus.* Edited by Moses Hadas. New York: The Modern Library, 1942.

Tasso, Torquato. *Jerusalem Delivered.* Translated by Edward Fairfax. London: Centaur Press, 1962.

Ward, Robert. *Animadversions of Warre; or, A Militarie Magazine of the*

Truest Rules, and Ablest Instructions, for the Managing of Warre. London, 1639.

SECONDARY SOURCES

Adair, John. *Cheriton, 1644: The Campaign and the Battle*. Kineton, Warwick: Roundtree Press, 1973.

Adamson, J. H. "The Creation." In *Bright Essence: Studies in Milton's Theology*, edited by William B. Hunter, Jr., et al. Salt Lake City: University of Utah Press, 1971.

———. "The War in Heaven: Milton's Version of the Merkabah." *JEGP* 57 (1958): 690–703.

Allen, Don Cameron. *The Harmonious Vision: Studies in Milton's Poetry*. Baltimore: Johns Hopkins University Press, 1954.

Arieti, Silvano. *Creativity: The Magic Synthesis*. New York: Basic Books, 1976.

———. *Interpretation of Schizophrenia*. New York: Basic Books, 1974.

Ashley, Maurice. *The Greatness of Oliver Cromwell*. London: Hodder and Stoughton, 1957.

Ashton, Robert. *The English Civil War: Conservatism and Revolution*. London: Weidenfeld and Nicolson, 1978.

Barker, Arthur E. *Milton and the Puritan Dilemma, 1641–1660*. Toronto: University of Toronto Press, 1942.

Barron, Frank. *Creativity and Personal Freedom*. New York: Van Nostrand, 1968.

———. *The Shaping of Personality: Conflict, Choice, and Growth*. New York: Harper, 1979.

———. "Diffusion, Integration, and Enduring Attention in the Creative Process." In *The Study of Lives: Essays on Personality in Honor of Henry A. Murray*, edited by Robert W. White. New York: Atherton, 1963.

Barzun, Jacques. *Clio and the Doctors: Psycho-History, Quanto-History, & History*. Chicago: University of Chicago Press, 1974.

———. "Biography and Criticism—A Misalliance Disputed." *Critical Inquiry* 1 (March 1975): 479–96.

Bate, W. Jackson. *Samuel Johnson*. New York: Harcourt, Brace, Jovanovitch, 1977.

Berry, Boyd M. *Process of Speech: Puritan Religious Writing and "Paradise Lost."* Baltimore: Johns Hopkins University Press, 1976.

Boswell, Jackson Campbell. *Milton's Library*. New York: Garland, 1975.

Bowra, C. M. *From Virgil to Milton*. London: Macmillan, 1948.

Brett-James, Norman G. "The Fortifications of London in 1642/3."In *London Topographical Record*. Vol. 14. Edited by Walter H. Godfrey. Cambridge: Cambridge University Press, 1928.

Broadbent, J. B. *Some Graver Subject: An Essay on "Paradise Lost."* New York: Barnes and Noble, 1960.

Brunton, D., and D. H. Pennington. *The Members of the Long Parliament*. London: Allen and Unwin, 1954.

Cole, Charles Woolsey. *Colbert and a Century of French Mercantilism.* New York: Columbia University Press, 1932.

Cope, Jackson I. *The Metaphorical Structure of "Paradise Lost."* Baltimore: Johns Hopkins University Press, 1962.

Crump, Galbraith Miller. *The Mystical Design of "Paradise Lost."* Lewisburg: Bucknell University Press, 1975.

Daiches, David. *Milton.* London: Hutchinson's Universal Library, 1964.

Darbishire, Helen, ed. *The Early Lives of Milton.* London: Constable, 1965.

Davies, Godfrey. *The Restoration of Charles II, 1658–1660.* Oxford: Oxford University Press, 1969.

DiSalvo, Jackie. "'The Lords Battells': 'Samson Agonistes' and the Puritan Revolution." In *Milton Studies IV*, edited by James D. Simmonds. Pittsburgh: University of Pittsburgh Press, 1973.

Dorian, Donald. "A Study of Milton's Ideas of War". Master's Thesis, Columbia University, 1929.

Eliot, T. S. "Milton (1947)." In *Milton Criticism: Selections from Four Centuries*, edited by James Thorpe. New York: Collier Books, 1969.

Empson, William. *Milton's God.* Norfolk, Conn.: New Directions, 1961.

Fallon, Robert Thomas. "Filling the Gaps: New Perspectives on Mr. Secretary Milton." In *Milton Studies XII*, edited by James D. Simmonds. Pittsburgh: University of Pittsburgh Press, 1979.

———. "John Milton and the Honourable Artillery Company." *Milton Quarterly* 9 (May 1975): 49–51.

———. "Milton's 'defenseless doors': The Limits of Irony." *Milton Quarterly* 13 (December 1979): 146–51.

———. "Milton in the Anarchy, 1659–1660: A Question of Consistency." *Studies in English Literature* 21 (Winter 1981): 123–46.

Ferry, Anne. *Milton's Epic Voice: The Narrator in "Paradise Lost."* Cambridge: Harvard University Press, 1963.

Firth, Charles Harding. *The Last Years of the Protectorate, 1656–1658.* 2 vols. 1909. Reprint. New York: Russell and Russell, 1964.

———. *Cromwell's Army.* London: Methuen, 1921.

———. "The Raising of the Ironsides." *Transactions of the Royal Historical Society.* Vol. 3. London: Longmans, Green, 1899.

Fish, Stanley. *Surprised by Sin: The Reader in "Paradise Lost."* New York: St. Martin's Press, 1967.

Fixler, Michael. *Milton and the Kingdoms of God.* London: Faber and Faber, 1964.

Fraser, Antonia. *Cromwell, The Lord Protector.* New York: Knopf, 1974.

Freeman, James A. *Milton and the Martial Muse: "Paradise Lost" and European Traditions of War.* Princeton: Princeton University Press, 1980.

Frye, Roland Mushat. *God, Man, and Satan: Patterns of Christian Thought in "Paradise Lost," "Pilgrim's Progress," and the Great Theologians.* Princeton: Princeton University Press, 1960.

———. *Milton's Imagery and the Visual Arts: Iconographic Tradition in the Epic Poems.* Princeton: Princeton University Press, 1978.

Gardiner, Samuel Rawson. *History of the Great Civil War, 1642–1649.* 4 vol. 1893. Reprint. New York: AMS Press, 1965.

———. *History of the Commonwealth and Protectorate, 1649–1656.* 4 vols. London: Longmans, Green, 1903.

Gilbert, Allan H. *On the Composition of "Paradise Lost": A Study of the Ordering and Insertion of Material.* Chapel Hill: University of North Carolina Press, 1947.

———. "The Theological Basis of Satan's Rebellion and the Function of Abdiel on *Paradise Lost.*" *Modern Philology* 15 (1942): 19–42.

Gregory, E. R. "'Lift not thy spear against the Muses bowre': Essay in Historical Explication." *Milton Quarterly* 11 (December 1977): 112–13.

Haller, William. *Liberty and Reformation in the Puritan Revolution.* New York: Columbia University Press, 1955.

———. *The Rise of Puritanism.* New York: Columbia University Press, 1957.

Hanford, James Holly. *A Milton Handbook.* New York: Appleton, 1954.

———. *John Milton, Englishman.* New York: Crown, 1949.

———. "Milton and the Art of War." In *John Milton: Poet and Humanist: Essays by James Holly Hanford.* Cleveland: Case Western Reserve University Press, 1966.

Harris, William O. "Despair and 'Patience as the Truest Fortitude' in *Samson Agonistes.*" *English Literary History* 30 (1963): 107–20.

Hazlitt, William. "On Shakespeare and Milton." In *Milton Criticism: Selections from Four Centuries*, edited by James Thorpe. New York: Collier Books, 1950.

Hexter, J. H. *The Reign of King Pym.* Cambridge: Harvard University Press, 1941.

———. "The Problem of the Presbyterian-Independents." *The American Historical Review* 44 (1938): 29–49.

Hill, Christopher. *Change and Continuity in 17th Century England.* London: Weidenfeld and Nicolson, 1974.

———. *Milton and the English Revolution.* New York: Viking, 1977.

Hosmer, James K. *The Life of Young Sir Henry Vane.* Boston: Houghton Mifflin, 1888.

Hughes, Merritt Y. *Ten Perspectives on Milton.* New Haven: Yale University Press, 1965.

———. "Milton and the Sense of Glory." *Philological Quarterly* 28 (1949): 107–24.

———. "The Christ of *Paradise Regained* and the Renaissance Heroic Tradition." *Studies in Philology* 35 (1938): 257–77.

Hughes, Merritt Y., ed. *A Variorum Commentary on the Poems of John Milton.* 4 vols. New York: Columbia University Press, 1970–1975.

Hunter, William B., Jr. "Milton and Richard Cromwell." *English Language Notes* 3 (1966): 252–59.

———. "Milton's Arianism Reconsidered." In *Bright Essence: Studies in Milton's Theology*, edited by William B. Hunter, Jr., et al. Salt Lake City: University of Utah Press, 1971.

———. "The War in Heaven: The Exaltation of the Son." In *Bright Essence: Studies in Milton's Theology*, edited by William B. Hunter, Jr., et al. Salt Lake City: University of Utah Press, 1971.

Hunter, William B., Jr., C. A. Patrides, and J. H. Adamson, eds. *Bright Essence: Studies in Milton's Theology*. Salt Lake City: University of Utah Press, 1971.

Hyman, Lawrence W. *The Quarrel Within: Art and Morality in Milton's Poetry*. Port Washington, N.Y.: Kennikat Press, 1972.

Jung, C. G. "Psychology and Literature." In *Modern Man in Search of a Soul*. New York: Harcourt, Brace, 1933.

Kastor, Frank. *Milton and the Literary Satan*. Amsterdam: Rodopi N. V., 1974.

Kelley, Maurice. *"This Great Argument": A Study of "De Doctrina Christiana" as a Gloss upon "Paradise Lost."* Princeton: Princeton University Press, 1941.

Kermode, Frank. "A Moderate New Notion." *New York Times Book Review*, 5 March 1978, p. 10.

Kerrigan, William. *The Sacred Complex: On the Psychogenesis of "Paradise Lost."* Cambridge: Harvard University Press, 1983.

Kirkconnell, Watson. *The Celestial Cycle: The Theme of "Paradise Lost" in World Literature with Translations of the Major Analogues*. Toronto: University of Toronto Press, 1952.

Kishlansky, Mark A. *The Rise of the New Model Army*. Cambridge: Cambridge University Press, 1979.

Knight, G. Wilson. *Chariot of Wrath: The Message of John Milton to Democracy at War*. London: Faber, 1942.

Kranidas, Thomas, ed. *New Essays on "Paradise Lost."* Berkeley: University of California Press, 1969.

Krause, F. Michael. *Milton's Samson and the Christian Tradition*. Princeton: Princeton University Press, 1963.

Labriola, Albert C. "'Thy Humiliation Shall Exalt': The Christology of *Paradise Lost*." In *Milton Studies XV*, edited by James D. Simmonds. Pittsburgh: University of Pittsburgh Press, 1981.

Labriola, Albert C., and Michael Lieb, eds. *"Eyes Fast Fixt": Current Perspectives in Milton Methodology. Milton Studies VII*. Pittsburgh: University of Pittsburgh Press, 1975.

Langton, Edward. *Satan, A Portrait: A Study of the Character of Satan Through the Ages*. London: Skeffington & Sons, 1945.

Le Comte, Edward. *Yet Once More: Verbal and Psychological Patterns in Milton*. New York: Liberal Arts Press, 1953.

Leavis, F. R. "Mr. Eliot and Milton." In *The Common Pursuit*. London: Chatto and Windus, 1962.

Lewalski, Barbara K. *Milton's Brief Epic: The Genre, Meaning, and Art of "Paradise Regained."* Providence: Brown University Press, 1966.

———. "Milton: Political Beliefs and Polemical Methods, 1659–60." *PMLA* 74(1959): 191–202.

Lewis, C. S. *A Preface to "Paradise Lost."* Oxford: Oxford University Press, 1942.

Lieb, Michael, and John T. Shawcross, eds. *Achievements of the Left Hand: Essays on the Prose of John Milton*. Amherst: University of Massachusetts Press, 1974.

Lieb, Michael. *Poetics of the Holy: A Reading of "Paradise Lost."* Chapel Hill: University of North Carolina Press, 1981.

———. *The Dialectics of Creation: Patterns of Birth and Regeneration in "Paradise Lost."* Amherst: University of Massachusetts Press, 1970.

———. "Further Thoughts on Satan's Journey Through Chaos." *Milton Quarterly* 12 (December 1978): 126–33.

Locke, Richard. "The Literary View." *New York Times Book Review*, 10 Jan 1978, p. 3; and 26 Feb 1978, p. 3.

Low, Anthony. *The Blaze of Noon: A Reading of "Samson Agonistes.* "New York: Columbia University Press, 1974.

Manning, Brian. *The English People and the English Revolution, 1640–1649*. London: Heinemann, 1976.

Martz, Louis L. *Poet of Exile: A Study of Milton's Poetry*. New Haven: Yale University Press, 1980.

Masson, David. *The Life of John Milton*. 6 vols. 1859–1880. Reprint. New York: Peter Smith, 1946.

———. *The Quarrel Between the Earl of Manchester and Oliver Cromwell*. Westminster: Nichols and Sons, 1875.

Mengert, James G. "Styling the Strife of Glory: The War in Heaven." Unpublished paper delivered at the Milton Tercentenary Conference, University of Wisconsin—Milwaukee, 1974.

Miller, David M. *John Milton: Poetry*. Twayne English Author Series. Boston: Twayne, 1978.

Mohl, Ruth. *John Milton and His Commonplace Book*. New York: Frederick Unger, 1969.

Mulder, John R. "The Narrator in *Paradise Lost*." Unpublished paper delivered at the Milton Tercentenary Conference, University of Wisconsin—Milwaukee, 1974.

Nicolson, Marjorie Hope. "Milton's Hell and the Phlegraean Fields." *University of Toronto Quarterly* 7 (1938): 500–513.

———. *John Milton: A Reader's Guide to His Poetry*. New York: Noonday, 1963.

Notestein, Wallace. "The Establishment of the Committee of Both Kingdoms." *American Historical Review* 17 (1912): 484–89.

Parker, William Riley. *Milton, A Biography*. 2 vols. Oxford: Clarendon Press, 1968.

———. "The Date of *Samson Agonistes* Again." In *Calm of Mind: Tercentenary Essays on "Paradise Regained" and "Samson Agonistes,"* edited by Joseph A. Wittreich, Jr. Cleveland: Case Western Reserve University Press, 1971.

Parnes, Sidney J., and Harold F. Harding, eds. *A Source Book for Creative Thinking*. New York: Scribner's, 1962.

Patrick, J. Max. "Milton's Revolution Against Rime, and Some of Its Implications." In *Milton and the Art of Sacred Song*, edited by J. Max Patrick and Roger Sundell. Madison: University of Wisconsin Press, 1979.

———. "Significant Aspects of Milton State Papers." *Huntington Library Quarterly* 33 (1970): 321–30.

Patrides, C. A., ed. *Approaches to "Paradise Lost."* London: Edward Arnold, 1968.

Patrides, C. A. "The Godhead in *Paradise Lost.*" In *Bright Essence: Studies in Milton's Theology*, edited by William B. Hunter, Jr., et al. Salt Lake City: University of Utah Press, 1971.

Patterson, Annabel. *Marvell and the Civic Crown.* Princeton: Princeton University Press, 1978.

Pearl, Valerie. *London and the Outbreak of the Puritan Revolution.* Oxford: Oxford University Press, 1961.

———. "London's Counter-Revolution." In *The Interregnum: The Quest for Settlement, 1646–1660*, edited by G. E. Aylmer. London: Macmillan, 1972.

———. "Oliver St. John and the 'Middle Group' in the Long Parliament. August 1643-May 1644." *English Historical Review* 81 (1966): 508–15.

Peter, John. *A Critique of "Paradise Lost."* New York: Columbia University Press, 1960.

Pope, Elizabeth. *"Paradise Regained": The Tradition and the Poem.* New York: Russell and Russell, 1962.

Price, Alan F. "Incidental Imagery in *Areopagitica.*" *Modern Philology* 49 (1952): 217–22.

Prothero, G. W., and E. M. Lloyd. "The First Civil War, 1642–7." *The Cambridge Modern History*, 3:302–35.

Radzinowicz, Mary Ann. *Toward "Samson Agonistes": The Growth of Milton's Mind.* Princeton: Princeton University Press, 1978.

Raikes, G. A. *The History of the Honourable Artillery Company.* 2 vols. London: Richard Bentley, 1878.

Rajan, Balachandra. *"Paradise Lost" and the Seventeenth Century Reader.* New York: Oxford University Press, 1948.

Raleigh, Walter. *Milton.* London: Edward Arnold, 1900.

Revard, Stella P. *The War in Heaven: "Paradise Lost" and the Tradition of Satan's Rebellion.* Ithaca: Cornell University Press, 1980.

———. "Milton's Critique of Heroic Warfare in '*Paradise Lost*' V and VI." *Studies in English Literature* 7 (Winter 1967): 119–39.

Richmond, Hugh H. *The Christian Revolutionary: John Milton.* Berkeley: University of California Press, 1974.

Rosner, Stanley, and Lawrence E. Apt, eds. *The Creative Experience.* New York: Grossman, 1970.

Roston, Murray. *Milton and the Baroque.* Pittsburgh: Pittsburgh University Press, 1980.

Rudrum, Alan, ed. *Milton: Modern Judgments.* London: Macmillan, 1968.

Ruthven, K. K. *Critical Assumptions.* Cambridge: Cambridge University Press, 1979.

Samuel, Irene. *Plato and Milton.* Cornell Studies in English, vol. 35. Ithaca: Cornell University Press, 1947.

Sensabaugh, George F. *That Grand Whig, Milton.* Stanford: Stanford University Press, 1952.

Shawcross, John T. *With Mortal Voice: The Creation of "Paradise Lost."* Lexington: University of Kentucky Press, 1982.

———. "A Survey of Milton's Prose Works." In *Achievements of the Left Hand: Essays on the Prose of John Milton*, edited by Michael Lieb and John T. Shawcross. Amherst: University of Massachusetts Press, 1974.

———. "Irony as Tragic Effect: *Samson Agonistes* as the Tragedy of Hope." In *Calm of Mind: Tercentenary Essays on "Paradise Regained" and "Samson Agonistes,"* edited by Joseph A. Wittreich, Jr. Cleveland: Case Western Reserve University Press, 1971.

———. "The Chronology of Milton's Major Poems." *PMLA* 76 (1961): 345–58.

———. "The Hero of *Paradise Lost* One More Time." In *Milton and the Art of Sacred Song*, edited by J. Max Patrick and Roger Sundell. Madison: University of Wisconsin Press, 1979.

Skinner, B. F. *About Behaviorism*. New York: Knopf, 1974.

———. *Cumulative Record: A Selection of Papers*. 3d ed. New York: Appleton-Century-Crofts, 1972.

Smart, John S. *The Sonnets of Milton*. Glasgow: Miclehouse, Johnson, 1921.

Smith, Logan Pearsall. *Milton and His Modern Critics*. Oxford: Oxford University Press, 1940.

Solt, Leo F. *Saints in Arms: Puritanism and Democracy in Cromwell's Army*. Stanford: Stanford University Press, 1959.

Spencer, T. J. B. "*Paradise Lost*: The Anti-Epic." In *Approaches to "Paradise Lost,"* edited by C. A. Patrides. London: Edward Arnold, 1968.

Stein, Arnold. *Answerable Style: Essays on "Paradise Lost."* Minneapolis: University of Minnesota Press, 1953.

———. *Heroic Knowledge: An Interpretation of "Paradise Regained" and "Samson Agonistes."* Hamden, Conn.: Archon Books, 1965.

———. *The Art of Presence: The Poet and "Paradise Lost."* Berkeley: University of California Press, 1977.

Summers, Joseph H. "Milton and the Cult of Conformity." In *Milton: Modern Judgments*, edited by Alan Rudrum. London: Macmillan, 1968.

———. *The Muse's Method: An Introduction to "Paradise Lost."* London: Chatto and Windus, 1962.

Sundell, Roger H. "The Prologues in *Paradise Lost*: Progress of a Prophet and His Vision." Unpublished paper delivered at the Milton Tercentenary Conference, University of Wisconsin—Milwaukee, 1974.

Swardson, H. R. *Poetry and the Fountain of Light*. London: Allen & Unwin, 1962.

Tayler, Edward W. *Milton's Poetry: Its Development in Time*. Pittsburgh: Duquesne University Press, 1979.

Thorpe, James. *John Milton: The Inner Life*. San Marino: The Huntington Library, 1983.

Tillyard, E. M. W. *Milton*. London: Chatto and Windus, 1961.

———. *Shakespeare's History Plays*. New York: Macmillan, 1947.

———. *The Epic Stream in the English Novel.* London: Chatto and Windus, 1958.
———. "A Note on Milton's Humour." In *Studies in Milton.* London: Chatto & Windus, 1951.
———. "Milton and the Epics." In *The Miltonic Setting, Past and Present.* London: Chatto and Windus, 1938.
Toliver, Harold E. "The Splinter Coalition." In *New Essays on "Paradise Lost,"* edited by Thomas Kranidas. Berkeley: University of California Press, 1969.
Tuchman, Barbara. *A Distant Mirror: The Calamitous Fourteenth Century.* New York: Ballantine Books, 1978.
Underdown, Donald. *Pride's Purge: Politics in the Puritan Revolution.* Oxford: Clarendon Press, 1971.
Valency, Maurice. *In Praise of Love.* New York: Macmillan, 1961.
Wagenknecht, Edward. *The Personality of Milton.* Norman: University of Oklahoma Press, 1970.
Waldock, A. J. A. *"Paradise Lost" and Its Critics.* Cambridge: Cambridge University Press, 1962.
Walker, G. Goold. *The Honourable Artillery Company, 1537–1947.* Aldershot: Gale and Polden, 1954.
Walzer, Michael. *The Revolution of the Saints.* Cambridge: Cambridge University Press, 1965.
Webber, Joan M. *Milton and His Epic Tradition.* Seattle: University of Washington Press, 1979.
Weber, Burton Jasper. *Wedges and Wings: The Patterning of "Paradise Regained."* Carbondale: Southern Illinois University Press, 1975.
Wedgwood, C. V. *The Thirty Years War.* New Haven: Yale University Press, 1939.
Whiting, George Michael. *Milton's Literary Milieu.* New York: Russell and Russell, 1964.
Wilding, Michael. *Milton's "Paradise Lost."* Sydney: Sydney University Press, 1969.
———. "The Last of the Epics: The Rejection of the Heroic in *Paradise Lost* and *Hudibras.*" In *Restoration Literature: Critical Approaches,* edited by Harold Love. London: Methuen, 1972.
Williams, C. M. "The Anatomy of a Radical Gentleman: Henry Marten." In *Puritans and Revolutionaries: Essays in Seventeenth-Century History Presented to Christopher Hill,* edited by Donald Pennington and Keith Thomas. Oxford: Clarendon Press, 1978.
Williams, Charles. *The Figure of Beatrice.* London: Oxford University Press, 1943.
———. Introduction to *The English Poems of John Milton.* Edited by H. C. Beeching. The World's Classics, vol. 182. London: Oxford University Press, 1940.
Wittreich, Joseph A., ed. *Calm of Mind: Tercentenary Essays on "Paradise Regained" and "Samson Agonistes."* Cleveland: Case Western Reserve University Press, 1971.
Wolfe, Don M. *Milton in the Puritan Revolution.* New York: Thomas Nelson, 1941.

Woodhouse, A. S. P. *The Heavenly Muse: A Preface to Milton*, ed. Hugh MacCallum. Toronto: University of Toronto Press, 1972.

Woolrych, Austin. "Milton and Cromwell: 'A Short but Scandalous Night of Interruption'?" In *Achievements of the Left Hand: Essays on the Prose of John Milton*, edited by Michael Lieb and John T. Shawcross. Amherst: University of Massachusetts Press, 1974.

———. Introduction to vol. 7 of *Complete Prose Works of John Milton*. Edited by Robert W. Ayers. New Haven: Yale University Press, 1980.

Wooten, John. "The Metaphysics of Milton's Epic Burlesque Humor." In *Milton Studies XII*, edited by James D. Simmonds. Pittsburgh: University of Pittsburgh Press, 1979.

Worden, Blair. "Milton Among the Radicals." *Times Literary Supplement*, 2 December 1977, p. 1395.

Wright, B. A. *Milton's "Paradise Lost."* New York: Barnes and Noble, 1962.

Young, G. M. *Charles I and Cromwell: An Essay*. London: Rupert Hart-Davis, 1954.

Index

Abdiel, 134, 217–20, 228–29, 233, 243
Adam, 140, 145, 148, 156, 161, 185, 211–12, 215, 224
Adamson, J. H., 224
Agincourt, 38, 230
Anarchy, period of, 101, 107, 113–15, 246
Angels:
—loyal: and cannon, 237; obedience of, 212–15, 244–45; as soldiers, 144
—as military figures, 134–35
—as political figures, 136
—rebel: comic, 228; council in mid air, 187, 193, 143–44; council in Pandemonium, 136, 158–61; in Hell, 174–79; and pain, 229–30; as parody of man, 170
—relationship with Son, 225
Arianism, 170, 225
Arieti, Silvano, 18, 21
Ariosto, Lodovico, 10, 12
Aristotle, 204
Arminianism, 130
Arthur, Arthuriad, 37–39, 91–97, 132, 241–42
Artillery Garden, 35, 46, 55, 57
Ashley, Maurice, 79
Ashton, Robert, 23, 75, 78n, 88n
Austerlitz, 206

Babel, Tower of, 171
Bacon, Francis, 32
Barriffe, William: 46n; *Militarie Discipline*, 58–60
Barron, Frank, 18, 18n
Barzun, Jacques, 7, 19n, 169
Baxter, Richard, 80
Beelzebub, 158, 160, 162, 175
Behaviorism, 27
Belial, 158–60, 178, 180–81
Beverning, Hieronymous van, 190, 191, 199
Blake, Robert, Admiral, 141–42, 142n
Blake, William, 17
Booth, Sir George, 114, 121
Bordeaux, Antoine de, 146
Bowles, Edward, 83
Bowra, C. M., 139n, 222
Bradshaw, John, 102
Browne, Sir Thomas, 31
Buckingham, George Villiers, Duke of, 31, 38
Burton, Robert, 32
Butler, Samuel, *Hudibras*, 172
Byron, George Gordon, Lord, 32

Cardenas, Alphonso de, 146, 148
Chaos, 135, 143, 145, 147, 156, 200, 224
Charles I: and the church, 75; in custody, 86; execution, 86, 87, 90, 100, 101; and five members, 41, 47, 75n, 216; and HAC, 46; at Newark, 174; at Nottingham, 42–43, 53; at Reading, 44, 49; at Second Newbury, 80–81; source for Satan, 9; surrender, 84; and Thirty Years War, 30–31; and Treaty of Newport, 91; at Turnham Green; in Westminster Palace, 104
Charles II: 106, 115, 121–23; in France, 141–42, 146–47, 148; (Prince of Wales) and HAC, 46. *See also* Restoration
Chivalry, 205, 242, 242n. *See also* Milton, John, on
Christ: and David's throne, 193–94, 199; as God or man, 188, 198; as heir and king, 225; at Last Judgment, 179; and Parthia, 194–97; on pinnacle of Temple, 188, 198; and rejection of learning, 195, 198; and Rome, 196–97; and Satan, 186–98; as soldier, 144–45, 208, 211, 220; temptations of, 186–88; victor in Heaven, 145, 198. *See also* Son
Civil Wars: 36, 42–43, 89–90, 136, 213, 216, 225
—battles: Alton, 56; Basing House, 55–56; Brentford, 43, 44, 61; Chalgrove Field, 49; Cheriton, 48; Cropredy Bridge, 53; Edgehill, 43, 61, 80; First Newbury, 48; Gloucester, 49, 53, 55, 174; High

Wycombe, 49, 55; Lostwithiel, 174; Marston Moor, 44, 53, 67, 72, 76, 80, 92; Naseby, 83, 92; Roundway Down, 49, 52, 174; Second Newbury, 48, 49, 56, 77, 80–81, 87n, 213; Turnham Green, 43, 44, 47, 49, 54–55, 61, 63, 64
—operations: Arundel Castle, 44; Birmingham, 49; Colchester, 89; Hull, 124, 130; Kent, 48; Lichfield, 49; Newcastle, 76; Newport-Pagnell, 44
Clarendon, Edward Hyde, Earl, 219
Clio, 251
Colbert, Jean Baptiste, 190
Committee of Both Kingdoms, 77–78, 81, 83
Commonwealth, period of, 101
Council of State: 107n, 152, 161–62; Commonwealth, 101–3; Protectorate, 103–4, 119, 191
Crawford, Lawrence, Major-General, 76–77
Criticism: biographical, 7–8, 15n, 151; experiential, 9, 15–16, 22–30, 133, 164–66, 167; experiential analogies, 8, 149–53, 164, 173n; historical, 8, 9, 11, 15, 164; New, 8, 14; psychoanalytic, 16–19, 20, 21, 26, 27, 164; structuralist, 15
Cromwell, Oliver: 89; death, 106; dissolves Rump, 103, 162; Dutch negotiations, 191–92, 199; Dutch war, 159; French treaty, 141–46; in Ireland, 106; and Ironsides, 10, 67, 92, 95; as king, 108; as Lord Protector, 101, 103, 110, 161; and Manchester, 76–77, 81–82, 159, 213; at Marston Moor, 53, 67; at Naseby, 83; and New Model Army, 83, 108; and Pride's Purge, 91; source for Satan, 9, 10, 16, 127, 172–73; on war, 79–80; and Western Design, 107, 136. *See also* Milton, John, on
Cromwell, Richard, 101, 106
Ctesiphon, 194–96

Dagon, 237, 239, 240
Dante 129n
Davies, Godfrey, 23, 117n, 133n
Dell, William, 83
Devil, the, 167, 205
Diggers, 128
DiSalvo, Jackie, 237–38, 248
Dunkirk, 107, 142, 145–46, 149–50

Eden, 140, 156
Eliot, T. S., 13, 14
Empson, William, 22, 153, 172n, 227n, 251
Essex, Robert Devereux, Earl: 43, 47, 49, 66, 78, 81, 82, 94, 165; as Lord General, 50; and Parliamentary divisions, 50–53
Eve, 157, 161, 169, 200
Evil: as mirror (twin) of good, 68, 185–89, 199–201, 228, 234; powerful, 228, 234; self-defeating, 179–85, 230, 234. *See also* Devil; Satan
Experience and art:
—creative process, Chap. 1, 138–39, 164–66
—parallels between: Anglo-Dutch negotiations/Christ and Satan, 189–90, 198–99; argument for rebellion, Parliament/Satan, 219–20; battle, Puritan-Royalist/Samson-Harapha, 244; civil wars/war in Heaven, 140, 217; Council of State/council in Pandemonium, 152; Cromwell/Samson, 238, 241; Cromwell/Satan, 161–62, 172–73; Dunkirk/earth as foothold (bridgehead), 145–46, 149–50; governments, change in, 161–63; human warfare/war in Heaven, 216–34; Manchester/Belial, Mammon, 159; military obedience/obedience to God, 214–15, 248; Milton/Samson, 235; New Model Army/council in Pandemonium, 157; New Model Army/Samson, 235, 244, 249; Parliament, divisions/council in Pandemonium, 136, 152, 158–59; Parliamentary armies/defeated angels, 174; Philip IV/Satan, 144; Phlegraean Fields/Hell, 207; political structures, 152–64; Raphael/Admiral Blake, 142n; secondary attack/war in Heaven, 213; Spanish war/war of good vs. evil, 140–52 (balance of power, 146–49); temporal/spiritual battle, 28, 67, 70, 139–40, 151–52
Fairfax, Sir Thomas, General, 50, 76, 83, 89, 91, 106, 110

Ferry, Anne Davidson, 21
Firth, Charles Harding, 84
Fish, Stanley, 200, 237n
Fleetwood, Charles, General, 89, 110, 114–15, 246
Fowke, John, 88
France, treaty with, 107, 141, 146
Freeman, James A., 5, 10, 26n
Freud, Sigmund, Freudian, 17, 18, 21, 26, 27
Frye, Roland M., 10, 155n, 167n, 222n, 247

Gabriel, 140, 147, 184, 213, 215, 239
Gardiner, Samuel Rawson, 49, 53
Gettysburg, 177, 206, 209, 210n
Gill, Alexander, 32
Glastonbury Abbey, 93–94
God: as absolute monarch, 155; creation *egressus-regressus*, 224–27; creation ex deo, 224–27; and Dagon, 237, 240; description of, 222; glory of, 213, 221–27; laughter in Heaven, 169, 171–72; as Louis XIV, 223; and Michael, 211–15; obedience to, 211–15, 244–46; omnipotence, 170, 171, 180, 182, 207–10, 215–16; in *PR*, 208; predicts man's triumph, 148–49; one with Son, 225–27; war aims, 220–27; wicked, 22, 153.
Graves, Robert, 13

Haller, William, 67, 72n, 84
Hanford, James Holly, 10, 14, 39, 57, 61, 64, 70, 96, 158n
Harapha: challenged, 239; as chivalric knight, 132, 239; as Homeric hero, 241; and Samson, 240–44; and Satan, 239, 248; as soldier, 239
Harrington, Sir James, 56, 87n
Hartlib, Samuel, 60
Hazlitt, William, 168
Heaven, government of, 155–56, 163, 225–27. *See also* War in Heaven
Heimbach, Peter, 104n
Hell: government of, 156–64; parody of Heaven, 157, 163, 168–69
Herbert, George, 31
Hexter, J. H., 51, 75n
Hill, Christopher, 10, 11, 15n, 105n, 112, 113n, 216, 251
Hobson, John, 55–56, 60
Holles, Denzil, 43, 55–56, 60, 61
Holy Trinity, 170
Homer: 12, 16, 135, 165, 204, 234; as source for war in Heaven, 207–10, 217
Honourable Artillery Company, 45–48, 55, 56–60
Hopton, Sir Ralph, 44
Hotham, Sir John, 124, 130
Hughes, Merritt Y., 12, 195n, 221

Imagery, function:
—military: 4, 135–38; in early poetry, 32–39; disobedience-obedience, 137, 211–15; evil, definition of, 164–65, 172; evil, powerful, 137; evil, self-defeating, 181; as parody of warfare, 202–6; in prose, 68–71, 125–26; in war in Heaven, 227–28—political: 4, 135–38; disobedience-obedience, 163–64; evil, definition of, 155, 164–65, 172
Imagery, military, pervasive in *PL*, 134–35, 204
Independents: dominate New Model Army, 82–83; dominate war effort, 83; majority in Committee of Both Kingdoms, 78; and war, 75–76. *See also* Parliament, divisions
Ireton, Henry, 90–91, 85

James I, 30, 38
James II, as Duke of York, 46
Johnson, Samuel, 202, 222
Jones, Inigo, 31, 100
Jung, C. G., Jungian, 17, 26, 29, 138

Knight, G. Wilson, 10
Kris, Ernst, 26

Lambert, John, General, 89, 110, 113, 114–15, 116, 121, 246
Laud, William, archbishop of Canterbury, 41
Leavis, F. R., 13, 14
Lee, Robert E., General, 177, 209
Levellers, 106, 112, 219
Lewalski, Barbara, 186, 194n, 197
Lewis, C. S., 168, 170, 171, 182, 209
Lieb, Michael, 6, 161, 169

Lithgow, William, 48
Lockhart, William, 149
London: and civil wars, 40, 44–45; Committee for General Rising, 52, 66; Common Council, 48, 52; demonstrations, 40–41, 87–89; fortifications, 45, 48–49, 65; military situation, 1643, 49, 70; Militia Committee, 47; occupied by Monk, 115, 118; occupied by New Model Army, 44–45, 87; and parliamentary divisions, 1643, 50–51; and Parliamentary Puritans, 47; and Presbyterians, 88–89. *See also* Milton, John, on
Louis XIV, 142

Machiavelli, Niccolo, 39, 85, 132
MacKellar, Walter, 196
Major-Generals, rule of, 108, 109, 112
Mammon, 158–60
Manchester, Edward Montagu, Earl: 50, 82; and Cromwell, 76–77, 78, 81, 159; at Second Newbury, 48, 79–81, 213
Marathon, battle of, 230
Marten, Henry, 49, 51, 75n
Martz, Louis L., 235
Mary, Mother of Christ, 186
Masson, David, 10, 32, 54n, 79, 88
Mazarin, Cardinal, 141, 142
Michael: as commander, 134, 145, 148, 212, 246; as prophet, 127, 157, 179; and Satan, 229, 243, 247; as soldier, 184, 208, 211, 228; strength limited by God, 211–15, 244; as tutor, 212
Michelangelo, 164
Milton, Christopher, 53
Milton, John, on:
—chivalry, 93–96, 129–30, 132, 150, 241–42
—Cromwell, 63, 95, 108–12, 120–24, 127, 173
—good old cause, 133n
—governments, 119–24, 152n, 153–54, 157, 163, 217–20
—kings: 89, 96, 155, 251; Charles I, 152–53, 241–42; "single person," 114, 119, 120–24
—learning, 20, 64, 195
—London, 40, 54, 87–89
—New Model Army: 13, 63, 72–73, 79, 86, 90, 91, 95–96, 98, 109, 112–13, 116–20, 137, 205, 214, 251; conflict with Rump, 106, 116–20; and "short but scandalous night," 114n
—old age, 195, 195n, 236–37
—pacifism, antiwar, antimilitary, 2, 14, 22, 109, 111–12, 127–28, 135, 173, 194–95, 203. *See also* Pacifism
—Parliament(s): 54, 90–91, 112, 116–20, 153; Barebones, 108
—Presbyterians, 75, 87, 89, 90, 124, 129
—Protectorate, 13, 108–9, 112–13, 119, 120–24, 153
—Scots, 89, 132
—"single blow," 243
—soldiers, 5, 34–35, 63, 108, 110–11, 116–20, 124–33, 174, 238, 241–42
—Trained Bands, 61, 89
—warfare, 2, 42, 61–64, 70–71, 82, 108–9, 124–33, 150–52, 159–60, 203–7
—wars: Dutch, 111, 159; Ireland, 106; Thirty Years, 31–32, 35n, 37–39
Milton, John, works:
—chronology, 3n, 4, 235n
—*Poems of Mr. John Milton*, 87
—poetry (*See also* Sonnets below): *Ad Patrem*, 33; *At a Vacation Exercise*, 37; *Comus*, 33–34, 36, 67–68; *Elegia Prima*, 34; *Elegia Tertia*, 32n; *Elegia Septima*, 33n; *Elegia Quarta*, 32, 32n, 35–36, 35n; *Epitaphium Damonis*, 37, 39; *In quintum Novembris*, 67: *L'Allegro*, 31, 34, 36; *Lycidas*, 24, 37, 62, 243; *Mansus*, 37; *On the Death of the Bishop of Ely*, 33: *On the Morning of Christ's Nativity*, 23, 33, 34, 148n; *On the new Forcers of Conscience*, 24, 75, 87; *Paradise Lost*, passim; *Paradise Regained*, 3n, 14n, 82, 143–45, 148–49, 162, 186–201, 237; *The Passion*, 39; *Samson Agonistes*, 3n, 11, Chap. 8; *Upon the Circumcision*, 34
—prose: *Animadversions*, 42n; *An Apology against a Pamphlet*, 42n, 54, 54n, 68, 93–94; *Areopagitica*, 39, 61, 68–70, 88, 125, 185; *Ar-*

ticles of Peace, 91n, 103, 106, 109; *Brief Notes*, 106, 116, 123; *Commonplace Book*, 57, 59, 127–28, 130, 150n; *Considerations touching the Likeliest Means*, 106, 114n; *De Doctrina Christiana*, 106, 130–31, 153, 222, 245; *Defensio Secunda*, 54n, 62, 72–73, 88–89, 91n, 105, 108, 110–11, 123, 124, 125, 132, 214, 241; Divorce tracts, 54, 60–61, 87; *Eikonoklastes*, 89, 103, 124, 130, 160, 181, 223n, 242; *The History of Britain*, 90, 91–99, 132; Letters, private: Carlo Dati, 40–41, 54; Peter Heimbach, 104n; Moses Wall, 113n; *Letter to a Friend*, 73, 113n, 116–17, 121–22; *Of Education*, 61, 64–67, 80; *Of Prelatical Episcopacy*, 42n; *Of Reformation*, 41, 68; *Of True Religion*, 133, 195, 236; *The Present Means*, 116, 120, 133; *Prolusion I, V, VII*, 36; *Prolusion III*, 65n; *Proposalls of Certaine Expedients*, 116, 118; *Pro Populo Anglicano Defensio*, 88, 91, 103, 110, 112, 124, 131, 155, 181, 218; *Pro Se Defensio*, 105, 125–26, 159n; *The Readie & Easie Way*, 89n, 106, 116, 118–24, 133, 154, 163; *The Reason of Church Government*, 42n; State Papers, 101, 104–5, 142, 142n, 192, 192n, 198–99; *The Tenure of Kings and Magistrates*, 56, 72n, 125, 218; *A Treatise of Civil Power*, 106, 113n; Trinity MS, 96

—sonnets (numbered as in *CW*): *Captain or Colonel* (8), 61–64, 110, 248; *Cromwell, our cheif of men* (16), 25, 90n, 111–12, 125; *Cyriac, whose Grandsire* (21), 91, 126, 237; *Daughter to that good Earl* (10), 23, 54; *Fairfax* (15), 23, 89–90, 111–12, 137; *Giovane piano* (6), 33n; *How soon hath time* (7), 24; *I did but prompt the age* (12), 23; *Lady that in the prime* (9), 23, 54; *Lawrence of vertuous Father* (20), 24; *Methought I saw* (23), 12; *On the Late Massacher in Piemont* (18), 23; *Vane, young in yeares* (17), 59, 111–12, 192; *When Faith and Love*, (14), 23; *When I consider* (19), 24, 236–37

Milton, John (the elder), 31, 53
Mohl, Ruth, 127–28
Moloch, 158–60
Monk, George, General: 106, 114–15, 116, 119, 133, 246; as Duke of Albemarle, 133
Montrose, James Graham, Earl, 76
More, Alexander: 169, 219; *Supplementum*, 125–26
More, Sir Thomas, 128
Mortalism, 11–12
Mosaic Code, 153
Mylius, Hermann, 101n, 103n

Navigation Act, 190, 198
Nephates, Mt., 181
Netherlands, Spanish, Flanders, 141, 144, 149
Netherlands, United, Dutch: in Elizabethan era, 38; commercial power, 146, 190; independence, 141; negotiations with England, 190–93, 198–99. *See also* Wars, Dutch
New Model Army, Army of Saints: Chap.3, 63, 94–95; chaplains, 83; and chivalric tradition, 95; Committee of Safety, 115, 117; and Council of State, 108; and Cromwell, 83, 108; divisions within, 115, 117, 246; and English Republic, 73, 107, 126; and Independents, 82–84; march through London, 86, 87, 89; occupation of London, 44–45, 87, 90; organization of, 48, 67, 81–83, 83n; obedience of, 214, 246; and Parliament, 90–91; as political force, 84–86, 91, 107–8, 136, 154; religious fervor of, 73, 84–85; and Rump, 106, 115–18; source for Samson, 238, 244, 249. *See also* Milton, John, on
New Model Ordinance, 83
Nicolson, Marjorie Hope, 2, 26n, 37n, 64, 206, 207, 243n
Notestein, Wallace, 78

Ormond, James Butler, Earl, 106, 109

Pacifism, antiwar, antimilitary, 2, 127–28, 131, 136–37. *See also*

Milton, John, on
Pandemonium, 136, 152, 157, 158–61, 178, 199
Paradise of Fools, 169
Parker, William Riley, 13, 23, 38n
Parliament, Long Parliament: army, commanders inept, 65–66, 80, 94; army, divisions within, 49, 76–77, 101n; army, Associations, 50, 67; Barebones, 108; Committee of Safety, 77; and Confession of Faith, 88; convened, 40; Convention, 115, 118; dissolved, 118; divisions, Presbyterian-Independent, 74–75, 75n, 88n, 91n; divisions, war and peace, 49–50, 51–53, 158–59; and king, 40; and New Model Army, 85–86, 90–91; Pride's Purge, 84, 86, 90–91; Rump, 86, 102, 103, 153; Rump and Council of State, 102; Rump and Committee for Propagation of the Gospel, 112; Rump dissolved, 109, 110; Rump and New Model Army, conflict, 106, 115–18; Rump and New Model Army, remodeling, 108, 114–15, 133; Rump recalled, 106, 114; Short, 40
Parthia, 194–97, 196n
Patrides, C. A., 225–26
Patterson, Annabel M., 11
Pearl, Valerie, 23, 41n, 57, 87, 88n
Pennington, Isaac, 46n, 47n, 88
Peter, John, 183, 203n, 232
Peters, Hugh, 83
Philip IV, 141
Philistine officer, 239, 246–47
Phillips, Edward, 54, 60
Phillips, John, 126
Plato, 25
Polybius, 150, 151
Portugal, 189
Powell, Mary, 46, 53, 54, 87, 94, 129
Presbyterians: English, 74; majority in Parliament, 76; majority in England, 76; and New Model Army, 72, 88; Scot, 73–74; and war, 76. *See also* Milton, John, on; Parliament, divisions
Protectorate, period of, 101, 114. *See also* Milton, John, on
Protestant League, 136, 191
Pym, John, 50, 51–53, 60, 73, 75, 173n
Pyrenees, Peace of, 149

Quietists, 128

Radzinowicz, Mary Ann, 11, 120n, 236n, 238n
Rajan, Balachandra, 183
Raleigh, Walter, 170
Raphael: and cannon, 231; as diplomat, 143; on reconnaissance, 135, 142n, 178, 214–15; as tutor, 140, 211–12, 215, 220
Reformation, 139
Republic, English, 73, 86, 100, 101, 106, 107
Restoration, 86, 101, 106, 129, 137, 153, 165, 235. *See also* Charles II
Revard, Stella P., 5, 14n, 203n
Revelation, Book of, 209, 211
Richardson, Jonathan, 25
Rome, 150, 196–97
Roston, Murray, 6
Rupert, Prince, 1, 34n, 43, 44, 48, 49, 52, 61, 66, 165
Ruthven, K. K., *Defensio Regia*, 217–19

Saltmarsh, John, 83
Samson: Chap. 8; as fallen leader, 238–40; and Gabriel, 239, 244; and Harapha, 240–44; as Hercules, 340–41; and loyal angels, 244–45; and Michael, 244; as Nazarite, 239, 247; and patience, 239, 241, 248; and Philistine officer, 239, 246–47; and Raphael, 244; as soldier, 238; and violence, 238, 239
Sarajevo, 216
Satan: Chap. 6, 20; and Abdiel, 217–20, 233, 243; as antagonist of God, 167–68, 172; and Christ, 186–98, 237; commander, 71, 138; commander, failure as, 232–33; commander in Heaven, 184, 230–31; commander in Hell, 134, 173–79; as courtier, 155, 186, 93; and Cromwell, 172; and Death, 183; as deceiver, 167, 172, 185–89, 192–99; as diplomat, 142–43, 185–89, 192–99; and Eve, 169, 186; as fallen man, 168, 172, 179–85; as fool, 168–72; free to act, 140, 208; function in *PL*, 16; and Gabriel, 184; Godlike, 228; and Harapha, 239, 248; as hero, 168, 170, 174, 183; and

Michael, 184, 229, 243; as mirror of good, 168, 172; and omnipotence, 230; as parody of God, 170; poetic decline of, 179, 183–85; as political figure, 138, 161, 162; powerful, 167, 172; psychological deterioration of, 179–83; rules earth, 137, 143, 147–48, 187; self-defeating, 167, 172, 179–85; and Sin, 183; as soldier, 141, 183–85; sources for, 9; speeches of, 176–78, 181; as spy, 141; volunteers, 160
Scotland; in Civil Wars, 44, 73–74, 76, 77; union with England, 192, 199; war with England; 92, 106, 107
Scythians, 194–96
Secretary for Foreign Languages, Latin Secretary: Marvell as, 103; Milton as, 42, 98, 100–105, 136, 142, 189, 199, 251; Weckherlin as, 103
Self-Denying Ordinance, 82
Shakespeare, William, 124, 200, 204, 206
Shawcross, John T., 92n, 142n, 156–57n
"Short but scandalous night," 114n
Sin, 183, 208
"Single person": 114, 119; Charles II as, 121–23; Cromwell as, 120; Lambert as, 121; Monk as, 123
Skinner, B. F., 26
Skippon, Philip, General, 46–47, 83, 89
Smith, Logan Pearsall, 14–15
Soldiers: image of, 27–28; in 17th century, 5, 28, 31–32, 34, 34n, 39, 67, 238; in 20th century, 73, 131, 137. *See also* Milton, John, on
Solemn League and Covenant, 74, 113
Son, the: as angel, 226; at Creation, 135, 227; one with God, 225–27, 228; as soldier, 233; victor in Heaven, 145, 180, 198, 210–11, 225, 234; volunteers, 155, 227. *See also* Christ
Sophocles, 180
Spain. *See* Experience and Art; Wars
Spenser, Edmund, 95
Stein, Arnold, 15n, 19–20, 20n, 195, 202, 233n, 251
St. John, Oliver, 111n, 124, 190, 198
Strafford, Thomas Wentworth, Earl, 41, 75n
Strickland, William, 111n, 124, 190, 198
Summers, Joseph H., 14, 171n, 203

Tacitus, 16, 196
Tasso, Torquato: 150; *Jerusalem Delivered*, 200
Thurloe, John, 103, 104, 105n, 145, 147
Tillyard, E. M. W., 14n, 20, 21, 38, 95, 180n
Tolstoy, Leo, 206
Towse, John, 47
Trained Bands: 41, 45–48, 54–56, 66, 87, 94; and London fortifications, 48; Presbyterian control of, 88–89; at Turnham Green, 43, 61. *See also* Milton, John, on

Uriel, 140, 155, 187, 200

Vane, Sir Henry, 76, 77–78, 83, 111
Venn, Sir John, 57
Virgil, 12, 135, 204, 207, 234
Voltaire, 180

Waldock, A. J. A., 20, 168, 176, 181, 214n, 200, 232
Wall, Moses, 113n
Waller, Sir William, General: 48, 49, 50, 53, 55, 66, 66n, 78, 81, 82, 174, 213; as Lord General, 52; Milton as adjutant-general to, 60
War in Heaven: Chap. 7; cannon, 10, 12, 169, 202, 211, 231–33, 245; causes of, 216–17; as comic, 172, 202–6, 230; deficiencies of, 207; exchange of hills, 202, 208, 232–33; function in *PL*, 16; as lesson in sin, 212; as power of evil, 174; as realistic combat, 228–34; relative combat power, 231; war aims, 217–28
Ward, Robert: 16, 39; *Animadversions of Warre*, 57–59
Wars: Bishops, 38, 40; Caribbean, 107; Dutch, 106–7, 111, 136, 59, 189–92; English, as a source, 16; Ireland, 84, 106; Ireland, Drogheda, 13, 92, 110, 132; Scotland, Worcester, 92, 106, 107; in 17th century, 28, 128–29, 139; Spain, 107, 136, 141–42, 149–50; Spain,

Battle of Dunes, 142; Thirty Years, 30–32, 32n, 35n, 39, 128, 139, 141; Thirty Years, Magdeburg, 43; in 20th century, 127; World War I, 206; World War II, 43. *See also* Milton, John, on; Soldiers
Waterloo, 206
Webber, Joan, 157n, 204n, 236, 251
Wedgwood, C. V., 23, 30
Westminster Assembly of Divines, 24, 74, 87
Westphalia, Treaty of, 146
Williams, Charles, 168, 170, 171, 222n, 251
Williams, Roger, 192
Wolfe, Don M., 102, 110, 154
Wollaston, John, 47, 55
Woodhouse, A. S. P., 120n, 235
Woolrych, Austin, 13, 101n, 120n
Wright, B. A., 1–2

Young, Thomas, 32, 35